THE GUN
IN AMERICA

The Gun in America

The Origins of a National Dilemma

Lee Kennett
and
James LaVerne Anderson

Contributions in American History
Number 37

GREENWOOD PRESS

New York • Westport, Connecticut • London

Library of Congress Cataloging in Publication Data

Kennett, Lee B
    The gun in America

    (Contributions in American history; no. 37)
    Includes bibliographical references and index.
    1. Firearms—History. 2. Firearms—Laws and
regulations—United States—History. 3. Firearms
industry and trade—United States—History. 1. Anderson, James L. II. Title.
HV8059.K45   363.3   74-5990
ISBN 0-8371-7530-5

Library of Congress Catalog Card Number: 74-5990

First published in 1975
Paperback edition 1976

Greenwood Press, Inc.
88 Post Road West, Westport, Connecticut 06881

Manufactured in the United States of America

10 9 8 7 6 5

Contents

Illustrations

Preface

Most authors introduce their books with a statement of intent. The present work might well begin with a disclaimer. It is not a history of American firearms, nor is it a proposed solution to the "gun problem." On both of these subjects there is already a considerable literature. But between the technical and antiquarian works on the gun itself, and the recent and partisan writings on gun control, there is a broad, largely unexplored field for historical inquiry. We have tried to measure the gun as an ingredient in our national experience, and to determine why and in what ways it has become both a fixture and a shibboleth in American life. In following this course we have sought to keep to a minimum the technological complexities surrounding firearms themselves and the statistical and rhetorical maze of the modern gun control controversy.

Like most historians, when we began we had a number of preconceptions. In the course of research many of these fell by the wayside, and there we left them. The historian does not usually go to such lengths in asserting the scrupulousness of his method but when he seeks to shed light on such a burning topic as we have chosen, his work may generate heat of its own. Whatever flaws the reader may find in this book, they do not proceed from an *a priori* approach. Where the evidence seemed to lead we have tried to follow.

We have divided our work along lines of interest and competence. Professor Kennett supplied the materials on the European background, the arms industry, and the American experience with firearms since 1900 (Chapters 1, 4, 7, 8, and 9). Professor Anderson contributed the chapters on earlier American history and constitutional issues (2, 3, 5, and 6). The conclusion, written by Professor Kennett, incorporates our common findings.

THE GUN
IN AMERICA

1 Firearms in the European Experience

*T he three great elements of mod-
ern civilization: gunpowder,
printing, and the Protestant religion.*

—Thomas Carlyle

On the morning of April 30, 1524, French and Spanish forces clashed near the Italian town of Gattinare. The engagement was not a major one; if it is remembered at all it is only because it was the chevalier de Bayard's last battle. The celebrated *chevalier sans peur et sans reproche* was leading a charge against the Spanish that morning when he suddenly toppled from his horse, mortally wounded. The stricken warrior was carried from the battlefield by his men, who propped him against a tree, his face toward the enemy. He clasped his sword before him and made his last confession to his page. French and Spanish officers stood in a respectful circle as he expired. In life, Bayard had been curiously out of place: the embodiment of chivalrous virtues in an age of grasping kings and hireling armies. The manner of his death

3

seemed to underscore the anachronism of his life: the most famous knight in Christendom had been felled by the bullet of a nameless Spanish footsoldier.

Those crude firearms of the Italian wars were indeed the symbols of change, but they were also very real agents of change. Writing about those same wars, the historian Sismondi could scarcely find language strong enough to tell his readers how the new weapons had changed society for the worse:

> The invention of firearms has had far more disastrous consequences for the human race than either plagues or famines. It has subjected the strength of man to calculation. It has reduced the soldier to the level of the machine. It has taken the value from all that was noble, from all that was the individual character. It has increased the power of despots and diminished that of nations; it has taken from cities their security, from walls the confidence they inspired.[1]

Historians today no longer moralize or make such sweeping assertions, but there is still some truth in what Sismondi wrote. Firearms did help transform European society and not merely in the military sense. The presence of the new arms, even the menace of their presence, was to influence the political and social structure of early modern Europe in a number of ways.

The fundamental question concerning arms as instruments of coercion and their use in society had been posed long before the advent of gunpowder. That question, examined by political thinkers at least as far back as Plato's day, was: to whom should the guardianship of the state be entrusted? It had long been observed that in the democratic states of antiquity the mass of armed citizens protected their *polis*, while despotic governments entrusted their safety to hired soldiers. Machiavelli reminded his contemporaries that "Rome remained free for four hundred years and Sparta eight hundred, although their citizens were armed all that time."[2] While any acquaintance with ancient history provides ample evidence that this problem of guardianship and the instruments of coercion necessary to it was resolved in a variety of ways, one is tempted to conclude that during the medieval period the question fell into abeyance because of the ascendancy of the feudal nobility.

This generalization, like those of Sismondi, masks a more complicated picture. The so-called military monopoly of the feudal nobility was not absolute; moreover, the whole question of who should bear arms was sometimes the subject of clamorous debate. In one of the few studies on arms-bearing in the Middle Ages, a German scholar has found the question argued "throughout the entire middle ages and into the sixteenth century." There was notably a long-standing difference of opinion between countryside and town: "While in the countryside the social decline of the peasantry made the bearing of arms more and more a prerogative of the landed nobility, in the towns it was obstinately defended as a natural consequence of a more general liability to military service."[3] What is more, medieval monarchs attempted, albeit with only indifferent success, to regulate and even prohibit the bearing of arms.

By the sixteenth century the feudal order was clearly fading. In part its demise was hastened by changes in military technology, foremost among them the increasing use of the new weaponry to which Bayard fell victim.

Politically, the era is distinguished by the rapid development of the nation-state, particularly in Western Europe. Firearms and strong monarchies thus came into fashion at roughly the same time, and for many historians this is more than a coincidence. V. G. Kiernan has argued, for example, that "firearms were essential to the rise of the modern state."[4] The arguments that can be marshalled for this thesis are imposing. The new weapons drove the knight from the battlefield, though his primacy there had already been challenged. Nor could he any longer find sanctuary in a feudal stronghold, for the new monarchs had also invested in siege artillery. The crown's new arsenal gave it an intimidating superiority in its law and order efforts in both town and countryside and helped maintain "the king's peace."

The feudal aristocracy understandably resented the new weapons, and this resentment manifested itself in various ways. In the fifteenth and early sixteenth centuries there were instances in which enemy soldiers captured with firearms were summarily put to death for employing barbarous and ungentlemanly weapons.[5] Montaigne, writing in the sixteenth century, expressed the hope that firearms might soon be abandoned for the traditional sword.[6] The sword, particularly, remained the weapon of the gentleman, indeed the symbol of gentility. It was worn as a badge of status and was preferred by duelists well into the eighteenth century. The cult of the sword, and of the *arme blanche* in general, was preserved in warfare as well since military leadership remained largely aristocratic. As late as 1817 a writer on military organization denounced the use of firearms, which caused "brave men to perish from blows delivered at a distance by cowards."[7]

This long-standing prejudice against firearms does

not seem to have been confined to the nobility. An eminent authority on the evolution of warfare has suggested that a taint of diabolism clung to gunpowder, so that "a consciousness of sinful responsibility weighed on our sixteenth-century ancestors far more heavily in connection with firearms than in connection with old accepted weapons, such as bows, lances, and swords."[8] A recent Italian writer suspects that the dearth of information on the first firearms can in part be attributed to an aversion to the new arms in literary circles, "an aversion proportionate to the military, political and social upheavals firearms were causing."[9] Even after the gun was accorded *droit d'entrée* on the battlefield, some of this aversion remained. In the eighteenth century the use of firearms was limited by the customs of war. Monarchs and jurists, as well as soldiers, objected to the use of poison bullets and other unorthodox projectiles on the battlefield. In 1718 an English inventor named James Puckle sought a patent for a cannon that would fire conventional round projectiles at Christians and square ones at Turks.[10] In naval warfare the firing of langrage (nails, scrap iron, etc.) into a ship's rigging was also condemned.[11] There were other taboos: the air gun, familiar to every American boy, was held in law and custom to be a fiendish weapon, used by assassins, poachers, and other malefactors. When Austria equipped some of her troops with this weapon during the Napoleonic wars, the French executed prisoners who had used them. Napoleon held them to be contrary to the laws and usages of civilized war.[12]

In the main, rulers were pragmatic about the new arms. Rightly used they could be a strong prop to the new state; in the wrong hands they could imperil its existence. It is not surprising, then, that early modern dynasts gave considerable attention to firearms. In France and England particularly, the growth of the state and the evolution of policy regarding the ownership and use of firearms seem to be intimately connected. During the sixteenth, seventeenth, and eighteenth centuries, while the American colonies were evolving, these policies were taking shape. By the time of the American Revolution the process was largely completed. Though there were nuances from one European nation to the next, the policies were roughly similar. By the end of the eighteenth century they constituted what might be called a European tradition in these matters, a tradition that still stands in marked contrast to attitudes on this side of the Atlantic.

Nowhere, perhaps, did arms regulation seem a more natural and traditional prerogative of the state than in France. A recent French legal text asserts categorically: "Because of the dangers which they constitute to the public order, the security of the state, and the security of persons, the production, trade, possession, and bearing of arms and munitions has always been, in French positive law, the subject of regulation."[13] This tradition of regulation, already pronounced in the sixteenth century, was closely related to the needs of the monarchy. The French king and his councillors were well aware that the preservation of the regime depended first and foremost on the efficiency and loyalty of those it chose to arm in its behalf, whether the threat came from foreign enemies, internal factions, or from the sort of routine criminality that has always filled police blotters. The constitution of the armed forces was thus a major preoccupation of the crown and the point of departure for understanding its policy regarding arms.

The Bourbon rulers of the sixteenth century had several options in creating a military establishment. First, the king might rely on the feudal nobility that had earlier dominated the battlefield. He might also employ the mercenary armies that had challenged the feudal knights. A third alternative was some type of national conscript army, for which ample precedent existed in the ancient *arrière-ban* or feudal levy, comprising both noblemen and commoners. A final choice was a professional army, paid and maintained by the monarch for his exclusive use.

All of these solutions were tried, often simultaneously. As late as 1674 Louis XIV called out his great vassals for war, much as his Valois forbears had done. But times had changed; the host was a pale shadow of its former self and totally unfit for war. A general who inspected them urged the king never to call out his nobility again, since they formed "a body incapable of action and more proper to stir up disorders than to remedy troubles."[14] The idea of a national conscript army was largely abandoned too, perhaps because warfare now required long training of soldiers. There was an economic consideration as well, since the monarch disliked taking the productive peasant class from their labors.

By the end of the seventeenth century the *armée du roi* had emerged as an essentially professional force, based on long-term enlistments so far as the enlisted men were concerned. Ample room was made for the nobility, since they officered and led the army. The tradition of foreign mercenaries, notably Swiss and German mercenaries, survived in a number of foreign regiments. Thus, in a sense the military establishment of Louis XIV and his successors was a compromise; the guardians of the state, however, were royal servants, not the people themselves. What was true for the army was essentially true for the navy and such police organizations as the *maréchaussée*.

The notion of universal military service did survive, both in theory and in practice, for behind the army stood the militia. But its role was largely that of a reserve, to be utilized only in time of grave crisis. It was never allowed to compete with the regular army or to usurp its functions. It underwent constant mutations, none of which made it more than an unwelcome burden on the population on which it was imposed. By the middle of the eighteenth century it was little more than a recruiting pool for the regular army. In 1726 the monthly assemblies of militia companies in peacetime were abolished, and after 1778 even the yearly assemblies were suspended. By the time of the French Revolution the militia scarcely existed, save on the registers of the ministry of war.[15]

The decline of the militia can easily be attributed to the same military considerations that doomed the conscript army: such poorly trained forces were seldom useful for anything other than home guard duties. But there were also some very great political risks involved in training the masses in the art of war; at least so ran the argument. It was widely held by sixteenth-century political theorists that a national or citizen army was incompatible with monarchy. Jean Bodin, perhaps the most famous of these theorists in France, was particularly outspoken on this point. It was all very well, he argued, to arm the general population in a democratic state, where equality was the rule. But a monarchical government like that of France, resting on a hierarchy of social orders, would court disaster if it trained the masses in war. Unless kept constantly engaged against foreign enemies, they would seek with their newfound force to usurp the position of their betters at home. From this no end of mischief would follow:

> The slave asks only to be unfettered; once removed from his shackles, he desires liberty; once freed, he asks the right of the bourgeois; from bourgeois, he wishes to be made a magistrate; when he is in the highest rank of magistrates, he wants to be king; once king, he wants to be the only king; finally, he wants to be God.[16]

The wise course, Bodin argued, would be to confide guardianship of the state to the nobility, or failing that, to a professional army. The mass of the population would be prohibited from bearing arms.[17] The misgivings of Bodin and other philosophers were echoed in other quarters; the French nobility complained to Francis I that mobilizing peasants and putting weapons in their hands had made them "disobedient and contrary."[18] As an essentially popular force in its composition, and hence a potentially democratic one, the militia was undoubtedly the object of mistrust. Indeed, we are told that as the eighteenth century progressed, this monarchical distrust became "more manifest."[19] By 1743 a minister of war noted that "all their arms have been taken from them some time ago."[20] These were locked up in royal arsenals, to be issued only for the period the militia assembled.

The disarming of the militia was part of the monarchy's long effort to disarm its subjects, especially its potentially troublesome ones. It was in accord with this policy that Richelieu deprived the Huguenots of their fortresses and set about the systematic demolition of feudal strongholds. The impulsion toward this policy is understandable, since the realm had been badly shaken by the religious civil wars of the sixteenth century and by sporadic outbursts on the part of the nobility, culminating in the Fronde, that confused uprising of the mid-seventeenth century.[21] In the interest of public order, minority groups and privileged elements were urged to rely on the protection of the crown, not upon their own devices. In the case of the Huguenots, this reliance was to be ill placed; in 1685 Louis XIV withdrew the state's protection and began a policy of persecution.

In the case of the nobility, the monarchy was a good deal more conciliatory. It is true that sporadic efforts were made to disarm them too; as evidence one can cite several royal decrees in the sixteenth century. An edict of Francis I, for example, prohibited the bearing of arms by "all persons, gentlemen or others, under penalty of death."[22] The government likewise issued prohibitions against dueling, which had become almost a craze in aristocratic circles at the beginning of the seventeenth century. (It has been estimated that during 1589-1607 some 4,000 Frenchmen were killed in these encounters.)[23] All evidence tends to indicate that these measures were so many dead letters, and that the nobility continued to own and bear arms, right down to the Revolution of 1789. This privilege was conceded by Louis XIV and his successors. By the time of the Sun King the nobility had become a much less factious lot, attuned for the most part to the genteel life of Versailles, whether they had the privilege of residing there or not. Tradition, always a strong force in the old monarchy, accorded arms to the nobility as a symbol of its warlike origins—the oldest noble families were referred to as the *noblesse de l'épée*, the nobility of the sword. That military tradition still survived, since the nobles led the king's armies.

The privilege of bearing arms was closely linked in origin to another prerogative enjoyed by the nobility —their monopoly of hunting rights. This had been the pastime of the warrior since medieval times. As a recent study has shown the chase was viewed as a sort of training for war: "In the opportunity hunting exertions gave for maintaining the readiness of the weapons bearing class, it was a surrogate for war."[24] This privilege, denied to the masses, was maintained despite a great deal of popular resentment. That resentment was to surface in a spectacular way in 1789, when the French peasants declared open season on the pigeons and rabbits that had ravaged their fields with impunity for several centuries.

What the monarchy accorded to the aristocracy it denied to the mass of Frenchmen. The peasant or craftsman needed no weapons to defend the realm, since he was excused from this task. Nor could he justify owning them for sporting purposes, since he had no legal right to hunt. Finally, since an imposing array of royal officers was charged with the protection of his life and property, he did not need to undertake this protection himself. In the well-ordered monarchy to which the Bourbons aspired, the state could better defend its subjects than they could defend themselves. Denied deadly weapons, criminals would be less dangerous and the honest citizens less likely to do irreparable harm in moments of rashness or temper. From 1500 to 1789 there were repeated legal reminders that the population at large could not possess or use arms, especially firearms. The Isambert collection of French laws, though far from complete, contains some thirty of these prohibitions.

Their text tells us something about their inspiration, for most of them dwell at length on "murders, affrays, tumults," etc., occasioned by the indiscriminate possession of deadly weapons.

We may assume that the government was sincere in the belief that banning arms would reduce the crime rate, but it would be ingenuous to conclude that this was the only reason for the reiterated prohibitions. What the laws did not say, but what the king knew very well, was that his subjects were all too capable of insurrection and rebellion. A number of recent studies have demonstrated how real this danger was, and how fragile was the peace and order of the realm. A poor harvest, a tax levy, an unpopular official—any of these things could produce sudden and widespread disorders that would have to be put down by force. Writing of the situation in the early seventeenth century, the historian Hanotaux finds: "All contemporaries are in agreement in declaring that in France arms are no longer given to the people, for fear that they will rise up against their oppressors."[25]

When the people assembled in armed bodies, the authorities moved quickly to disarm them by persuasion, or failing that, by force. A royal official sent to investigate troubles in Saint Jean-de-Luz in 1671 reported: "When I arrived here the first time I found the whole population in arms, making common head; having taken the first step, they were capable of all the rest. I disarmed them in a quarter-hour."[26] The task was not always this easy.

When widespread civil disorders did come, and elements of the population that normally had no arms found weapons in their hands, the danger was a double one: the arms not only made them formidable, but they also gave the rebels an exalted sense of their status. Writing of French peasant rebellions of the seventeenth century, the historian Mousnier finds little evidence of any desire among the insurgents for profound political or social changes. But he does note: "The only evidence of a desire for social change, for equality, might be the sword worn at their sides even as they worked, the sword which was the social symbol of the gentleman."[27]

Another historian notes the appearance of this same phenomenon in the Fronde. He views the generalized wearing of arms in this turbulent period as "a democratization of manners, and an ardent desire to bridge, at least symbolically, the distance between the people whom Saint Simon describes as *'du néant,'* and persons of quality."[28] The government of Louis XIV took particular umbrage at the bourgeois who paraded themselves with swords and pistols. The government was determined to make them "disabuse themselves and return to being good merchants and worthy businessmen."[29] This was the shibboleth raised by Bodin: armed masses of men bent on social leveling. To the government and privileged orders of the old regime the danger must have seemed very real.

As the firearms became more efficient and more widespread, and therefore from the government's point of view more dangerous, they became the objects of special concern. As early as 1561 an edict ordered all inhabitants of Paris who owned firearms to turn them in to the city hall within twenty-four hours.[30] This measure was followed by a host of others addressed to the problem of guns; in almost every case unauthorized bearers of such weapons were subject to the death penalty. Pocket pistols, because of their concealable nature were the object of stern prohibitions right down to the end of the eighteenth century. There was also manifest a tendency to establish state controls over manufacture and distribution, partly because firearms and munitions were strategic commodities. Thus, the production of gunpowder became a state monopoly (and remains so today). Likewise the monarch selected a group of entrepreneurs to work exclusively for his needs in firearms, with the physical plant supplied by the king and production carefully supervised by his agents.

Royal efforts went beyond purely military considerations. The edict of 1561, previously cited, required all Paris gunmakers to provide lists of all the arms they had in their shops and of all they had sold. They were prohibited from selling any arms in the future, except to persons whose names and addresses were known to them. We may assume that in the turbulent city of Paris, at least, the government was attempting a primitive form of registration. As time passed, royal intervention in the gun trade became more pronounced. By the eighteenth century laws appeared prohibiting the export and import of firearms. Finally, in 1783, the state moved directly to regulate the domestic production of civilian arms, by providing that all such weapons manufactured in the chief arms center of Saint Etienne be subjected to inspection and testing under royal auspices. Local agents of the crown had already begun to require licenses for their shipment out of the region.[31] In sum, by the time of the American Revolution the French monarch had adopted a comprehensive policy of regulation and prohibition which covered virtually every aspect of the industry.

Turning to English history in this same period, one might expect to find quite a different tradition regarding the ownership and use of firearms. Even the most casual student of English history will recall that the famous Bill of Rights of 1689 contained a provision granting to Protestants the right to bear arms "for their defence." Some historians find this but one example of a long-standing "permissive" attitude that did not change until quite recently. The author of a recent article in a British law journal holds that there was no real restriction on the right to bear arms until the time of the Boer War: "Indeed," he argues, "the right to carry arms would have been defended as a traditional privilege of Englishmen. The people, it could be said, ought not be be deprived of an ultimate prerogative—the means to resist unjust government by force."[32]

English policy regarding the bearing of arms, like that in France, was tied to the military exigencies of the new state. Here we are at once struck by an apparent contrast. English panegyrists of the eighteenth century frequently spoke of their island as being defended by "freeborn Englishmen," arrayed in frequent wars against the "janissaries" and "pandours" of Continental monarchs. That image captivated the historians of the nineteenth century and still has vitality today. A recent writer has insisted that throughout the centuries England's salvation depended upon the spontaneous and selfless efforts of all classes:

> The merchant in the marketplace, the blacksmith at his forge, the cowherd in his byre, the ploughman at his furrow, the yeoman in his hall and the squire in his manor, these were the men who could and often did rally to the defense of the homeland; and what the Iceni did in A. D. 61 was done by bank clerks, laborers, stockbrokers and shopkeepers in A. D. 1914. The difference was only one of degree. The character of the driving force has not changed.[33]

This assessment accords well historically with the fact that England was slow to develop a professional standing army. Its inception came much later than in France. Military historians often cite Henry VII's handful of Yeomen of the Guard as the germ of the British army. That germ was slow to grow, for a variety of reasons. As an essentially maritime power, England expended more effort on her fleet. Her insularity likewise made a constant posture of defense unnecessary. Moreover, it is probable that the slender financial resources of the Tudors would have put a permanent force of any size beyond their means. Thus it was that Henry VII and subsequent monarchs continued to rely on the ancient obligation of all Englishmen to bear arms when need arose. This concept of universal liability was a strong one: it can be traced back to the Assize of Arms of 1181, and beyond that to the Anglo-Saxon fyrd or militia. This system sufficed, for home defense at least, well into the Stuart era.

The mid-seventeenth century was as troubled for England as it was for France. The English Civil War brought into being a new force: this was the New Model Army, the military wonder of its day. It is described in the classic treatise of C. H. Firth as "a compact, well-organized body, working like a machine, and directed by a single will."[34] But the New Model brought in its wake the dictatorship of Oliver Cromwell, and that experience produced an aversion to standing armies so strong that it was transmitted to the American colonists. A standing army of sorts was retained by the later Stuarts, along with the militia. These two bodies constituted "a sort of equipoise in the state, the one under the king's control, the other obedient to the county aristocracy."[35] Both bodies were used on occasion for internal police functions, though the army's role in quelling disorders became the more prominent in the eighteenth century. This internal peacekeeping role was all the more important in England since the country was underpoliced by Continental standards. Once a situation went beyond the limited competence of the constable or the justice of the peace, the only solution was to "call out the militia" or, failing that, the army.

Since the militia, in some form or other, remained a fairly constant element in the machinery of order, it would be well to inquire whether this body were indeed composed of the mass of Englishmen. For Elizabeth's reign and the early Stuart period we may rely on the excellent monograph by Professor Lindsay Boynton. He found that the militia was, in its inception, a genuinely popular body, since into the 1570s the musters called out all able-bodied commoners between the ages of sixteen and sixty. But from the 1570s onward, the government showed a marked tendency to draw a small number of men from the manpower pool, mustering them more frequently and giving considerable attention to their training. The criteria for selecting these men for the train bands were political as well as physical. The crown sought to enroll men of property, tied by self-interest to the maintenance of order—men who were in the then-current expression "well affected" toward monarch and church. These troops could also be expected to contribute to the costs of their arms and equipment.(There was a simultaneous effort on the part of the authorities to store these centrally rather than leave them in the hands of individuals.) The selective nature of the train bands led Professor Boynton to observe: "There was a deep-

seated apprehension among the ruling classes about putting such dangerous weapons into the hands of the people at large."[36]

The practice of calling upon the well-to-do for armed
assistance also appears in the *posse comitatus*, a kind of
scratch force organized by the local sheriff or justice of
the peace. At the end of the eighteenth century it takes a
third form—volunteer organizations. Formed with governmental sanction, they have been described as "armed
associations of the wealthier classes to put down by force
the unrest of the poor."[37] We must conclude that, while
Elizabeth and her successors did indeed confide guardianship of the state to their freeborn subjects, they
showed a marked disinclination to choose those guardians among the baseborn.

We have noted that the French monarch was particularly anxious to disarm potential elements of opposition
in his realm. This same phenomenon also occurred across the Channel. English Catholics were subjected to a
series of disabilities, among them a prohibition from
bearing arms. Local authorities took it as one of their
regular duties to search the houses of "Papists" for arms.
This task was sometimes performed by Protestant vigilantes as well.[38] The Catholics of British-ruled Ireland
were even more feared because of their numbers. The
British lodgement there was that of a small minority
imposing its will upon the mass of Catholic "Irishry."
Elizabeth's government worried, for example, about the
presence of Catholics in the military establishment there
and sought to replace them.[39] If the Irish in uniform and
under military discipline were a threat, the indiscriminate ownership of firearms by the population at large
would be an even greater one. The dimensions of the
threat became apparent in 1689, when the Catholic

James II, having been deposed by his English subjects, arrived in Ireland at the head of a small army. The island rose for him and made him its master for a time. William III had to mount a major military effort in order to defeat James at the Boyne in 1690. The Catholics continued a bitter resistance until 1696.

Against this background we can easily understand why the Irish Parliament passed, in 1695, an act "for the Better Security of the Government, by Disarming the Papists." The law was a severe one; on or before March 1, 1695, all Catholics were required to surrender all "arms, armour, and munitions, of what kind soever the same be," under threat of severe penalties. To ensure that the disarmament was complete, the justices of the peace, mayors, and sheriffs on the island were empowered to carry out searches; in cities these might be done both day and night. The authors of the act were also concerned lest Catholics learn to make firearms of their own, for a provision was added whereby gunsmiths were prohibited from taking on "popish" apprentices. In addition, all apprentices in the trade were required to take an oath of loyalty to William III.[40] In 1739 these regulations were strengthened by a new law requiring searches for arms at least once a year. Now Catholics were prohibited from owning even parts of weapons, such as blades and gunlocks. Finally, Protestant servants in the employ of Catholics were denied the right to keep weapons. It is noteworthy and as we shall see characteristic of English legislation that the only persons excepted from these provisions were Catholic noblemen, who might possess "a sword, a case of pistols, and a gun."[41]

By the eighteenth century Scotland, or at least its Highlands, became an area of dissidence at least as troublesome as Ireland; this was in large part because the

Hanoverians had acceded to the English and Scottish thrones. In the Highlands particularly, there was a strong residual loyalty to the Stuart descendants of James II. Stuart pretenders relied heavily on this support in their attempts to overthrow the Hanoverians in 1715 and 1745. A glance at the statutes shows that the Hanoverians had worried about these turbulent folk from the moment of their succession. Hardly was George I on the throne before he commanded his officials in Scotland "to search for and seize all arms, ammunition, and other warlike stores, in the custody and possession of any person who the said lieutenants, or any two or more of their deputies, shall judge dangerous to the peace of the realm."[42] The insurrection of 1715 inspired an act which blamed the Highlanders for "riots, robberies and tumults," and prohibited possession by them of any "broadsword, target, poynard, whingar, or dirk, side pistol or gun, or any other warlike weapon."[43] After the 1745 uprising these prohibitions were repeated, but this time, with the area under military occupation, numerous searches and seizures were carried out. Exempted from the general prohibition were peers and commoners with an annual income of £400 Scots. These privileged few might keep "three firelocks, three pairs of pistols, and three swords."[44] As in the case of Ireland, the crown showed a marked deference toward the upper classes, even though their political reliability was open to question.

So far we have dealt with the government's attitude toward admittedly suspect elements. How did it view the possession of arms, and especially firearms, by loyal English Protestants? The first legal expression of Tudor policy, and the germ for subsequent legislation, was a statute of 1504, regulating the use of crossbows. By its terms, none might use this weapon "except he be a lord, or have 200 mark land," though certain other individuals might obtain a royal license to use it.[45] In the reign of Henry VIII handguns were added, since they, like cross-bows, were regarded as exceptional weapons. A law of 1541, still enforced in the eighteenth century, limited free use of these arms to noblemen and those common-ers with incomes of at least £100 per annum; they might keep them in their homes, hunt with them, and carry them as they traveled. Town-dwellers might also keep them, but "to use and shoot in the same as a butt or bank of earth only." That this was a concession to the militia is manifest, since the avowed purpose of this provision was to aid in "the defence of the realm." Crossbows and firearms were also authorized for inhabitants of remote and frontier areas (notably the Scottish border), but only for self-defense, not for hunting. None might keep or use a gun of less than "three-quarters of one yard" in length; this was clearly an effort to outlaw concealable firearms.[46]

The period of the English Civil War, like the roughly contemporaneous Fronde in France, had the practical effect of temporarily disseminating weapons among clas-ses that did not ordinarily use them. As we might well suspect, this led to certain egalitarian tendencies among those who now found arms in their hands. Speaking of the soldiers in Cromwell's army, an historian has ob-served:

Before they enlisted in the New Model these lads, whether they were peasants or craftsmen, would have had to endure any violence and any grossness from so-called gentlemen, drunk or sober, without question or redress. Now, with swords in their hands, they were helpless no longer. The sword had won back for them what they obstinately believed to be their birthright as freeborn Englishmen.[47]

By the end of the Protectorate repressive measures were frequent.[48] Thus in 1659 householders throughout the country were required to submit lists of all lodgers in their houses and of all arms and ammunition there. Arrests and seizures of arms were authorized when local authorities found "just cause for suspicion and danger to the commonwealth."[49]

With the Restoration the traditional policy of permitting firearms only to the nobility and the well-to-do was confirmed. A statute of 1670 followed closely the guidelines of Henry VIII, though now qualified commoners had to possess £150 in annual income.[50] Gone were the Henrician concessions to town-dwellers and to those who lived in remote areas. The Bill of Rights appeared nineteen years later, with its provision that "the subjects which are Protestants may have arms for their defence suitable to their conditions and as allowed by law."[51] There is no indication that this declaration had any practical effect on enforcing the 1670 statute, at least as regards firearms. The contradiction is more apparent than real, since whatever other arms the masses might possess the government had duly indicated in law that firearms were not "suitable to their condition."[52]

The statute of 1670 closely linked the right to own and use firearms to the right to hunt, a question regulated by the game laws. These enactments, often harsh in themselves, were rendered doubly so when enforced by a country magistracy that was drawn from the squirearchy, and was thus anxious to defend a monopoly in which it shared. Just how heavily this sort of justice was weighted against the accused we learn from an outraged but prudently anonymous writer of 1753: "If a person be falsely accused of killing a partridge, the intrinsick worth of which is not above the value of a groat, it shall be made to cost him *fifty, sixty,* or *eighty* pounds, or more, to shew his innocence on so important an occasion. Yet we call ourselves *free*; we boast of our laws! We boast of our liberties!"[53]

These laws made poaching a hazardous business indeed, particularly when used in conjunction with other penal provisions. Thus, illegal hunting by three or more constituted a riot, for which the penalty prescribed was death. Obviously, this legislation had an inhibiting effect on the ownership of firearms, since the mere possession of "engines" for taking game was sometimes the basis of prosecution. That the intent of the game laws was at least in part to keep the masses disarmed was no secret. The eminent jurist Sir William Blackstone conceded that they aided in "the prevention of popular insurrections and resistance to government by disarming the bulk of the people."[54]

The constitutional status of the Bill of Rights and its provision concerning the "right" to bear arms is a matter best left to legal historians. What concerns us here is the degree to which the government did in fact limit the ownership and use of firearms. If we descend to the level of local justice and examine the whole body of regulations that guided the justice of the peace in his work, we must conclude that he had at his disposal a considerable panoply of regulatory and prohibitive powers. Beyond the laws specifically relating to firearms and hunting, there were powers of search and seizure, numerous acts against going armed at night, and an old common law prohibition against "going armed in terror of the people."[55] Though English judges did recognize the right of any Englishman to defend his life and home against malefactors, the legal guides hastened to add that "the safest way is to be armed in the assistance of the King's officers and ministers of justice."[56]

By the end of the eighteenth century, then, the British crown had a long-established policy of regulation and prohibition, directed not only against avowedly dissident elements but also against the lower orders of English society in general. It is indicative that the crown accorded free possession of firearms only to the nobility and the upper middle classes, the same elements with which it had come to share political power.[57]

The policy of arms regulation was thus roughly the same in France and England, though somewhat more rigid in the former where class lines between the nobility and the third estate were more carefully delineated. However repugnant its motives may seem today, such a policy is completely understandable in the context of pre-1789 Europe, with its paternal governments, social hierarchies, and restless masses. Indeed, it could hardly have been otherwise: a monarch could scarcely risk confiding the ultimate coercive power in the state to those same masses to whom he denied political power or representation, for what seemed to him eminently good and valid reasons. An examination of the pattern of regulation in other European countries would exceed the scope of the present study;[58] we must therefore take the English and French experience as roughly representative of a general European tradition.

To the arguments developed so far a very serious objection can be raised. Regardless of the laws, did the mass of Europeans still manage to possess arms, particularly firearms? The question is a valid one and calls for an answer. It is always dangerous to confuse the law with the fact, particularly in an earlier period when enforcement was more difficult and concern for legality perhaps more casual than it is today. In fact, as a general rule the more frequently a prohibition was reiterated in law, the more likely it was not being observed. An answer is not easy to find, since what was concealed from the authorities is also concealed from the modern researcher.

It is probable that into the seventeenth century firearms were not generally held, legally or otherwise, because of their inefficiency, costliness, and general scarcity. The shoulder arms with which Elizabeth equipped her train bands were matchlocks in which the gunpowder was ignited by means of a cord or match, which the soldier had to keep burning. These arms were so cumbersome and crude that some of Elizabeth's captains urged a return to bows and arrows. Yet, they cost the queen about thirty shillings each, a price that would put them out of reach of all but the affluent.[59] The matchlock was succeeded by the wheel lock, which made its appearance in the sixteenth century and was widely used in the seventeenth. This weapon was more efficient, since ignition was provided by sparks thrown off as a serrated metal wheel spun against a piece of pyrite. But its mechanism was intricate and expensive, so much so that a recent authority suggested that when it first appeared its cost "placed it within the reach only of princes and rich lords."[60]

The wheel lock was in its turn superceded by the flintlock ignition system, which came into general use in the seventeenth century and reigned supreme into the early nineteenth. It had the efficiency of the wheel lock and the added advantage of being cheaper to produce. By the end of the eighteenth century, production techniques had been so perfected that colonial powers could export countless cheap flintlock muskets for the overseas trade. It has been estimated that the French alone traded at least 200,000 of these to the North American Indians in the hundred years ending in 1763.[61] It seems only fair to concede that what a Chippewa brave could afford was within the means of most Europeans, and that by the eighteenth century the economic restraint against the widespread acquisition of firearms had largely ended.

Even so, what evidence there is indicates that until the end of the eighteenth century most Europeans did not possess firearms, clandestinely or otherwise. There were some illegally held arms, particularly in rural areas. These in many cases came from militia arsenals or were acquired from deserters, who had a habit of taking their muskets with them when they decamped. Wherever major military operations had taken place a residue of arms and equipment usually fell into the hands of peasants. Those who lived in remote and frontier areas had more arms, either with governmental permission or because powers of enforcement were weak or nonexistent there. This would be the case for the Highlanders, the inhabitants of the isolated Vendée region of France, the Russian Cossacks, and the armed populations that helped guard the eastern frontiers of the Hapsburg domains. Finally, there were the patently criminal elements—highwaymen, smugglers, and the like—who frequently went armed.

With these exceptions, there is little evidence of widespread possession of arms. A recent writer on English social history is categorical about the situation there in the mid-seventeenth century: "Though poachers swarmed over the land, only a handful of yeomen Englishmen and those who did not rule possessed even the slightest knowledge of how to handle firearms."[62]

What was true of the countryside seems to have been true of the city. The author of a treatise on the London police, writing in 1800, proposed the careful regulation of "dangerous and suspicious trades" in order to reduce the crime rate. Pawnbrokers and horse dealers figured on the list, but there was no mention of gunmakers.[63] Since the gunmaking trade was centered here, we must assume that its clientele was quality folk above reproach.

In France there is striking evidence of the disarmed state of the population in the 1760s when a man-eating wolf terrorized the Gévaudan region. The widespread panic and the sizable reward offered for the "Beast of Gévaudan" put the whole population under arms, but these were for the most part farming implements or crude pikes, with very few firearms.[64] Parisians were similarly without arms in 1789; one of the first acts of the revolutionaries there was to seize them.

We have further evidence of the disarmed state of the people in general in the rural upheavals of the seventeenth and eighteenth centuries. These were frequent and often bloody and protracted, but were generally marked by an absence of firearms, at least in the hands of the insurgents. Even when these uprisings produced full-fledged civil war, the rebels were poorly armed. This was notably the case with Pugachev's Rebellion in Russia in the 1770s. According to a recent study, "the distinctive trait of the insurgent forces was the small number of firearms."[65] Of the 2,000 men in one of Pugachev's units, only ten were armed with muskets.[66] One cannot help but contrast this force with the New England farmers who were assembling at Lexington at about the same time.

Urban riots were also marked by a lack of firearms in the hands of the rioters. Nor did the typical eighteenth-century mob seek out these weapons. Their favorite targets were prisons, bakeries, distilleries, and the homes of unpopular officials, not gunshops or armories. But we should note a distinct change at the end of the eighteenth century, with what Professor George Rudé has called the political riot, marked by widespread arming of the crowd.[67] In the upheaval that led to the storming of the Bastille, the Paris rioters seized some 30,000 arms from public and private sources.[68] The decision of this revolutionary crowd to take up firearms, and thus transgress the customary limits of mob behavior, might be considered evidence of a resolve and sense of mission absent in prior disturbances.

The people, then, were disarmed in law and in fact at the end of the eighteenth century. The events at Lexington and Concord, and more spectacularly in the Paris of 1789, must have smacked of revolution in more ways than one. But this vision of the people in arms did not come without some preparation, at least on the intellectual level. The notion that the citizen armed was the best guarantor of his own liberties had never vanished from the realm of speculation. This principle, it was said, had underlain the greatness of republican Rome and Periclean Athens, societies with which every educated European was familiar. The idea had thus been part of the cult of antiquity. In the eighteenth century philosophers and writers resurrected it into a liberal dissentient view with a new immediacy. A society of free men armed, they argued, still offered the best guarantee against tyranny. Edward Gibbon, for example, could not resist this digression in his famous history of Rome: "A martial nobility and stubborn commons, possessed of arms, tenacious of property, and collected into constitutional assemblies, form the only balance capable of preserving a free constitution against enterprises of an aspiring prince."[69] As the century wore on, the argument became more strident. It was left to an American, Joel Barlow, to speak out most strongly. He accused the princes of Europe of having disarmed their peoples "as an essential part of their military system," in order to keep all matters of state out of their reach. But as a revolutionary in what had become an age of revolution, Barlow spoke also of the future: "The people will be universally armed; they will assume those weapons for security, which the art of war has invented for destruction."[70] This idea was not to prevail in the Europe of Barlow's day, though on the other side of the Atlantic it was to thrive.

The explanation lies in the differing fortunes of those two spectacular popular upheavals of the period, the American and French Revolutions. The Revolution in America was a success, both militarily and politically. The French Revolution which made a far deeper impression on European thought, was not a success, at least in the short term. The French revolutionaries could hold the rest of Europe at bay for nearly a decade, but they could not agree on a viable form of government to represent them. Their Revolution was attended by a succession of political experiments and episodes of violence; many of its early partisans, both in France and elsewhere in Europe, became disillusioned. In 1799 the distracted country received its fourth constitution in a decade; and with it the despotism of Napoleon. By the time of his fall all of Europe was united against him and against the "democratic contagion" that had brought him to power. In the decade after Waterloo the armed masses were more feared than ever. While the fear was strongest on the Continent, it was also felt in England where Parliament in the winter of 1819 passed the so-called "Six

Acts." This battery of laws was designed to stifle uprisings by imposing curbs on the press, public meetings, and
the use of firearms. One of the acts banned drilling and
training in the use of arms; another authorized searches
and seizures of weapons in private houses. The Duke of
Wellington, a firm supporter of the measures, hoped
they would forestall "the universal revolution which
seems to menace us all."[71]

In Western Europe, at least, the climate of reaction
eventually gave way to a more liberal age. Paternal governments became representative ones as the franchise
was extended. The nobility lost many of its privileges.
Finally, the military concept of the nation in arms reappeared. By 1880 almost every country in Europe had
adopted some form of universal military service. With
these changes the old fears tended to vanish, and much
of the restrictive arms legislation was rescinded. This was
the case in England and France.[72] Hence, it may be
suggested that the ownership and use of arms were
closely related to regime and society, with access to
weaponry an indicator of political and social status. The
argument is a familiar one today, since it is frequently
made by those who oppose rigid gun control in the
United States.[73] The European experience until the
nineteenth century seems to bear out this contention.

The nation, like the individual, is the sum of its experiences, and the restrictive policies of earlier centuries
have left their mark. They appeared virtually with the
first firearms, establishing the competence of the state in
such matters from the beginning. Subsequent constitutional developments did not destroy that competence.
The result has been that modern Continental governments, even democratic ones, can find ample precedent
for controls of their own. Even in England common law

rights and the declaration of 1689 have not prevented their imposition.

The early measures also helped set certain patterns in the formative period of modern European society. The ordinary European weathered the turbulence of earlier times without a gun at his side. By the time he could possess one freely, much of the need for it was gone, at least in terms of self-defense. The "king's peace" had given way to an improved mechanism of law and order symbolized by the Bobbie and the gendarme. Even hunting, opened to the lower classes in the nineteenth century, never quite shook off its aristocratic past. As proof, one has only to compare the English sporting magazine *The Field* with its American counterparts.

Perhaps this legacy, both in law and custom, explains why the gun never became an important totem in Europe's popular culture or a dominant symbol in its folklore. In a negative way this same legacy is a key to understanding the uniqueness of the American dilemma, for it was not to be transplanted to the New World.

2　The Origins of a Weapons-Bearing Society

They which builded on the wall, and they that bare burdens with those that laded, every one with one of his hands wrought in the work, and with the other hand held a weapon.

—Nehemiah 4:17

In its most flattering light, the English colonization of North America reveals a genius for adaptation and improvisation that remains a part of the American character. But a closer look at the American colonial experience shows it to be strewn with the debris of discarded visions and unworkable institutions. These were the remains of abortive attempts to transplant directly the practices or dreams of the Old World to the New, resulting from the misreading of what was needed in America. These Europeans arrived ill-prepared, both mentally and physically, to face the conditions of the wilderness. They seldom adopted native ways or attempted to understand the Indians. Aliens in this strange land, the English came seeking their fortunes either individually or corporately.[1] The need for survival and protection soon blotted out the preconceived ideas of rapid wealth. It was only gradually that seventeenth-century colonizers learned the lesson so obvious to modern historians: if the European was to survive and prosper in the New World, he had to adapt himself and his institutions to a strange land.[2] An important area wherein such a realization came was in the possession and use of firearms.

The North American continent was not just different, it was positively hostile. Though the paid panegyrists of the Virginia and Plymouth Companies painted the new settlements as lands of "milk and honey," an undeniable air of tragedy and desperation clouded the early colonies. The first English lodgement, that on Roanoke Island, vanished without a trace. Of the first settlers at Jamestown, only 30 percent were alive at the end of a year. To the north, the first colonists at Plymouth Bay held on just as precariously. All of these settlements required constant transfusions of men and supplies.[3]

Nature herself presented formidable obstacles. Harsh winters, spring floods, and malarial summers provided a calendar full of natural disasters. Even the soils and growing seasons were different. Furthermore, the forest abounded in predators. To the English settlers, more accustomed to the seemingly tranquil lands of England, a fearful note must have been struck by the bears, wolves, and panthers. Of course, the indigenous population added to the fear of the unknown woods.[4] The term *Indian summer* was originated to define weeks of warm weather in the fall when the natives attacked.

Nor were the colonies a haven from the scourge of war. From the fear of a Spanish attack on Roanoke Island to the surrender of Canada by the French in 1763, almost two centuries of intercolonial competition developed. Though this struggle was at times more keen in the Caribbean, North America was the scene of considerable action. The French, Spanish, Dutch, English and even the Swedes struggled for control of North America. The Indians, of course, were inexorably drawn into the struggle. These conflicts were often extensions of wars on the continent, but they exceeded the limits of traditional warfare. The Indians fought by different rules. To them, bravery was allied with cruelty; torture or enslavement of prisoners served as the symbols of victory. To meet this challenge, European ways were changed. The continent, the native population, the wildlife, and, in fact, the European alignment of nations, would never again be the same.[5] Thus, the battle was joined, and in the end won, by settlers who were supported by their determination, religious beliefs, and superior firepower. The musket, along with the ax and the plow, vanquished the wilderness. America, as Philip Sharpe wrote, "was born with the rifle in its hand."[6]

The firearms available to the colonists during the early colonial period were cranky and imperfect. The first weapons brought to America were either the expensive wheel lock or the simpler matchlock. Relatively few wheel locks even came to the New World, as their complexity and expense made them ill suited to the American environment. The weight of both of these weapons was so great that they usually had to be fired from a support, thus making field use difficult. Edward Winslow of Plymouth advised: "Bring every man a musket or fowling piece. Let your piece be long in the barrel, and fear not the weight of it, for most of our shooting is done from stands." But tastes soon changed. In 1621, the more experienced Virginia colonists were already doing away with these heavy weapons.[7]

The more popular weapon in the early seventeenth century was the simpler matchlock, but it too had disadvantages. The colonist must have found it difficult to stalk hostile Indians or game in the New England forests while at the same time protecting a lighted match. On at least one occasion, attacking Indians caught the Pilgrims with their matches out, defenseless. If the match ignited the charge prematurely, the colonist might be injured by his own weapon, as was John Smith when he was severely burned by his matchlock. Successful firing of these guns required perfect weather conditions, dry powder, and a stationary target, none of which was easily found in the American wilderness. Because of their unreliability, matchlocks were never used in great numbers and rapidly disappeared. By the late seventeenth century, both Massachusetts and Connecticut outlawed matchlocks because they were obsolete. The weapon that had been carried by both Captains John Smith and Miles Standish was not designed for America.[8]

The third firearm to be used, and the one which achieved greatest popularity, was the snaphance, a forerunner of the flintlock. This weapon, with an ignition system based on a piece of flint striking a frizzen causing a spark to ignite the powder, was used with modifications into the nineteenth century.[9] Within several years of settlement, John Smith reported that there were snaphances in Virginia. The number of this style of firearm seems to have been high even in the early days. The Massachusetts Bay Company chose the snaphance as the major weapon for that colony. Governor William Bradford reported in 1645 that the Plymouth militia was "well-armed all with snaphance pecces."[10] At first, these

weapons were not rifled. New England colonists, following the lead of English gunmakers, continued using the
smoothbore as their major weapon longer than those in
the middle or southern colonies. The latter areas preferred the rifled weapons brought from Germany or
manufactured in the middle colonies.[11] The succession
of weapons shows that the colonists wished to adopt the
best firearms, even ahead of their European counterparts.

The American colonists secured the most modern armament available from Europe, and then creatively improved it. Their modifications led to new types of
weapons and stimulated a new industry. Most of the
seventeenth-century weapons were European imports,
including a sizable number of muskets for trade with the
Indians. These imported weapons were still cumbersome and, due to their large bore, a considerable amount
of lead and powder was required for each shot. Colonial
governments, hesitating to spend money for powder and
shot, required that each man furnish his own.[12]

An early contribution of the frontier was a weapon
uniquely adapted to its primitive conditions. This new
type of firearm was developed in the region surrounding
Lancaster, Pennsylvania, in the early eighteenth century.
German gunsmiths, who had brought their knowledge
of the Jäger Rifle to America, modified it to conform to
American needs. In Germany, this weapon was a massive
ornamental rifle with a short barrel and large bore. Colonial gunsmiths reduced the caliber to conserve powder
and lead, lengthened the barrel, and removed much of
the excessive ornamentation. They created a rifle which
the American frontiersmen found lighter and more
economical to use. Furthermore, the owners discovered
the advantages of using a greased patch to seat the bullet

tightly in the barrel. The former method had been the hammering of the bullet into place. The new procedure greatly reduced loading time. Thus, American ingenuity created a practical solution and the American rifle took its place in history.[13]

Carl Bridenbaugh has written that traditionally the arts and crafts tended to deteriorate in the colonial wilderness. The history of the Pennsylvania rifle does not conform to this thesis. Although the American gunsmiths almost never matched their German counterparts in ornateness, their Pennsylvania rifle was of equal quality and more functional. To those who admire the beauty of the long rifle, it is apparent that the craft did not suffer in America, that, rather, functionalism was emphasized. Though there was a lack of German silver and carving on the stock, the tiger stripe walnut stock with its brass furniture and long slender style produced an equal aesthetic quality. Because of its clean style, this rifle is a prized possession today. The Pennsylvania-Kentucky style rifle became the first firearm on which American men lavished great love and attention.

Lancaster, with its German population, became the production center for the American long rifle. Marin Meylan, Peter Leman, and members of the Henry family were all in the gunsmith business by the early 1720s. Leman established one of the early gunsmith dynasties; the Henrys were one of the most prominent families ever involved in firearms production in America.[14] In discussing the role of these men, Roger Burlingame has written that "our nation is a monument to the skill of their patient hands."[15]

From the small gunsmith shops in Lancaster, the Pennsylvania rifle became the product of thousands of hands over the century. Some of the rifles so produced were shoddy and poorly made, because there was no rigid guild system to preserve the purity of the weapon. American economic development was in its embryonic stage in the colonial period; hence, no attempts were made to create larger producers. Every man operated alone, his rifles a tribute to his skill or lack of it. Since local governments purchased very few weapons, no standard sizes were developed. No two muskets were ever the same. The lands of the barrels, the length, and of course, the caliber all varied from weapon to weapon. Each part was handmade and carefully fitted. A bullet mold was custom made for each rifle. A new piece was hand-fashioned to replace any part that broke.[16]

Because these weapons were extremely susceptible to damage, the gunsmith became one of the earliest trained professionals in American society. Records from almost every colony indicate the presence of gunsmiths. An unknown man was listed as a gunsmith in Virginia by 1628, Eltwed Pomeroy was established in Massachusetts in 1630, and Bennett and Packson were working in Maryland by 1635. Apparently, these men maintained firearms brought from Europe. At this time, little actual production of firearms seems to have been done in the colonies. There are no figures in existence today showing the number of weapons shipped to America, nor are there any indigenous production figures. Nevertheless, the American colonists rapidly made the wheel lock and matchlock obsolete, adopted the snaphance, and, from that time, gunsmiths became necessary. By the eighteenth century, gunsmiths were located in practically every town. Although there were never a great number of gunsmiths, they played an important role in society. The citizens of Williamsburg, for example, elected such a tradesman as their mayor.[17]

Understandably, colonial assemblies were constantly concerned over the availability of gunpowder. The Virginia House of Burgesses instructed the colonists not to shoot needlessly, in order to conserve powder. The South Carolina Assembly adopted the novel solution of taxing each vessel that entered the port, the tax being payable in gunpowder. Assemblies offered bounties for the production of saltpetre and gunpowder. Since gunpowder was a greatly needed item, governmental officials concerned themselves on many occasions with instructing the colonists on its use and also attempted to stimulate its production. The earliest production seems to have started in Massachusetts by 1675.[18]

The spread and use of firearms and their rapid evolution proceeded from the urgent demand for weapons. Colonists adjusted to the environment by turning chiefly to products of the land, crops and game, first to exist and then to accumulate wealth, after finding that the silk culture and gold mining did not provide a viable economic base. Harvesting the bounty of nature directly by fishing, hunting, and trapping added considerably to the necessities of life and to the growth of commercial exports.

In this unsettled wilderness, game animals were more a public bounty than a private possession.[19] It was a product available to be harvested by those willing to do so. In America, hunting was not to be the private domain of only the rich and well-born; this change reflected an emerging egalitarian concept.

Although there are no accurate statistics concerning the number of animals in America or the number killed, the totals must have been staggering. In 1770 where some figures are available, more than 800,000 pounds of dressed deerskins valued at £57,738 were exported. This

means that deerskins ranked fifth in the value of commodities exported from the American colonies behind
tobacco, grain, indigo, and whale oil.[20] Since deer were
usually taken by hunting, this figure gives us a crude idea
of the volume of hunting as an economic enterprise. To
the early colonists, the supply of wildlife must have
seemed inexhaustible.

With thousands of colonials shooting at wild birds and
animals for food, profit, and practice, Connecticut responded in 1677 by passing the colonies' first wildlife
law. Massachusetts created a closed season on deer in
1694 and Virginia instituted the first doe season in 1738.
Since game animals were the major supply of fresh meat
for many colonists, these laws were in response to potential problems. The harvest had to be taken regularly and
had to be allowed to reproduce. Legislators assumed the
right to regulate what a man could and could not kill.[21]

As a result of the need to hunt for food, as well as the
growing commercial market for furs, most American
males became familiar with firearms. An Anglican minister, remarking on the effect of this hunting, wrote that
"the great quantities of game, the many kinds, and the
great privileges of killing make the Americans the best
marksman in the world."[22] Another wrote: "there is not a
Man born in America that does not understand the Use
of Firearms and that well. . . . It is almost the First thing
they Purchase and take to all the New Settlements and in
the Cities you can scarcely find a Lad of 12 years That
[does not] go a Gunning. . . ."[23] A third writer recorded
that when a boy was twelve "he then became a fort soldier, and had his port-hole assigned him. Hunting squirrels, turkeys, and raccoons, soon made him expert in the
use of his gun."[24] The average colonial, who would have
been unacquainted with firearms in Europe, thus be-

came the daily user of a potentially powerful weapon. More importantly, he became an expert marksman.

Arms were essential to secure food, and of equal importance in providing security. The building of forts and blockhouses, the mounting of a guard, and the maintaining of weapons, all served to protect the community. Armed vigilance was a necessity. The omnipresent fear, real and imagined, of the American Indian compelled the colonists to maintain a constant guard over their homes and businesses. The carrying of a firearm became commonplace. De Crevecoeur wrote, "the surrounding hostility immediately puts the gun into their hands."[25]

Colonial fears of the Indians were based on terrifying experiences with aggressive tribes. From Opechancanough's two attacks on the Virginia frontier, through the Pequot War and King Philip's War to the Cherokee raids on South Carolina and the Pontiac upheaval in 1763, Indian wars were a severe threat to the establishment of stable colonies in many areas. The results of these wars were lives lost, settlements destroyed, and opportunities shattered. It was not unusual to see the Pilgrims at Plymouth assemble at the rolling of drums, and march to church with firearms, which were then laid next to them while they prayed during the service.[26] This vigilance against a much-feared enemy lasted almost three centuries, and caused the American settlers to seek visible security. They could reach out to control what was within a musket shot.

The sound of the early guns when fired was frightful and intimidating. This psychological advantage was frequently used in dealing with the Indians. From Hernan Cortez's invasion of Mexico, through several centuries of confrontation, Europeans employed these weapons to awe unknowing Indians. In 1669, the French explorer

Nicholas Perrot fired his musket and gunpowder to convince the Potawatomie Indians of his power.[27]

The early Virginians likewise demonstrated their firearms in front of the local Indians. One Virginian wrote that "only the best marksmen were to be allowed target shooting when Indians were about for, . . . if they see your learners miss what they aim at, they will think the weapons not so terrible."[28] In another instance, the Virginians wished to demonstrate their weapons superiority over the Indians. Thus, a gentleman set up a wooden target for his advantage in a match between himself and an Indian. When the Indian pierced the target with his arrow, the chagrined Englishman then used armour. This the Indian failed to penetrate. At the first Thanksgiving celebration at Plymouth, Standish put on a shooting exhibition for the benefit of the Indians.[29] In each of these situations the Europeans used firearms to show their superiority and thus intimidate the Indians.

With firearms becoming a necessity for survival in the early colonies, local colonial governments became involved in the legal regulation of arms. The European idea that only gentlemen had the privilege to bear arms had been brought to America, but of necessity this philosophy changed rapidly. In the first company to Virginia, 54 of the 105 adventurers were labeled as gentlemen with the right to possess firearms. Because the struggle for survival was so desperate, these new colonies could not afford the luxury of allowing some men to spend all their time guarding the remainder of the settlers. In a sense, the concept of a standing army for protection was abandoned because of the critical survival problem. Men had to perform more than one task, and from this necessity evolved the concept of the armed citizen-soldier.

Within the first four years of arrival, the Virginia government moved to arm every man. Solicitations were sent to England asking that each new settler be armed with a gun and powder. James I of England thought nothing of dispatching boatloads of arms to America, while preventing citizens of the British Isles from having them. John Smith wished that every man be equipped with a musket, ten pounds of powder, and forty pounds of lead. A settler became both a worker and a soldier.[30] Actually, Governor Lord De La Warr was responsible for creating a military society in Virginia. In his Martial Laws of 1611 "all targeteers were ordered to carry either flint or wheel lock pistols."[31] Survival dictated that the old social distinctions of arms ownership give way to the practical necessities of creating a new colony. Every man needed to be armed to defend the colony; thus was born a new concept of civic responsibility.

Once the idea that only gentlemen could be armed was destroyed, colonies were created based on the new premise of an armed citizenry. The colony of Georgia was originally developed with the idea that small, yeoman-type farmers would diligently work their fields until an emergency arose. Then they would assemble with their muskets, marching off to fight the Spanish and Indians of Florida. By creating and fostering an armed society, England did not have to provide troops for protection for many years.[32]

After determining that all men needed arms, the colonial governments moved to formalize the military establishment. Virginia did so after the Indian massacre of 1622. A militia concept was adopted which encompassed every able-bodied man between the ages of sixteen and fifty. In 1631, the Massachusetts Court of Assistants ordered that every town enroll all men, except ministers and magistrates, in the militia. These men were to supply their own weapons. A year later all men were required to possess a firearm and those who did not were to be hired out as servants. The governmental approach was to compel the citizens to arm themselves rather than to provide a standing army, which was expensive. Thus created, the Massachusetts militia consisted of nonuniformed men who provided their own arms and elected their own officers.

Other laws were passed to further clarify the use of firearms. Since firearms were used as alarms for danger, the Massachusetts government forbade nonemergency firing of a musket at night, because of the panic it might cause.[33] New laws appeared encouraging hunting so that the colonists sharpened their aim at private expense, as local governments had limited budgets and the English government only rarely provided arms or ammunition. A Virginia law of 1637 encouraged men to practice so that they could kill the wild animals and Indians that lurked in the forests.[34] During times of conflict, such as King Philip's War in New England, the government resorted to confiscation of surplus firearms. Other laws permitted wealthy men to buy their way out of militia service by furnishing three guns for the public use.[35]

Eventually, every colony except Pennsylvania created a militia based on such guidelines. Pennsylvania was founded by the pacifist Quakers, who refused on many occasions to vote money to provide arms for defense. Later, a split developed in Pennsylvania between the Quakers, who lived in the eastern sections of the colony, and the westerners, who were predominantly Scotch-Irish. The westerners became very bitter over the government's failure to defend them. Ironically, when the backwoods Paxton boys threatened Philadelphia in

1763, some Quakers actually mustered arms to repel them.[36]

Since no standing army existed, the colonial leaders responded to the challenge of being surrounded by enemies, and created a universal military service. Musters were held, officers were elected, and men provided their own weapons. Although the colonial governments pressed hard to arm all men, in fact many men never provided suitable arms for mustering days. Those who did arm themselves selected a gun that served both purposes, a sturdy weapon for private use and one that could be used at muster. The militia drilling regularly on town greens kept armed men constantly in view. The militia laws issued during the colonial period are the origin of the legal concept of the armed American citizen.[37]

The arming of colonial society took on added significance in the late seventeenth century. John Shy, who has studied the American colonial militia, stated that it was "an instrument of either order or insurrection, depending on circumstances."[38] As the colonists were experiencing their first signs of nervousness through an emerging subconscious feeling of diverging loyalties, armed men became important in many of the upheavals of colonial America. In Virginia, the failure of Governor Sir William Berkeley to use the militia against the Indians precipitated an uprising in 1676 led by Nathaniel Bacon, Jr. In the end, Bacon and his armed men attacked the capital at Jamestown.[39] Berkeley lamented: "How miserable that man is, . . . that Governes a People wher six parts of seaven at least are Poore Endebted Discontented and Armed."[40]

Years later, in 1689, a band of New York militia captains rallied around Jacob Leisler in their conflict with the Stuart Dominion of New England. This recourse to arms for the redress of supposed grievances continued into the eighteenth century. The spectre of civil war seemed imminent until negotiations resolved some of the problems. Other armed encounters took place in North Carolina, Maryland, and Pennsylvania.[41]

By the beginning of the eighteenth century, civilization was established along the east coast, and so the active carrying of firearms declined. The long gun which was the predominant firearm of the colonial period was suitable to field and forest use, but it had little application in the emerging city. Thus, during the colonial period, the urban areas were relatively free of the consistent use of firearms. No longer did a resident of Philadelphia, Boston, Newport, or New York need to be constantly armed. Of course, firearms were still visible on muster days and many colonists went hunting in the surrounding vacant land. While the Indian menace had created an armed situation, as towns were established and the frontier receded the use of firearms declined. This change is reflected in the numerous riots and insurrections of the colonies in the eighteenth century. Generally, the use of firearms appeared only when the militia or groups of armed frontiersmen were involved. In most of the urban disorders of the eighteenth century, firearms were a scarce commodity. The mobs of Boston or New York strongly resembled their European counterparts, using stones, clubs, and swords in their affrays.[42]

The distinction is clear: rural citizens in the eighteenth century were more likely than their urban counterparts to turn to firearms. The different weapons used by mobs in New York during the 1760s and 1770s supports this point. In the land riots which occurred in rural New York, in the 1760s, the persons involved used firearms. However, in a major encounter in New York City during

March 1770, guns were not involved. In 1770 in Boston, with the almost continuous conflict between the mob and British troops, scarcely any of the mob was armed with a gun. Only after the Boston Massacre did some Bostonians even consider arming themselves. In addition, the groups from the country which moved to the support of the Boston citizens came with their firearms.[43] In any event, where firearms were used during civilian disorders, the rioters who used them were legally entitled to possess them.

While governments sought to arm citizens, social distinctions dictated restrictions on the use of firearms. On at least one occasion, the Massachusetts government confiscated arms from a dissident religious group. In the aftermath of the Antinomian controversy in 1637, the Massachusetts leaders ordered seventy-six followers of Anne Hutchinson and the Reverend John Wheelwright disarmed. However, if any of the seventy-six men were willing to recant their beliefs in "the seditious libell," they would be allowed to keep their firearms. Thus, conformity in religious belief was a qualification for the possession of firearms in this situation. To the Massachusetts Bay leaders, only the "right people" were to have firearms. This is the clearest example in our colonial history where the government which had commanded the men to be armed also exerted the right, unchallenged, to confiscate firearms from dissenters.[44] Too, this was one of the few instances in colonial America where Europeans restricted fellow Europeans from possessing arms.

The use of firearms by white indentured servants clearly shows the differing social concerns of the colonials. While there was religious discrimination in this regard, there was no evidence of class distinctions. There was no fear shown of armed white servants. With almost 70 percent of the white settlers immigrating to America under some form of work contract, the colonies were populated by such arrangements. Some of the immigrants, of course, were transported criminals. Despite the diversity of European migration, the colonial leaders were not concerned whether white servants or former convicts possessed firearms. They could serve in the militia using their master's musket. When they reached the end of their indentured servitude, these white servants received their "freedom dues." The colony of Virginia included a musket in the list of freedom dues, which usually contained clothes, land, corn, money, and tools. A freeman was to be an armed citizen who owned his own gun.[45]

A quite different approach was taken concerning black servants. They were placed in an analogous position to the peasantry of Europe and were forbidden weapons because they were outside the established order of colonial society. An early sign of the emerging restrictions on Africans brought to this country was the passing of laws prohibiting them from possessing firearms. In 1640, the first recorded restrictive legislation passed concerning blacks in Virginia excluded them from owning a gun.[46] The fear of slave uprisings, which developed in the South in the latter part of the seventeenth century, was mirrored in various laws dealing with the use of guns by blacks. An example of such strictures was passed in South Carolina in 1712. In "An Act for the better ordering and governing of Negroes and Slaves," the legislators wrote two articles particularly relating to blacks and firearms. First, a black was prohibited from carrying a firearm beyond the limits of his master's plantation without his written permission. Further, the white men were ordered to keep their guns, "in the most private and least frequented room in the house."[47] Several southern colonies ordered all white men to carry firearms to church for fear that the slaves might select this peaceable time to revolt.[48] The pattern of discrimination was firmly set and the only time it was changed was during a time of acute danger to the colony. In such times, blacks were occasionally employed in the militia, carrying firearms along with the whites.[49]

The dispersion of firearms to the American Indian was another source of developing conflict and legal action in colonial America. The dilemma was caused in the colonies because the firearms trade was militarily risky, but at the same time economically tempting and, paradoxically, secured European dominance. Prior to meeting the white settlers, the American Indian was not dependent on any outside source for power. Once the European had introduced the Indian to firearms, he became technologically dependent for weapons, powder, lead, and repairs.[50] Peter Kalm noted the problem in 1750 when he wrote:

> The Europeans have taught the Indians in their neighborhood the use of firearms, and so they have laid aside their bows and arrows. . . . If the Europeans should now refuse to supply the natives with muskets, they would starve to death . . . or they would be irritated to such a degree as to attack the colonists. The savages have hitherto never tried to make muskets or similar firearms, and their great indolence does not even allow them to mend those muskets which they have. They leave this entirely to the settlers.[51]

The trading of firearms aroused much early concern

among various colonizing governments. In 1622, a Royal British proclamation was issued against the practice. Speeches were made on the floor of Parliament expressing concern over the firearms trade. Sir Ferdinando Gorges, an early promoter of America, warned against the loss of white superiority by giving the Indians an equality in weapons. Finally, in 1630, the Privy Council formally prohibited the firearms trade.[52] As late at 1641, the government again ordered: "In trucking or trading with the Indians no man shall give them for any commodity of theirs, silver or gold, or any weapons of war, either guns or gunpowder, nor any other munition, which might come to be used against ourselves."[53] Local officials closer to the situation took precautionary and legal steps to prevent Indians from obtaining firearms. In 1628, the leaders of Plymouth Colony formally expelled Thomas Morton, "a carousing trader," for having sold firearms to the Indians.[54]

Another American colonizing power of the seventeenth century, the Netherlands, attempted for years to control this trade. The position of the Dutch in New Amsterdam was obviously important in the development of the Indian trade. Dutch leaders became so exasperated at the flow of firearms to the Indians that in 1638 they imposed the death penalty for participants in such trade. In 1648, Governor Peter Stuyvesant attempted to use the law. He arrested several men who were later convicted and sentenced to death for their part in selling firearms to Indians. Certain local citizens protested, which brought a reduced sentence.[55] Finally, the States General declared in 1650: "This evil [trading guns to the Indians] had now reached such a stage that it could not be forbidden without danger of a war."[56] The Indians and traders had reached a position concerning firearms in which the Indians threatened war to secure weapons and the traders risked a blazing frontier for a profit. Finally, the States General limited Dutch settlers to the ownership of matchlock guns only, simply as a means of keeping more sophisticated weapons from falling into the hands of the Indians during a raid.[57]

European colonial officials complicated their own problems by arming the Indians as allies. "When the Europeans came into North America, they were very careful not to give the Indians any firearms. But in the wars between the French and English, each party gave their Indian allies firearms in order to weaken the force of the enemy."[58] The Virginia legislature distinguished between Indians who were allies and those who were potential enemies. Allied Indians were entitled by law to firearms, gunpowder, and in some instances repairs of their weapons.[59]

The Indians readily realized the benefits of firearms in their own wars. This was why the Algonquians invited Champlain to accompany them in their attack on the Iroquois. Massasoit accepted terms with the Pilgrims in order to obtain their support and firearms against the Narragansetts.[60] LaSalle wrote in 1680: "The Savages take better care of us French than of their own children. From us only can they get guns."[61] The possession of guns affected the tribal balance of power throughout America. The first tribes to acquire muskets usually succeeded in establishing their dominance over the neighboring tribes. This was one of the principal reasons why the Iroquois federation became so powerful. The indigenous population fell not only under the influence of European colonizers, due to their desire to obtain firearms, but also into the power sphere of the Indians who acquired firearms first.[62]

Profit also created an overwhelming motive for Europeans to provide arms to the Indians rather than comply with trade laws. Indians willingly paid twenty beaver pelts per gun. The Dutch received an equivalent of more than forty modern American dollars per pound for gunpowder. The current European cost per pound of gunpowder was $1.26. Such a profit overcame the scruples of many traders who sacrificed the military superiority of their colony and the lives of some of their fellow colonists to sell firearms to the Indians. In addition, the prospects of trading for firearms no doubt stimulated the Indians to kill more game to obtain the furs that were so important to the trade; thus the wildlife was greatly depleted. This large-scale commerce had a great impact on the Indians, wildlife, and colonies. The Dutch, French, English, and Americans traded hundreds of thousands of muskets to the Indians in less than two centuries. France alone sent more than 200,000 muskets for the Indians during the century ending in 1763.[63]

The English colonists in America diverged from other European nations in developing a frontier policy. From the fifteenth century, as European monarchs contested their rivals for power, colonial development, in terms of the prevailing economic theory of mercantilism, became part of the imperial struggle. Nearly every European monarchy from this time tried to spread into its own hinterland, and more adventurous kings dispatched explorers around the world. As the age of reconnaissance became the age of settlement, Europeans came into conflict with the indigenous population. The Swedes, Dutch, Portugese, Russians, Austrians, Spanish, French, and English all faced the problems of what was to become known as frontier defense. The first three groups adopted the outpost method. Small enclaves were established in hostile territory where trading posts were created. At these centers, goods were exchanged with the native population in order to attract the desired products for the European markets. These outposts were usually strong militarily but the traders seldom controlled the territory outside their immediate area.[64]

Russia, Austria, and, later, Argentina used an alternative approach to the fortified outpost system as defense for their frontier. Russia and Austria were concerned about encroachment from the Turks, Tatars, and other groups. As a result, both established chains of fortified villages peopled by military colonists. The Russian version was the famous Cossacks. Loyal to a central government, these military frontiersmen worked for centuries, rising to meet the defense needs of the times. They constituted a caste created for frontier defense. Argentina adopted much the same type of frontier in the nineteenth century using the mestizo gauchos.[65]

Spain employed a series of missions and presidios on its northern Mexican frontier to control that area. In addition, Roman Catholic missionaries worked hard to convert local Indian tribes. They developed their own society, in some instances absorbing cultural and institutional elements of the native population. These Spanish frontiersmen, living on the fringes of society, carried out their functions of protection, religious conversion of the Indians, and working various frontier industries.[66]

France, as it moved into Canada, employed a combination of several frontier solutions to cope with its problems of defense. The Bourbon monarchy maintained close control over the expansion of New France. As the colony developed, a special breed of frontiersmen, the *coureurs de bois*, evolved. These men pushed the French frontier far into the interior. To protect this frontier land the royal government used Indian tribes as a military force, attempted to build the population, and formed a very effective local militia from the colonists.[67]

The English lodgement in North America was only one of many expansionist movements conducted against a primitive but often hostile indigenous population. Its distinction lies in the fact that its survival rested not upon a specially recruited, quasi-military class, nor upon well-defined forces carefully organized and kept well in hand by the colonizing power.[68] Though the Redcoats played an undeniable role, the American system was an almost casual autodefense system, resting theoretically on the entire male population. The militia, the chief embodiment of this policy, lacked training, organization, and, most importantly, a professional sense of identity; in these qualities it was inferior to the militia of French Canada. But these very weaknesses had important social consequences. Colonial society continued to find the elements of self-preservation within the people generally. This concept helps explain the diffusion of firearms in that society, where they were ubiquitous, readily at hand, and unthinkingly accepted. The frontier had led the American to believe his personal safety lay with his gun; by 1776 he would take it up as a symbol of civic obligation.

3 The Heritage of the Second Amendment

A well-regulated militia being necessary to the security of a free state, the right of the people to keep and bear arms shall not be infringed.

**—Second Amendment,
U.S. Constitution**

On April 19,1775, the British regulars encountered a small contingent of American militiamen drawn up on the green in Lexington, Massachusetts. What followed could not be termed a great battle, yet the action was pregnant with consequences. As a popular phrase goes, "Here once the embattled farmers stood, and fired the shot heard 'round the world.' "[1] Militarily, it was the beginning of the American Revolution. Philosophically, the assembled militiamen represented a facet of colonial development that would be a legacy to American constitutional theory. The concepts supporting this group would be enshrined in the language of the Second Amendment to the federal Constitution. From that time

57

to the present, diverse people and groups, for political, personal, or philosophical reasons, have attempted to determine what is meant by the phrase "The Right to Bear Arms."[2]

Two different paths of thought led to the Second Amendment. The first, concerning the practical use of firearms by the colonists, was discussed in the preceding chapter. The second path centered around the philosophical development of ideas concerning the civilian soldier and weapons ownership. By 1775 Americans had possessed arms for generations. This strong tradition of firearms ownership established the role of the militia in society, acted as a symbol of pretensions among the colonists, stimulated resentment toward the British regular army.

Every English colony in North America except Pennsylvania had its own militia. Although the exact number of available troops is unknown, by 1774 the number theoretically would have been over 500,000 men, a total larger than any European army at that time. Of course, in peacetime this number shrank and many of the available men never served. We do know that, out of a population of two and one-half million people in America during the Revolutionary War, between 100,000 and 400,000 men participated at some time in that struggle.[3]

The colonial militia had enough success through its 150-year history to inflate the military egos of Americans and strengthen their commitment to citizen soldiery. The militia had fought most of the intercolonial struggles until the 1740s when England finally began to dispatch regular troops to America. Moreover, the militia had confronted the Indians with relative success for this same period. Twice the American militia had captured the French stronghold of Port Royal in Nova Scotia. Its greatest accomplishment came in 1745 when an expedition consisting of 4,000 men, led by a lawyer and a merchant from New England, surrounded and attacked the great French fortification at Louisburg. When the French surrendered their position, the Americans had achieved a tremendous victory, one which buoyed their opinions of the prowess of the citizen-soldier.[4]

During the French and Indian War, opinions on the ability of the American militia soldier began to change and be debated. The center of the controversy was a twenty-two-year-old militia colonel from Virginia named George Washington. After his defeat and surrender at Fort Necessity in Pennsylvania on July 4, 1754, Washington became the symbol in Europe of the inept and inexperienced militia officer found in the American wilderness.[5] Washington, himself a local hero, covered the disastrous retreat of the British army after Braddock's defeat in 1755. He soon demanded equality in rank with British army officers. Washington's demands reflected the American militia officers' confidence that they were competent officers. It rankled the young Virginia officer that he, as a colonial colonel, had to take orders from a British regular army captain. On this issue, Washington finally resigned from further service during the French and Indian War.

Such disagreements between colonial officers and English officers, coupled with the British views of the American militia, served to heighten the irritation between the two groups. One can imagine the shocked reaction of the Earl of Loudon, commander-in-chief of the British forces in North America, during the French and Indian War when he saw American militiamen "firing their guns at random after drill, sleeping on sentry duty, and taking pot shots at game while they were marching."[6] These were not the actions of a well-drilled professional army. Naturally, the British felt the need to bring discipline to the unkempt Americans who wished to fight, so England actively recruited colonials for British regiments and formed the Royal Americans.[7]

During the 1760s, following the French and Indian War, several provocative actions occurred which eventually led to America's break from England. One of these actions was the stationing of British regular troops in the American cities of Boston and New York. This event, coupled with other inflammatory incidents, led to protests, philosophical discussions on the nature of a standing army, and the Boston Massacre. A body of opinion was formed which constituted the other path to the Second Amendment.

The philosophical discussions stemmed from English arguments stimulated by the Glorious Revolution in England. Certain English political philosophers attacked the concept of a standing army because it could be used to thwart the liberties of the people. The English Radical Whigs "challenged anyone who denied the people's right of revolution."[8] To protect these rights, they and other contemporary political theorists endorsed the idea of citizen-soldiers. After all peaceful methods of securing redress of grievances had been attempted, a call to arms was a final means of protecting individual rights. These philosophers were not considering an individual's right to rebel, but only that of the body politic.[9]

With these ideas as background, the Boston Town Meeting, stimulated by the arrival of British troops in peacetime, argued: "The Raising or keeping [of] a standing army within the kingdom in time of peace, unless it be with the consent of Parliament, is against the law."[10] Andrew Eliot, a Bostonian, observed: "Our people begin to despise a military force."[11] To Samuel Seabury, a standing army was "the MONSTER."[12] The sending of these troops to America provided not only the grist for colonial propaganda, but stimulated awareness of the dangers inherent in a standing army.

Pamphleteers and orators used historical examples to illustrate how despotic rulers had used standing, professional armies to subvert the liberties of the people. Others relied on the British writer, John Trenchard, who wrote a pamphlet in 1697 entitled *Argument, Shewing, that a Standing Army is Inconsistent with a Free Government.*[13] James Lowell summarized the feeling of many colonists when he wrote in 1771: "The true strength and safety of every commonwealth or limited monarchy, is the bravery of its freeholders, its militia."[14]

This reliance on citizen-soldiers, as opposed to a professional army, became the hallmark of the emerging American national conscience. Don Higginbotham has written: "He [the soldier] was a free man, a property owner, and a voter, not a military hireling accustomed to obeying commands."[15] The militiaman symbolized the American nation—crude, unorganized, undisciplined, but ready to protect his rights. Such sentiments were reflected in the words of European philosophers of the period such as Voltaire, Turgot, Quesnay, and Rousseau.[16] The point was obvious: a thinking man was a thinking soldier. As Walter Millis phrased it, "the citizen, rather than a mercenary who bore arms in the state's service, was establishing new claims upon the state and new power over its institutions."[17]

The arguments opposing the stationing of British troops in American towns and favoring the civilian militia served to strengthen American opposition to a standing army and the quartering of troops. Jefferson carefully wrote into the Declaration of Independence protests against a standing army in times of peace, the quartering of troops, the use of mercenaries, and the removal of control of the military from civilian hands.[18] Later strictures against the quartering of troops would be written into the Third Amendment to the Constitution, while the ideas favoring the citizen militia would be protected in the Second Amendment. Both of these ideas came as a direct result of the debate over American rights prior to the outbreak of the Revolution.

Americans, buoyed by ideas about the worth of citizen-soldiers and objecting to British interference, started to drill in the late summer of 1774. With these groups marching, the British commander in Boston, General Thomas Gage, became increasingly uneasy. When he dispatched troops to Cambridge in September 1774 to seize powder, the alarm went out and reportedly more than 20,000 men answered the call before the rumor of the shelling of Boston proved false. The point was clear: armed Americans were willing to answer the call to fight British troops. From this time forward, arms were collected, powder stored, cannons purchased, and officers elected. Committees, conventions, and provincial congresses met to raise citizen troops.[19]

Washington responded to the call by assuming command of an independent militia company; others in Virginia were rushing to arms and writing enthusiastic comments about the militia. According to Richard Henry Lee, Fincastle, a western Virginia county, was going to furnish "1,000 rifle men that for their number made [the] most formidable light infantry in the world." He continued to boast, "there is not one of these men who wish a distance less than 200 yards or a larger object than an orange. Every shot is fatal."[20]

During this period prior to the actual outbreak of war, the presence of armed men drilling, assembling at rumors, and harassing royal officials provided the protection behind which the patriot political leaders worked. Walter Millis has pointed out:

> It was the militia which met the critical emergency, or, in less formal operations, kept control of the country, cut off foragers, captured British agents, intimidated the war-weary and disaffected or tarred and feathered the notorious Tories. The patriots' success in infiltrating and capturing the old militia organizations . . . was perhaps as important to the outcome as any of their purely political achievements.

By their actions, Millis continues, the militia prevented any effective counter-revolution from developing.[21]

While the militia organization provided the shield, the colonies and England moved toward an open break. Finally, General Gage issued orders to seize the powder at Concord and the war commenced. After the confrontation at Lexington and Concord, the militias of New England poured toward Boston where they bottled up the British troops and fought the Battle at Bunker Hill. To this point, the army was a creation of coalescing independent militia companies.[22]

The Second Continental Congress, meeting in Philadelphia in May 1775, wrestled with the difficult problem of what to do about an army. Having so long fought the British concept of a standing army, to create one now seemed almost contradictory. Yet, realizing the emergency and the need to act, the Congress created an American army, commanded by Washington but under the overall control of the civilian Congress. The Congress did select one of its own as the commander-in-chief. Enlistments were for the duration of the war, a congressional committee was appointed to oversee the operation of the army, and Washington was expected to keep Congress informed. Although the spectre of a military dictatorship was raised on several occasions during the remainder of the eighteenth century, with this congressional action and Washington's strong support of civilian control it never bore fruit.[23]

The American Revolution, initiated by the conflict at Lexington and Concord, developed an argument between the concepts of the citizen-soldiers and the trained professional in terms of equipment used and the methods of fighting battles. The Americans used more rifles, relied on individuals firing at individual targets, and tended to fight from behind shelter. The British, conforming to eighteenth-century rules of war, used muskets, massed volleys of fire by command, and tended to obtain close contact with the enemy by charging with bayonets. The American style of war was personal, the British impersonal. Thus, a basic animosity developed between the professional soldiers and the American riflemen.[24]

Americans soon realized that dependence on militia troops alone or avoiding the European methods of warfare would not produce victories. In the end, each side adopted some of the other's methods in order to win. England recruited Tory Americans to fight Americans, hired Jäger troops from Germany who had knowledge of the use of rifles, and employed Indians to harass the Americans. One small British contingent even used a breechloading rifle. The Americans, on the other hand, learned to drill, tried to copy the English Brown Bess musket, and charged with bayonets.[25]

Regardless of these changes, the Americans hoped to turn their use of firearms to their own psychological advantage. Americans attempted to impress the British troops with their skills with firearms. Merrill Jensen, citing a Bostonian, wrote: "A 'countryman' who watched an entire regiment of British soldiers miss a target, and when invited to try, hit the target three times running. The British were astonished, whereupon the man said, 'I'll tell you *naow*. I have got a boy at home that will toss up an apple and shoot out all the seeds as it's coming down.' "[26]

The Americans' ability with a rifle was an important asset. A correspondent informed the *Virginia Gazette* on July 22, 1775, that

one of the Gentlemen appointed to command a company of rifle-men, to be raised in one of our frontier counties, had so many applications from the people in his neighborhood, to be enrolled for the service, that a greater number presented than his instructions permitted him to engage, and being unwilling to give offence to any, thought of the following expedient; viz. He, with a piece of chalk, drew on a board the figure of a nose of the common size, which he placed at the distance of one hundred and fifty yards, declaring that those who should come nearest the mark should be enlisted, when sixty odd hit the object,——[General Gage, take care of *your* nose.][27]

This statement could be dismissed as backcountry

bragging had British officers themselves not worried about the high quality of American marksmanship. General William Howe spoke about the "terrible guns of the rebels." One Virginia rifleman deserted to the British; inside their lines, he demonstrated his prowess with a rifle and was finally sent to London to continue his demonstrations. Washington commanded his soldiers to wear hunting shirts because this garment symbolized the rifleman. Jefferson summed up the case for the American army when he wrote, "every soldier in our army [has] been intimate with his gun from his infancy."[28]

A persistent myth credits the Pennsylvania rifle with winning the war. English generals had commented on the use of the rifle during the French and Indian War. During the Revolution, that weapon saw much use, sometimes with telling effect, but military leaders regarded it as more of an expedient than a solution. The smoothbore flintlock musket was still the essential infantry weapon, and would reign supreme for another half century. While the rifle was more accurate, this advantage was lost in pitched battle, where smoke often obscured the enemy. In such engagements, sheer volume of fire decided the day, and the smoothbore musket could be loaded and fired three times more rapidly than the rifle. Civilian rifles pressed into service were fragile in construction, unsuited to the rigors of combat use; since they were of no standard caliber, supplying ammunition for them was a logistician's nightmare.[29] In a letter of 1776, the secretary of the Board of War left no doubt where the preference of the Continental Congress lay: "Were it in the power of Congress to supply muskets, they would speedily reduce the number of rifles, and replace them with the former, as they are more easily kept in order, can be fired oftener, and have the advantage of bayonets."[30]

The war lasted almost seven years. The factors contributing to victory were much more complex than a confrontation between free American citizen-soldiers and the paid professionals of Great Britain. Yet, it can be said that the Americans' long years of experience with firearms and the large size of their fighting force—more than 400,000 men—were essential ingredients in the eventual outcome. Of course, additional factors affected the result of the war: employment of European standards of warfare; use of American regular troops; French aid in terms of money, munitions, and soldiers; and British problems in providing constant support for their troops. But after the war, as the years passed, the idea of the citizen-soldier's important role in winning the struggle became firmly enshrined. Although Europeans continued to be unimpressed with the American militia, the result of victory strongly confirmed the American belief in its own citizen-soldiery.[31]

While the fighting was going on, the colonists established new governments. In most instances, they wrote constitutions to establish the new state governments. Many of these documents contained Bills of Rights as an expression of the writers' concerns about individual and corporate liberties. Using the English Bill of Rights of 1689 as a model, local authors embarked on their own expressions of rights.[32] From these revolutionary Declarations of Rights, the Second Amendment had its immediate origin. George Mason, writing the Declaration of Rights for Virginia, expressed the concerns of the citizens most clearly. He wrote:

That a well-regulated Militia, composed of the body

of the people, trained to arms, is the proper, natural, and safe defence of a free State; that Standing Armies, in time of peace, should be avoided as dangerous to liberty; and that, in all cases, the military should be under the strict subordination to, and governed by, the civil power.[33]

The militia was the instrument to safeguard the liberties of the corporate body of the state. Edmund Randolph, commenting many years later about this clause, wrote that "preferring militia to standing armies were the fruits of genuine democracy and historical experience."

In many of these state documents, the inherent right of revolution was protected. Jefferson wrote: "What country can preserve its liberties if its rulers are not warned from time to time that its people preserve the right of resistance. Let them take arms."[34] Other states followed Virginia's lead, incorporating similar statements into their constitutions, though varying the original wording. The Pennsylvania document stated that "people have a right to bear arms for the defense of themselves and the state."[35] The individual, however, was still linked with the state.[36] The Delaware convention, both reflecting and reacting to the long-time controversy in Quaker Pennsylvania, upheld the right not to bear arms, but stated that the duty of a citizen was to pay his share of defense. New Hampshire also followed this wording.[37]

To the men who drew up the revolutionary constitutions, the protection of the state was essential. They were responding to the old localism of the colonies that was to evolve in the United States as the doctrine of states' rights. There is little controversy among legal historians concerning the meaning of these clauses. Most of them agree with the obvious conclusion that the right to bear arms is closely linked with the corporate concept of the protection of the militia. The individual's right to bear arms had not been questioned, leaving no reason to believe that any of these writers would at this time have had cause to separate the two concepts. No national power, whether the royal government in England against whom they had revolted or the Congress, was to have ultimate control over their rights. To this end, the right of the state to maintain a militia was fully guaranteed in the Articles of Confederation.[38] The possession of arms, the protection of liberties, and the preservation of state localism were incorporated into the beliefs concerning the right to bear arms. There was no mention of the right to bear arms in the Articles. The implication of this omission was state control of the militia and the right to bear arms that this principle entailed.

With the signing of the peace treaty in 1783, the American Revolutionary War was over. The continuing impact of a firearms-wielding society was strengthened by success in the war. The reverence and hero-worship of the American marksmen continued. Despite some suggestions by Alexander Hamilton and George Washington about continuing a small standing army for defensive purposes, the Continental Army was allowed to collapse to less than 100 men. Since some political leaders were suspected of attempting to centralize the government and others had formed the military Society of Cincinnati, many politicians did not wish to perpetuate the idea of a standing army. With such fears, the state militia again became the instrument on which local officials relied. Moreover, the government of the Articles of Confederation was almost bankrupt and the idea of supporting a continental force was beyond the desires of most of the congressmen. For these reasons, both proponents of a stronger national government and those favoring state power supported the establishment of an efficient state militia. Militias were inexpensive and their cost was borne by the states and individuals.[39]

Washington, who suggested the idea of a small standing army supported by a well-organized militia, wrote: "every Citizen who enjoys the protection of a free Government, owes not only a proportion of his property, but even of his personal services to the defense of it. . . . [They ought to be] provided with uniform Arms, and [be] so far accustomed to the use of them." The militia, he continued, would become "the Van and flower of the American forces ever ready for Action and zealous to be employed whenever it may be necessary in the service of their country."[40] Though Washington envisaged a more modern concept with the central government providing the arms for the militia, too many congressmen were opposed to the idea. Elbridge Gerry, a future vice-president of the United States, sounded the cry: "If we have no standing Army, the Militia, which has ever been the dernier Resort of Liberty, may become respectable, and adequate to our Defence . . . but if a regular Army is admitted, will not the Militia be neglected, and gradually dwindle into Contempt? and where are we to look for Defence of our Rights and Liberties."[41]

To be sure, since men had participated in the armed revolt against England and had won, there continued to be the potential of civilian revolt in the years after the war. The Shays Rebellion in Massachusetts was caused by internal political problems and was staffed by former Revolutionary War soldiers. Armed men continued to defend their position and their rights, both in the original colonies and as they began battling their way west across the mountains.[42]

In the years before the federal Constitution was written, the arming of men and the type of army needed became political issues. Those who advocated a stronger federal government favored a reliance on some type of standing army. Those who favored the continuation of state power placed their faith in the state militia as the guardian of their position and liberties. It is from this political controversy that the Second Amendment to the Constitution was finally written and ratified.

By 1787, the armed American male had his firearm firmly clenched in his fist. Occasionally, he even threatened to use arms to establish a more powerful government, if the politicians would not. He arrived at this point in American history buoyed by the tradition of arms ownership and use, based on the colonial and revolutionary experience.

The right to bear arms was not a controversy in the Constitutional Convention. The struggle centered around control of the national army and state militias. After debating the issue on numerous occasions, often rather warmly, the members of the Convention adopted the premise that the president would be the civilian commander-in-chief, Congress would pass the necessary laws for the creation of a standing army, and there would continue to be state militias.[43] This last force would be under state control, but it could be called into national service "to execute the Laws of the Union, suppress Insurrections and repel Invasions."[44] The power to manage and regulate this militia was divided between the federal government and the various states, in order to provide checks on its use. To promote a degree of uniformity not found in state militias at that time, Congress had the power to organize, arm, and discipline the new militia. Beyond these distinct restrictions, the constitutional framers did not venture. The right of citizens to keep arms was neither admitted nor regulated. The concern was over the control of the army and the militia.

With the signing of the Constitution in September 1787, the conflict over ratification of the document moved into each of the thirteen states where conventions were called to consider the document. One issue broached in many of the conventions was the omission of a Bill of Rights. Many of the delegates, most of whom became antifederalist, believed there should be some guarantee of individual rights by the federal government. Those favoring ratification accepted the call for a Bill of Rights as the only means of securing the approval of the Constitution in several states.[45]

As each state met individually, suggestions for the Bill of Rights were made. The Pennsylvanians declared early that "the people have a right to bear arms for the defense of themselves and their own state, or the United States, or for the purpose of killing game and no law shall be passed for disarming the people or any of them, unless for crimes committed, or real danger of public injury from individuals."[46] This and other suggested amendments were not adopted by the Pennsylvania convention but were issued later as a minority report. However, they did point the way to other states, which incorporated such proposals in their ratifications.[47]

In the Massachusetts convention, Samuel Adams urged the adoption of his amendment reading, that the "Constitution be never construed to authorize Congress to . . . prevent the people of the United States, who are peaceable citizens, from keeping their own arms."[48] The

New Hampshire convention petitioned that "Congress shall never disarm any Citizen, unless such as are or have been in Actual Rebellion." This was the first actual proposed amendment concerning firearms approved by a state convention.[49]

The Virginians petitioned: "That the People have a Right to keep and bear Arms; that a well regulated Militia, composed of the Body of the People, trained to Arms, is the proper natural and safe Defence of a free State."[50] In the floor debate, Mason continued this argument, declaring, "I ask who are the militia? They consist now of the whole people, except a few public officers." Mason feared that a powerful central government might restrict militia membership to lower classes of society, thus making the militia unrepresentative in his eyes. He believed that all male citizens, except conscientious objectors, should be included in the militia.[51]

The New York convention proposed an amendment similar to that of Virginia, resolving: "That the People have a right to keep and bear Arms; that a well-regulated Militia including the body of the People capable of bearing Arms is the proper, natural, and safe-defense of a free State."[52]

The exact intent of these amendments suggested by the several state conventions seems cloudy. Clearly, they were concerned about protecting the state militia, as is shown in the preamble of the Virginia militia law of 1785: "The defense and safety of the commonwealth depends upon having its citizens properly armed and taught the knowledge of military duty."[53] Patrick Henry continued this reasoning in the Virginia Ratifying Convention when he stated: "The militia . . . is our ultimate safety."[54]

The proposals, as in the New York and Virginia

amendments, separated the right to bear arms concept from that of support for the militia. This is particularly true in the New York proposal, which specified that, first, all people have the right to keep and bear arms and, second, there should be a well-regulated militia composed of those *capable of bearing* arms. In literal terms, these conventions apparently hoped to protect the right of all citizens to be armed. It was in these proposals offered by the antifederalists that the individual right to keep arms was most clearly expressed.

The philosophical viewpoint on the militia is best understood in the context of when the Second Amendment was written. Many of the state politicians of the period had little faith in the national government. Even later, Joseph Story, associate justice of the Supreme Court in the nineteenth century, commented that "the militia is the natural defence of a free country against sudden foreign invasions, domestic insurrections, and domestic usurpations of power by rulers."[55] Many political leaders of both the eighteenth and nineteenth centuries considered preservation of the state militia to be the ultimate check and balance. Building on the inherent right of revolution to protect one's liberties when all other methods failed, proponents of the Second Amendment, in basic distrust and fear of the national government, firmly believed that the militia was the final recourse. Maryland's Luther Martin, a future associate justice of the Supreme Court, wrote: "The militia—[is] the only defence and protection which the states can have for the Security of their rights against arbitrary encroachment of the general government."[56] In this context the Second Amendment can be seen as the guarantee which eleven southern states used in 1861 as they resorted to an armed constitutional decision.

The new federal government was in operation on June 8, 1789, when James Madison introduced the amendments which became known as the Bill of Rights. At that time, the Second Amendment was part of his fourth section on civil rights, and contained a clause which protected men who had religious scruples against bearing arms from being compelled to join the militia.[57] Elbridge Gerry protested the religious clause because it gave "an opportunity to the people in power to destroy the Constitution itself. They can declare who are those religiously scrupulous, and prevent them from bearing arms." Gerry believed that the right to bear arms principle was intended "to secure the people against the maladministration of the Government."[58] The religious clause was the most controversial segment of the amendment and, in the end, was omitted in the draft of the amendments approved by the Senate. After debate in both houses, the Second Amendment was ratified, thus protecting the states with the statement, "A well-regulated militia being necessary to the security of a free State, the right of the people to keep and bear arms shall not be infringed."[59] No one protested the wording of this amendment and the states proceeded to ratify it.

Madison did not adopt the wording of several state resolutions. Instead, he placed the militia phrase first, followed by the right to bear arms statement as a clause connected to the original thought. The two ideas were linked in the Second Amendment, thus reverting to the wording of George Mason's Virginia Declaration of Rights of 1776.

By developing a constitutional guarantee which confirmed the founding and protection of the militia, the right to bear arms was given a philosophical and moral justification. The linking of the guaranteed militia with the right to bear arms is all-important to nineteenth and twentieth-century judicial decisions.

A continuing controversy has developed as historians, legal commentators, judges, and the public have questioned the meaning of the Second Amendment. A few have even gone so far as to discuss the location of commas in the statement. One critic has asserted that the amendment is now "obsolete."[60] As Daniel J. McKenna has explained: "The Second Amendment forbids Congress only from disarming citizens so as to prevent them from serving in the militia."[61] Walter Millis has suggested that, "through the state militia, the states planned to retain their control over national policy."[62] In fact, through legislation they had tried to insure "that the people would be more powerful than the government."[63] It was the shield against national power which the states' righters of the period, distrustful of the power of the federal Constitution, believed necessary to guarantee their liberties.

The Second Amendment was not adopted simply to protect the right to own firearms. This right had not been questioned, for it was viewed as a traditional privilege lying outside the Constitution and requiring Constitutional endorsement only. As a result of that position, many legal historians have concluded that the right is corporate rather than individual. This point was upheld by the Kansas Supreme Court in 1905 when it ruled that the word "people" is defined collectively.[64] Since the militia included all men, other commentators have reasoned that the right belongs to individuals. Still others have separated the right to possess from the physical act of carrying a weapon.[65] Hence, there is no consensus of opinion among legal scholars.

The meaning of the right to bear arms was not debated

until the nineteenth century when the courts ruled on various aspects of weapons ownership and use. Federal judicial interpretations of the Second Amendment have always been limited. During the first hundred years, only two U.S. Supreme Court cases made any reference to it. The first was the *U.S.* v. *Cruikshank* in 1876 and the second was *Presser* v. *Illinois* in 1886. Cruikshank was indicted on thirty-two counts, two of these counts alleging that he hindered blacks from possessing firearms. The point in contention was the guarantee of the right to possess firearms.[66] The court ruled that the right "of bearing arms for a lawful purpose is not a right granted by the Constitution nor is it in any manner dependent upon that instrument for its existence."[67]

The case against Herman Presser involved a paramilitary organization he led. He was arrested and convicted under an Illinois law prohibiting the creation and parading of a military group without a license from the governor. Presser contended that Illinois was violating the Second Amendment of the Constitution and thus appealed to the Supreme Court. The court held that the Second Amendment applied only to the federal government and not the states. The justices, however, went on:

> It is undoubtedly true that all citizens capable of bearing arms constitute the reserved military force or reserve militia of the United States as well as the States; and, in view of this prerogative of the General Government, as well as of its general powers, the States cannot, even laying the constitutional provisions in question out of view, prohibit the people from keeping and bearing arms, so as to deprive the United States of their rightful resource for main-

taining the public security, and disable the people from performing their duty to the General Government.[68]

The judicial interpretations of the Second Amendment do not clearly define the meaning of the phrase "the right to bear arms." There are no decisions supporting the unlimited right of the people to bear arms. The right has usually been viewed in terms of maintenance of the militia and the responsibility of citizens to defend the country. The police power of the state to regulate the use, possession, and carrying of firearms was implicit in the 1886 decision and was upheld by the court in 1894.

In the twentieth century, the Supreme Court has seldom consented to hear cases concerning the Second Amendment. In the few cases heard, it has usually focused on a broader point of law than merely an alleged infringement of the Second Amendment. Thus, in 1914, the justices heard an appeal from Joseph Patsone, an alien, who contended that Pennsylvania violated the due process clause of the Fourteenth Amendment when its assembly legislated that unnaturalized, foreign-born persons could not possess firearms or hunt. The court ruled that Pennsylvania was within its rights and did not violate the due process clause. Later, in 1935, the Supreme Court ruled as frivolous an appeal which alleged that Illinois did not have the right to reserve the use of concealed weapons to police officers, conductors, and baggagemen. In both instances, state police power to regulate the use of firearms was upheld.[69]

With the passage of the National Firearms Act in 1934, including provisions using the federal taxing power to regulate the sale of machine guns, the Supreme Court heard an argument against this new national regulation.

In 1939, *United States* v. *Miller,* the court ruled that the definition of firearms used in the act did not violate the Second Amendment and that the taxing power could be used to control the movement of certain kinds of firearms. Three years later, the court upheld the use of the interstate commerce clause to restrict the movement of firearms that had been established in a second act of 1938. The court stated that the Second Amendment was a guarantee to the states to prevent possible encroachment by the federal government.[70]

In recent years, the Supreme Court has not dealt with problems concerning the Second Amendment. Several of the other original ten amendments have found new life by the policy of selective incorporation into the guarantees of the Fourteenth Amendment. Through the judicial process, some of the Bill of Rights guarantees which originally restricted federal action have been extended to restrain the states; the Second Amendment has not been so treated. Bartlett Rummel, a judge of the Superior Court of the State of Washington and a past president of the National Rifle Association, has suggested the possible interpretation of the Second Amendment in this way.[71] However, the Supreme Court still views the Second Amendment as a device to protect the states from the federal government through the maintenance of a militia.

The state court decisions are even more varied. Following the ratification of the Second Amendment, most of the states followed with their own versions. Here the understanding of the concept becomes even more fragmented and dispersed. The wording in constitutions operative today varies among the thirty-five states which include some references to the right to bear arms. Some constitutions link the concept with the militia, while others vest the right solely in the individual. Several states reserve the right to regulate the usage, and nine specifically exclude concealed weapons. Many states have tied the principle to the common defense and the right of self-defense. Further, fifteen states today do not even give constitutional support to the right of their citizens to have or bear arms.[72] In these states, the only protection imposed would be the necessity of maintaining an armed militia. Where states do have some form of constitutional guarantee, the only common ground of definition seems to be the premise that states have the right to regulate but they cannot impair within the constitutional limitations of their own document.

Over the years, state courts have heard cases concerning prohibition of certain types of firearms, denial of the right of specific individuals to carry them, the sale of weapons, their transportation across state lines, weapon concealment, and the possession of these weapons in various places. Litigants have variously challenged state laws on weapons use and ownership as violations of the Second Amendment, state provisions protecting the right to bear arms, the Fourteenth Amendment guarantees of due process of law, and the immunities and privileges clause, as well as the equal protection clause of Article 4, Section 2, of the federal Constitution. Most state decisions have endorsed the militia concept and have upheld state police power to control various aspects of weapons use.[73]

The only restraints that state courts have imposed upon legislative actions have been decisions against unreasonable restrictions. In 1933, the New York Superior Court ruled that to require photographs and fingerprints for a pistol permit was excessive and unreasonable. Meanwhile, in Tennessee a state court held as uncon-

stitutional a municipal ordinance prohibiting the carrying of a pistol. Recently, in California a state court held
that, although the legislature can regulate the bearing of
firearms, it may lack the power to destroy the right entirely. Over the last two centuries, the courts have recognized the power of the legislature to control the use of
firearms, but have viewed absolute prohibitions as
unconstitutional.[74]

Popular opinion ranges from the belief that government can impose a ban on weapons to the assumption
that the Second Amendment guarantees absolutely the
right of citizens to possess and use arms. The latter assumption follows the wording of several of the proposed
amendments in 1788. Although there is little legal protection of the individual's unrestricted right to possess
and use firearms, Americans have continued to support
the tradition.

Long before controversy developed over the meaning
of the Second Amendment, Congress, in 1792, moved to
create uniform state militias. The Militia Law was passed
in that year, enrolling "every free, able-bodied, white
male citizen of the respective States (between 18 and 45)
in the militia. Each man was to provide his own weapons,
two flints, 24 rounds of ammunition for a musket or 20
rounds for a rifle. Slaves, freed Blacks, and Indians were
prohibited from serving."[75] The old colonial laws as well
as the continuing racial prejudice, were reflected quite
clearly in this new act. A second act followed, authorizing
the president to summon the state militia for federal use.
Both of these laws were employed in 1794 when
Washington dispatched state militias under federal authority against the Whiskey rebels in western
Pennsylvania.[76]

The use of the militia in western Pennsylvania served

to support the concept of the armed civilian being employed in times of emergencies. The militia had a special role in the American government. This role was a legacy of the revolutionary war period to future American generations. The fires of enthusiasm for the American marksman had burned brightly, and the militia, as Justice Joseph Story wrote, "was the palladium of the liberties of a republic."[77] Laws were still in effect in the nineteenth century ordering every able-bodied man to be armed. Moreover, state and federal constitutions, as well as political philosophers, supported the idea that armed men were the guarantors of their liberties. To the popular mind, this was what happened when the Minute Men met the British at Lexington and Concord in 1775. The visible use of firearms by militias, supported by constitutional and philosophical ideals, created a belief that the right to bear arms resided in individual men. The mere carrying and use of firearms in public provided the necessary popular support to link the beliefs with the practice. Americans continued to be armed both by law and by choice. The conflict over arms use did not develop until later.

The American use of firearms was distinctly founded in national pride. In the early nineteenth century Timothy Dwight wrote: "To trust arms in the hands of people at large, has, in Europe, been believed ... to be an experiment fraught only with danger. Here by a long trial it has been proved to be perfectly harmless.... If the government be equitable; if it be reasonable in its exactions; if proper attention was paid to the education of children in knowledge, and religion, few men will be disposed to use arms unless for their amusement, and for the defence of themselves and their country."[78]

4   An American Industry

If you buy a Colt's Rifle or Pistol, you feel certain that you have one true friend, with six hearts in his body, and who can always be re-lied upon.

—From a Colt advertisement, c. 1860

The fusillades at Lexington and Concord began a war that was in many ways the most perilous in American history. To contemporaries who watched the struggle between England and her rebellious colonies it seemed a contest between a giant and a pygmy. And in a purely technological sense that was in fact the case. England was already establishing her primacy in what later generations would call the Industrial Revolution; her colonies would today be termed *underdeveloped countries*.

As with most wars in our history, the conflict began with great resolve and little practical preparation. At the outset the patriots anticipated little difficulty in arming

83

themselves. The British embargo on shipments of munitions to the colonies, decreed in 1774, they held to be a
vain and futile gesture. The gunmakers of Pennsylvania
alone, they boasted, could supply all the weapons
needed.[1] Nor would many be required, for one American rifleman was the equal of five Redcoats.[2]

Patriotic propaganda could not long mask the grim
realities of American shortcomings. From the beginning
the war effort faltered from lack of supplies of all kinds,
but particularly from a dearth of arms and munitions.
The colonies had produced few pistols or swords, and
the mother country had supplied the muskets used in the
wars against the French. The Pennsylvania rifle, the
region's major contribution to weaponry, was essentially
a civilian arm, made in limited numbers for a purely
domestic market. Production was in the hands of hundreds of gunmakers scattered throughout the colonies.
Their methods were those of craftsmen, who often produced hardware and did general blacksmithing as well.[3]

With such modest domestic production, it is not surprising that one of the first acts of the revolutionaries was
to seize arms and powder belonging to the crown, an
action that precipitated the engagements at Lexington
and Concord. This expedient gave way to others as the
war continued. Agents of the Continental Congress and
the states competed for the arms available in Europe.
Revolutionary authorities confiscated the weapons of
suspect elements and solicited them from patriots. They
hurriedly signed contracts with local gunmakers for
thousands of stands of arms, most of which called for the
production of muskets patterned after the "Brown Bess"
carried by British troops. None of these measures completely solved the problem. In the critical summer of
1776 a fourth of Washington's men had no arms.[4] The

situation was somewhat better by the time of Yorktown, for nearly a hundred thousand weapons had come from French arsenals by then, but throughout the war small arms were in short supply.

In the years following Yorktown there were few signs of change. Military production came to a virtual standstill; Virginia and Pennsylvania closed the state armories they had opened during the war. For a time stocks left over from the conflict supplied the modest needs of the new republic. Commercial gunmaking resumed along traditional lines. The gunmaker hammered an iron ribbon into tubular shape and welded the seam to form the barrel. He smoothed its exterior surface with a grindstone and reamed out the interior to form the bore. If the barrel were to be rifled, he cut the necessary grooves in the bore. For the lock, the most intricate and demanding of the components, and for the other parts, he filed and fitted together rough castings and forgings. (Many locks came readymade from abroad, as did much of the iron and nearly all of the steel used in the trade.) With much fitting and shaping he assembled the arm. The whole process required much labor, no little skill, and the extensive use of hand tools. The final product was essentially hand-made and often custom-made, thus reflecting the tastes of both the gunmaker and his customer. Today collectors of such arms find in the best of them the same intuitive and scrupulous craftsmanship, the same charm of individuality, that the musician finds in an old violin. They were among the last creations of the pre-industrial age.

In the last decade of the century a movement began which was to transform the art of gunmaking and eventually, through a sort of technological "spin off," much of American industry. The impetus for change was once again war, or rather the threat of it. The French Revolution broke out in 1789 and within three years most of Europe was embroiled in a series of wars that would continue until Napoleon's final defeat in 1815. While the American republic sought to keep out of the struggle, it felt sufficiently apprehensive to modernize its armament. In 1794 Congress voted funds for the establishment of two national armories. With due regard for sectional sensibilities, the government built one installation in Springfield, Massachusetts, and the other at Harper's Ferry, Virginia (now West Virginia). The two armories had barely commenced production when war with France became a very real possibility in 1798. Congress acted once again, voting what was then the very large sum of $800,000 to buy more arms. The government's own facilities were limited and the need imperative, so the War Department turned to civilian contractors. In 1808 and subsequent years it issued further contracts.[5]

At this point something of a dichotomy developed in gunmaking. On the one hand, the great majority of gunmakers, supplying the civilian market, demonstrated considerable ingenuity and inventiveness in creating new and more efficient arms, but remained hampered in their work by primitive methods of production.[6] On the other hand, a select group, working under government contract, developed new techniques of manufacture for military weapons. The two sectors did not operate in total ignorance of each other's work; to be sure, the line that separated them was at best a blurred one. It is nevertheless true that in the 1830s innovative products and innovative methods of production began to merge. The fusion, personified by men such as Samuel Colt, would create an "American system" of manufacture that would astonish the world.

The government had an important role in this development. The War Department was not totally indifferent to the possibilities of perfecting weapons themselves; in 1817 it adopted in limited quantities a novel breechloading flintlock devised by John Hall. In the main, however, it remained conservative in such matters, and strongly under European influence. During the Revolution the Americans had sought to imitate their enemy, notably in armament. After the Revolution began a period of French ascendancy. A French officer named Du Portail created the American Corps of Engineers. Another, Simon Bernard, supervised American coastal fortification for a decade. Similarly, French small arms inspired American design for the next fifty years. But in the execution of its work the government gave contractors a relatively free hand. It advanced money against future deliveries, providing capital for the design and construction of gunmaking machinery. There is also a good bit of evidence that some of the new concepts of manufacture came out of the government armories themselves.[7]

Among the contractors of 1798 was Eli Whitney, fresh from a technological breakthrough with the cotton gin and a bitter defeat in defending the patent rights to it. Tradition has it that Whitney, applying his genius to the problems of arms manufacture, hit upon the principle of interchangeability. His biographers point to a dramatic demonstration he staged in 1801 before the secretary of war and a group of army officers. From the various parts of ten musket locks piled before him he selected the components at random, assembling one lock after the other.[8] More recently, it has been argued that he was but one of the innovative contractors, and perhaps not the most important.[9] Whatever share of credit properly belongs to him, it does appear that the "process oriented"[10] Whitney was intrigued by the techniques of manufacture.

The idea of interchangeable parts was not new, for many in both England and France had already experimented with the principle. In the 1780s Jefferson had noted the efforts of a French armorer named Blanc along these lines. The European experiments had shown that the idea was possible; the major achievement of the U.S. government and the gunmakers working for it was to make it practicable.[11] One reason the Continental experiments had not gone further was the inordinate amount of labor consumed in working metal to very close tolerances. In American manufacture this was overcome by the use of swages, forms in which parts could be forged, and jigs, devices which controlled the drills and files in their cutting. Along with these came more accurate gauges and other means of measurement. Even more significant was the introduction of power-driven machines that could work the metal faster, more accurately, and in the long run more cheaply than handworking. Many of the contractors had established themselves along waterways, partly to facilitate transportation in the pre-railroad era, partly so that waterpower could drive the grinding wheels and other machinery already used in gunmaking. These machines were soon followed by a new generation of machine tools, among them stock shaping machines, borers, lathes, and milling machines. An impressive number of these came into use at the Springfield and Harper's Ferry armories. These changes were not exclusively American. The same kind of development was going on in England and there was considerable borrowing in both directions.[12] Even so, Felicia Deyrup has concluded that by midcentury, "in the development of many and probably most arms machines America was ahead of Europe."[13]

The close working relationship between government and industry ended by the 1840s; by then the production of the federal armories satisfied the needs of the military establishment. Most of the contracting firms vanished, Whitney's being an exception. In their places others appeared, wedded to the new system of manufacture but oriented toward the commercial market. Technological development continued, particularly in machine tools, and spread rapidly to other industries. Samuel Colt's plant at Hartford was an especially fertile seedbed. One of his workmen, Christian Spencer, went on to develop the automatic turret lathe.[14] Another, Charles Billings, perfected the technique of drop forging.[15] In the 1850s Francis Pratt and Amos Whitney met in the Hartford plant, became friends and in 1860 went into business for themselves. Pratt & Whitney became a leading producer of machine tools and precision instruments. They played a critical role in the standardization of weights and measures. In the 1880s they built the Hollerith tabulating machine, the ancestor of the modern computer.[16] This technological extension soon revolutionized clockmaking and other trades, and it led to the sewing machine, typewriter, and internal combustion engine.

Samuel Colt himself epitomized the drive and innovative spirit of his age. He built his first revolver in 1832, before he was twenty. Lacking funds to launch his invention, he took to the lecture circuit, demonstrating nitrous oxide, or "laughing gas," under the name Dr. Coult. At the same time he obtained arms patents in the United States and Europe. Finally, in 1836, he was able to open a factory in Paterson, New Jersey, and begin production. The revolver was not a new idea, but had never been commercially successful. The pistols made in Paterson were complicated in mechanism and very expensive; buyers were few and the company was forced into bankruptcy in 1842.[17]

Many of Colt's early products found their way to Texas, where they soon gained a reputation. Captain Samuel Walker of the U.S. Dragoons became convinced of their value as military sidearms, and when the Mexican War broke out he prevailed upon the government to order a thousand of them.[18] Since the Paterson factory had closed by then, Colt arranged for them to be made at the Whitney plant. The new dragoon pistol was much simpler in mechanism and better adapted to serial manufacture. (It was also an enormous weapon, weighing nearly five pounds.) This time Colt's revolver was launched for good. Its inventor was a born salesman; he entered the commercial market and traveled across Europe demonstrating his weapon.[19] To meet the flood of orders that poured in he built the largest private armory in the world.[20] The new facility was completed in 1855, at a time when business was very brisk. During the Crimean War (1854-1856) British, Turkish, and Russian forces used his revolvers—Lord Cardigan carried one in the charge of the Light Brigade.

By 1860 Colt and others had transformed the industry. In addition to machine manufacture, the "patent" firearm came to the fore, with constantly improving designs entering the market. Competition was keen, and patent infringements and suits were common. Henry

Deringer's attempts to protect his name and trademark produced one of the landmark cases in the development of American copyright law.[21] Private capital was by now more readily available in the industry, and profits from other fields of manufacture were drawn into the arms trade. Parker Brothers, manufacturers of shotguns, had branched out from a modest start making coffee mills.[22] Oliver Winchester went from the production of shirts to that of rifles.[23] Private capital thus took the place of government money as contracting fell off and the military showed little interest in newer weapons. Though the revolver had proved itself, the official sidearm of the United States Army remained a single shot pistol. In 1860 the War Department adopted a policy against paying any royalties on patent firearms, which effectively ruled out their adoption.[24]

Then, in 1861, government and industry found themselves suddenly thrown together. The Civil War produced a demand for weapons that completely outstripped the capacities of government armories. The Harper's Ferry installation, having survived John Brown's raid, soon fell into Confederate hands. The government issued contracts for thousands of stands of regulation arms and patent firearms of all kinds were pressed into use. Agents of the federal government scoured the armories of Europe to supply their own needs and to keep the Confederates from getting arms.[25] In all, it has been estimated that the Union used some four million small arms, of which perhaps a million were imported.[26] The South was, of course, in an even more perilous situation; with its limited production facilities it probably produced no more than 70,000 shoulder arms. It relied heavily on importation and on what it could scavenge from the enemy after successful battles.[27] Pro-

duction increased enormously in the North as contractors, impelled by patriotism and profit, responded to the
government's call. In the initial haste to rearm, the federal authorities sometimes offered to pay too much and
sometimes awarded contracts to businesses which could
not meet contract terms. These blunders soon bred a
scandal that drove Secretary of War Simon Cameron
from office and sparked an official investigation. A governmental commission went over more than 100 contracts, involving claims of $50 million. It canceled some
and rewrote others, saving the government about $7
million.[28]

In addition to its role in expanding the small arms
industry, the war encouraged innovation. It was largely
responsible for the rapid switchover from percussion
arms to breechloading ones based on the principle of the
modern cartridge. Repeating rifles made their appearance. President Lincoln himself tested one of these
designed by Christopher Spencer and pronounced
it excellent.[29] Inventors redoubled their efforts in this
direction, filing some 500 patents in the years 1860-
1871.[30]

The war brought prosperity to the industry, but its
aftermath created severe problems. Many firms had
made heavy and long-term investments in expanded
facilities, so that with the cessation of hostilities and the
end of government business they faced a difficult transition. The Remington Company, which had accepted
contracts totaling some $29 million, suddenly found its
huge plant at Ilion, New York, idle when the government
canceled its orders, effective immediately, three days
after Appomattox. Remington survived, skirting the
edge of bankruptcy for several years while it financed

itself from the profits of its agricultural implement plant.[31]

The government had abruptly ceased being a customer. Now it compounded the difficulties of the arms industry by becoming something of a competitor, through its massive sales of surplus arms after the war. In some cases the firearms manufacturers could still turn a profit by buying up these arms and marking them up for resale. Remington was able to buy back from the army, for fifteen dollars each, rifles it had supplied at twenty-three dollars. Others were not so fortunate. Christopher Spencer, whose repeater President Lincoln had admired, now found himself in competition with his own arms in the form of surplus. His company failed in 1869 and was one of many that succumbed. Even Winchester, whose position was less perilous, weathered the depression of 1873 only by extensive price-cutting.[32]

The brightest prospect in the postwar period was foreign sales. The Franco-Prussian War (1870-1871) produced some contracts from the French government and drained off much of the surplus then on the market.[33] Beginning in the late 1860s a sizable boom developed in foreign sales and helped save those firms in a position to exploit it, notably Remington. The basic cause for this rush of business lay in the rapid evolution of firearms technology during the Civil War. Thanks to its stimulating effect in 1865 the United States possessed the most sophisticated military weaponry in the world and the most advanced methods of producing it. Consequently, as European armies converted to breechloading arms they could do no better than address themselves to American industry. A breechloading system devised by Henry Peabody became the basis for the infantry rifle

adopted by the British army in 1871.[34] Colonel Hiram
Berdan, who led a corps of sharpshooters during the
Civil War, designed the new rifle of the Russian army.[35]
The Turkish government, not to be outdone by its
neighbor, ordered 650,000 rifles from the Providence
Tool Company—at that time the largest order ever
placed with a civilian firm.[36] Remington reasserted itself
in a spectacular way with its rolling block rifle, a simple
and highly efficient breechloader. Orders for it flowed in
from Scandinavia to Egypt.[37] Smith & Wesson supplied
pistols to the Russian army, the Japanese navy, and the
Australian colonial police.[38] Dr. Richard Gatling, whose
gun was another product of the Civil War, marketed it all
over the world for forty years.[39]

In the tradition of Colonel Colt, American sales representatives demonstrated their wares wherever there
seemed to be a market. Samuel Remington himself
traveled for his firm, spending much of his life abroad.
W. W. Reynolds, a particularly enterprising salesman,
negotiated a series of contracts with the French government in the midst of the Franco-Prussian War, only to
find himself shut up in the besieged city of Paris. Un-
daunted, he purchased a balloon and left Paris by air.[40]
Thomas Emmett Addis, one of Winchester's roving
salesmen, made one of the first foreign sales in 1866,
when he delivered a thousand rifles and a half million
rounds of ammunition to the Juarez forces in Mexico.
When the Mexicans were slow to pay, Addis threatened
to sell to the forces of Maximilian. The Mexicans paid
and Addis returned with $57,000 in silver coins.[41]

Despite all the efforts of aggressive salesmen, the wars
of the period supplied the best advertising for American
arms. The Russian army found that while its Berdan
rifles were good the Winchester repeaters which the

Turks used against them were even better. At the battle of Langson the French were defeated by a Chinese force armed with Remington-Lee rifles.[42] The British took control of Egypt with camel-mounted Gatlings and crushed the Sudanese at Omdurman with the aid of Maxim machine guns.[43]

Arms producers also did a large business in ammunition. Winchester, which had some difficulty in getting military orders for its specialty, the lever action rifles, became a leading supplier of cartridges. By 1875 its plant had a manufacturing capacity of one million rounds a day. Its chief rival, the Union Metallic Cartridge Company (soon to be linked with Remington), had the same capability.[44] American hegemony in the field of armaments in the period was undeniable. In 1882 an expert on the industry wrote with some pride and only slight exaggeration: "It may be as well to remark here that with the single exception of the needlegun, [the arm of the Prussian infantry], every gun on a breech loading system used in Europe is of American origin, both in its principle and application; a large proportion being of American manufacture."[45]

The boom in foreign sales was of brief duration. Indeed, it could not last long, since it resulted from a temporary technological lag which was soon erased. Governments that dealt with American firms did so more from necessity than choice since it was never comfortable to rely on foreign sources for such critical needs as arms. European powers, particularly, expanded and modernized their armories as quickly as they could, a process that accelerated toward the end of the century with the arms race that preceded World War I. Even those countries that continued to use arms of American design preferred to produce them domestically under license.

In the 1880s armies which could afford them converted to repeating rifles, choosing whenever possible their own designs.

Oddly enough, this transformation too proceeded with American assistance. In this case it was the machine tool industry that facilitated the changeover through its own foreign sales.[46] Already in 1851 an American firm had supplied the machinery for the British government's Enfield Armory.[47] In 1873 Pratt & Whitney filled a $1.5 million order for gunmaking machinery to equip the arms plants of Bismarck's Germany.[48] The company subsequently made similar sales to many other European countries, as well as to China, Japan, Chile, Canada, and Australia. Then too, a number of American designers went to Europe to pursue their work. Hiram Maxim, one of a family of inventive geniuses, became associated with the British Vickers firm and was eventually knighted for his services. Another designer, B. B. Hotchkiss, opened an office in Paris. John Moses Browning, perhaps the most fertile genius of them all, eventually forsook his home in Ogden, Utah, for the Belgian city of Liège, producing designs that made the fortune of the Belgian Fabrique Nationale.[49]

By the 1880s some of the small arms firms were again in serious trouble. (A tariff which placed a 35 percent duty on imported arms helped insure the domestic market in 1883.) Some were simply victims of change. The Sharps Rifle Company found that its single shot rifles could no longer compete with repeating ones and closed its doors in 1881.[50] Eli Whitney's name disappeared from the industry in 1887 when Winchester accepted an offer to acquire the faltering Whitney Arms Company. Manufacturers who had expanded to meet foreign orders now had to diversify or face disaster. The Providence

Tool Company, which had armed much of Eastern Europe, turned its attention to the sewing machine. Remington which had been spectacularly successful in foreign sales, followed suit. Soon it was manufacturing a sewing machine, a reaper, a fire engine, and a trolley car. It bought the rights to produce the typewriter, a recent invention of Christopher Sholes. Most of its new products lost money, and the desperate company sold the rights to the typewriter just as it was beginning to catch on.[51] In 1886 the firm went into receivership; two years later it was acquired by Marcellus Hartley, who already owned the Union Metallic Cartridge Company. Hartley reopened the plant, retaining its name.

By the 1880s gunmaking had completed the transition from craft to industry. Technological change was the root cause. The firearm, once the product of the individual gunmaker, was now an item of machine production carried on in large plants. Even by midcentury the new "patent," mass-produced arms were having a significant impact on the market. With the advent of the cartridge era after the Civil War, their victory was complete. The gunsmith, driven from the field of manufacture, became essentially concerned with the repair and alteration of factory-made products, which he often sold as well. Concentration had become a hallmark of the industry as unsuccessful firms went out of business in the 1870s and 1880s. The more successful companies abetted in the process by buying out competitors in difficulty. Winchester pursued this policy steadily, acquiring the interests of Spencer (1868), American Repeating Rifle (1869), Adirondack (1874), Whitney (1888), and Burgess (1899).[52] For a brief period Winchester also owned half interest in Remington. The census of 1860 had listed 239 firms engaged in the production of small arms; the census of 1900 showed only 26. Most of the survivors were companies whose names still endure: Colt, Smith & Wesson, Winchester, Remington, Marlin, Savage, to name some of the more familiar.

The market remained competitive, though some companies nearly monopolized the demand for certain types—Winchester with its lever action rifles, for example. A number of "gentlemen's agreements" helped protect these specialties. Thus Colt refrained from extensive rifle manufacture and Winchester, in return, did not add pistols to its line of products.[53] More interesting was the agreement on ammunition sales. Winchester had entered the field early; Remington was now linked to Union Metallic Cartridge through Marcellus Hartley, who owned them both. These firms joined other ammunition makers in 1883 in setting up the Ammunition Manufacturers Association. Through it they succeeded in fixing prices, though they continued to compete in volume of sales.[54] Although the Sherman Anti-Trust Act of 1890 frowned on such practices, the association survived until 1907.

There were further changes in both manufacture and marketing toward the end of the century. Until about 1870 Smith & Wesson had virtually monopolized the manufacture of cartridge revolvers, through their ownership of the Rollin White patent covering cylinder design. (Automatic pistols would not appear in commercial quantities until the turn of the century.) When the Rollin White patent expired, dozens of other makers entered the lucrative field. Alongside the products of the more prestigious makers there soon appeared cheap revolvers of anonymous manufacture, stamped with names such as "Tramp's Terror," "Red Jacket," and "Little Giant." These arms, called "suicide specials" by collectors, were to have important social implications.[55] They were destined for an unsophisticated market and sold at very low prices, placing the handgun within reach of all. Colt's first revolvers had sold for upwards of thirty-five dollars; by 1900 the "two dollar pistol" was a fixture in American life.

The firearm and its manufacture had influenced other industries. Now the small arms market was stimulated in turn, particularly through the development of the linotype and the pulp paper process. These made possible new media: newspapers and magazines for the masses. With the popular press came modern advertising. Arms companies were not slow to exploit these possibilities. The briefest glance at the periodical press of the 1900 era will show that Colt's pistols and Marlin rifles competed for advertising space with Pear's Soap and Murad cigarettes. The purpose of this publicity was to lead the reader to the local store carrying the arms in question, since the established firms marketed through jobbers and retailers.

But the new media offered other marketing possibilities. With the development of the nation's railway grid and cheap postal rates it was possible not only to solicit business but also to transact it directly: the mail-order business was born. Aaron Montgomery Ward started his firm in 1872, followed by Sears in 1886. These two houses soon began advertising through their own catalogues, which the postal service classified as educational material and carried at the subventive rate of a penny per pound. Other mail-order firms continued to rely on newspaper and magazine advertising to sell their wares.[56] Prominent among these were firearms, particularly inexpensive revolvers which were light enough for mailing. The advertisements, in keeping with the times, were often flamboyant and deceptive. A $1.69 revolver offered in the June 1894 issue of *Demarest's Family Magazine* carried the bold legend "Smith & Wesson." Only on close examination would the reader find that these words were part of a phrase, the rest of which was in miniscule print. The entire phrase read simply "Smith & Wesson Cartridges Used." The ad also carried a superficially impressive endorsement: "I, P. W. McAllister, member of the City Council of Minneapolis, Minn., do hereby recommend this pistol and guarantee every statement of this firm."[57]

These mail-order practices were not appreciated by the more prestigious arms companies. They were also placed in something of a quandary when houses like Sears placed wholesale orders, since this would compete with their traditional marketing chain. When they filled these orders they found that the mail-order firms often would not honor the factory-set retail prices. Sears, for example, marked down Winchester products as "loss leaders." Winchester protested, to no avail, and finally refused to fill any more orders. Sears replied by placing orders through dummy firms, so the quarrel went on for several years.[58] It is probably safe to say that in their feelings about "cheap mail-order guns" the major small arms companies antedated Senator Thomas Dodd by a half century.

Despite these problems, the industry was fairly prosperous at the turn of the century and remained so until World War I. The Spanish-American War was too brief to provide much stimulus and foreign sales were small, so the market was primarily domestic and civilian. A survey by a correspondent of the *New York Daily Tribune* in 1892 found the industry humming. Local manufacturers had supplanted foreign firms in the cheap shotgun market, as a result of tariff protection. Foreign concerns had likewise lost ground in the production of inexpensive small caliber rifles destined for the sizable youth market. Annual domestic consumption was impressive: 750,000 pistols, 400,000 shotguns, and 500,000 rifles. "For a quiet, peace loving nation," the correspondent observed, "it is surprising how many firearms are sold in this country every year."[59] The 1900 census revealed that twenty-six producers had sold about $5.5 million worth of small arms, and had manufactured much of the $13 million worth of ammunition sold in that year. Their arms exports were valued at $681,000. Imports stood at about $900,000, but much of this was noncompetitive, being composed of muzzle loading guns, for which there was a lingering market, and unfinished barrels that the industry itself had ordered. Damascus barrels, whose variegated patterns resulted from the complicated hand forging of strands of iron and steel, were all imported. Barrels and other components came in free of duty; competitive arms had to surmount a tariff wall ranging from 25 to 75 percent ad valorem. The value of imported pistols, an American specialty, was a mere $2,000.[60]

The conflagration that began in 1914 had much the same effect as the Civil War. Foreign military orders skyrocketed, with especially heavy sales to the British and Russian governments. After 1917 the U. S. government became the industry's leading customer. Army ordnance discovered that it needed some four million Springfield rifles. It had 700,000 on hand and an armory capacity of 350,000 per year. The industry, it was hoped, would supply the rest. The government's business was profitable (just how profitable would be the subject of a Senate investigation), but once again it would create eventual problems. Winchester, for example, did slightly over

$100 million worth of business in military orders from 1915 to 1919, showing a net profit of about $6 million. At the same time it had spent about twice that amount on new plant and equipment.[61] While it could hope to dispose of some of the excess facilities when the war ended, the best solution was to find profitable activity for the increased capacity. There was no large pent-up civilian demand, since commercial production had continued during the war. Diversification was the logical measure to take. Remington added to its line such unlikely commodities as cutlery and cash registers, and Savage Arms brought out a washing machine. Winchester spread into the general hardware and sporting goods business and promoted a series of "Winchester Stores."[62]

The more recent history of the small arms industry can best be told as part of the gun control controversy treated in subsequent chapters. Having traced its development into the twentieth century, we might sum up some of its salient features—many of which it retains—and try to fix its historical role in what has been called the national "gun culture." For each of the handful of manufacturers currently producing small arms there were probably a hundred which vanished through bankruptcy, consolidation, or conversion to other fields of manufacture. While any industry has these ghosts, the gunmaking trade has had unique perils. Traditionally, it has been an industry with high overhead costs. The military market, foreign and domestic, produced short periods of intensive demand, followed by the proverbial lean years. The civilian market was the more steady of the two, but fickle in its changing tastes and its fascination for the new. Even so, there is probably some truth in the industry's assertion that it preferred civilian sales.[63]

What does seem clear is that the arms manufacturers,

whether by preference or not, have been oriented toward sales to the general public. Governmental policies gave the industry little choice in the matter. Even if the federal government had not opened its own plants, its orders would probably have been negligible for most of our history. Its conservatism played a part; the United States army underwent small arms changeovers infrequently, at least in comparison with European powers. It was one of the last to forsake the single shot rifle, for example, which was not replaced until the Spanish-American War. Even more important, the military establishment was modest and, in peacetime at least, was maintained on a minimal budget. This practice tended to set us apart from the other great powers, particularly after most of Europe adopted mass conscription in the decade following the Franco-Prussian War. In 1904 the United States stood at about 60,000 officers and men, making it slightly larger than the military establishment of Belgium and slightly smaller than that of Rumania. Our army was about a tenth the size of the French and German.[64] It was only on the eve of World War II that the peacetime draft became a feature of American life. Hence, it would be very difficult indeed to maintain that American arms companies had the same sinister relationship to government as Krupp, Vickers, and Schneider-Creusot allegedly had.

An industry with such an impressive record of development might be expected to have expanded geographically as the nation grew. To the contrary, the arms making trade has remained concentrated. The industrial northeast which was its cradle, especially Massachusetts, Connecticut, and New York, remains its stronghold. It was able to supply constantly widening markets without moving its base of operations partly because its commodities were not bulky and thus easily transported. By the time it shifted to machine production, the railways and steamship lines could handle its goods quickly and at low cost. This continuing concentration has made it a vital factor in the economy of a few states, while at the same time reducing the possibilities of political leverage or lobbying success at the national level.

Whatever impact the arms trade had on the evolution of the economy generally was confined to its technological contributions, particularly in creating the machine tool. Quantitatively, it never accounted for more than a tiny fraction of American industry. Felicia Deyrup, writing in 1950, noted: "Small arms production, in terms of numbers of employees, capital invested, value of product, or value added by manufacture, has in no census year exceeded 0.3% of total industry."[65] Recent research has shown that even the tremendous small arms production of the Civil War can scarcely be credited with stimulating iron production in the United States. The production absorbed only .025 percent of wartime iron output. Even if the metal required for the industry's machine tools is added, its total requirements were scarcely 1 percent of total wartime production of iron.[66] In this context Samuel Colt and Oliver Winchester must be considered captains of industry by courtesy title only.

Related to the modest size of the industry was the slowness with which it changed from the simple family concern to the modern corporate structure. Remington arms, founded in 1816, did not incorporate until 1865. The Remington family held the stock until 1886, when Marcellus Hartley made it his property. When Hartley died in 1902, he was succeeded by his grandson, who bought up the shares of the other heirs and became sole owner.[67] Only in 1933 did the company pass to Dupont.

(Winchester was added to the Olin interests two years earlier.)

With their small size and personal ownership, the arms companies were long able to manifest a benevolent, if self-serving, paternalism in their labor relations. Strikes were uncommon in the industry, partly because of the extensive use of the inside contract system, which some companies retained into the twentieth century. In this arrangement the management contracted with machinists and other skilled workers, supplying factory space, machinery, and raw materials. It also agreed to purchase, on a piece basis, the goods they would make or process. The contractor then hired the men for his department and fixed their wages. His profit consisted of the difference between the value of his sales to the company and his payroll costs, plus the daily wage he personally received, which was also fixed by the contract. It has been argued that this system encouraged initiative and made labor relations less thorny.[68]

Throughout the nineteenth century, the small arms industry possessed a staid respectability all its own. Its dominant figures enjoyed generally unimpeachable reputations; indeed, many of them were decidedly stern and sober of habit. The Remingtons founded a temperance hotel. Smith & Wesson, it is said, once halted production of one of their pistols when it was discovered the arm had found favor with prostitutes. But their public image was honorable chiefly because the American public attached no more opprobrium to their products than it did to sewing machines and typewriters. It was probably not until the Nye Committee investigations of the 1930s that any significant number of Americans came to attach a moral taint to the manufacture of arms. Until then the firearm had a generally positive image, and was advertised as such. Even in the 1920s the makers of the Thompson submachine gun would not hesitate to offer it to the well-to-do as "the ideal weapon for the protection of large estates, ranches, plantations, etc."[69]

Public acceptance, or at least lack of public outcry, influenced the industry in other ways. For one thing it kept it from being singled out as a target of government regulation. The industry did, and still does, set its own standards for quality and safety. In most European countries with any sizable small arms industry, government regulations require the testing of commercial arms by firing them with exceptionally heavy charges. This is generally done in installations called proof houses, operating under government supervision, the practice in some countries dates back to the seventeenth century. American firms still administer these tests themselves.

Domestic marketing continued virtually unhampered by federal regulation until the 1920s when pistols were banned from the mails. During the nineteenth century, arms exports seem to have been the only source of concern in Washington, and that only occasionally, as in the gun-running to Canada during its upheavals of the 1830s and to Mexico when civil strife broke out there. Such shipments were sometimes embarrassing to the government in its efforts to maintain a neutral posture. This was the case in the Franco-Prussian War and in the *Itata* incident, which involved the shipment of several thousand rifles to one of the political factions in Chile in the 1880s.[70] Even here the president did not receive standing authority to impose embargoes until 1898. Only in 1935 did neutrality legislation establish a comprehensive licensing system for munitions exports.[71]

In recent years it has been fashionable in "anti-gun" circles to lay much of the blame for the ubiquitous firearm, and for the violence in which it figures, at the door of those who made and sold it. Historically, there is little evidence to substantiate the charge. The national taste for firearms, in any event the national need for them, probably began with the Pilgrims. While the gunmaker fed that taste, and even whetted it, he dealt in a product whose utility and unexceptional nature have only recently been challenged. Early oriented toward volume production, and hence mass consumption, the industry placed a gun within the reach of every American and urged him to buy it—without any discernible qualm of conscience.

Nothing has been so revealing about the arms market as its popular nature. It has never been socially stratified, for example. In contrast, in England, the well-to-do would address themselves to one of the London gunmakers, where a gentleman would be measured for a shotgun much as he was measured for a suit; the less wealthy sportsman would have to content himself with a weapon made in Birmingham. The American product, whether revolver, automatic pistol, repeating rifle, or automatic shotgun, had as its hallmark functional efficiency. It offered accurate firepower, and plenty of it, to the proverbial man in the street. Thus, banker and bellboy would kill ducks with the same Marlin shotgun. Smith & Wesson revolvers, tucked in bureau drawers, served the defense of manor house and cold water flat. The ubiquitous gun is thus one of the more improbable indicators of the egalitarian nature of our society, and to many it is one of the most disturbing. The American firearms industry made an armed society possible. Its customers, millions of them in the past two centuries, have made it a fact of American life.

5 Firearms and the Frontier Experience: The Nineteenth Century

Be not afraid of any man,
No matter what his size;
When danger threatens, call
on me
And I will equalize.

—Inscription on a
Winchester rifle

Most American citizens entered the nineteenth century with firearms still at their sides. Men and boys carried arms into the farm fields to work. Arms were especially important for frontiersmen as they were now beginning to breach the wilderness west of the Mississippi River. Weapons were also needed as protection against the Indian danger which still existed at the outward edge of the frontier. The continued spread and use of firearms in nineteenth-century America was closely tied to the rapid expansion of the frontier. From a frontier nation of less than five million people in 1800 to an emerging world power spanning the continent in 1899, the United States matured, developed its own national character, and surged ahead of many European nations in industrial and technological improvements.

The spirit that buoyed much of this nationalistic enthusiasm for continent-taking started on a foggy morning in early January 1815 outside of New Orleans. A rough militia general from Tennessee bred in the frontier tradition had accumulated a motley army composed of riflemen, New Orleans dandies, and a few dozen pirates to challenge a landing by British troops who were veterans of the Napoleonic struggles. Through the morning fog, the British troops attacked the Americans in the proper European array of battle. When the fog and battle smoke cleared, 3,000 of the 5,000 British troops were dead or wounded. The American casualties were a mere handful.[1] A ditty called the "Hunters of Kentucky" recorded this historic event:

> But Jackson he was wide awake, and
> wasn't scared with trifles,
> For well he knew the aim we take
> With our Kentucky rifles. . . .[2]

The Battle of New Orleans confirmed Jackson as a national hero and enshrined the Kentucky rifle in the popular mind as the guarantor of the freedom of this nation.[3]

Williamson, in his history of the Winchester rifle, wrote, "Firearms, the axe, and the plow were the three cornerstones upon which the pioneer Americans built this nation. Of the three, firearms were the most dramatic and appealed most to popular imagination."[4] The nineteenth century was in many respects the age of firearms in America. They were the tools of politicians, hunters, frontiersmen, trappers, Indian fighters, Indians, outlaws, army men, women, prostitutes, and, increasingly, law enforcement agents.

The movement of the frontier west across the Mississippi River brought a continuation of the problems that had been with the pioneers since Jamestown two centuries before. They too faced the need for food, protection, and survival. Reacting to these concerns as their forefathers had, these nineteenth-century frontiersmen used a variety of firearms in their conquest of the wilderness. The great movement beyond the Mississippi River with its frontiers of ranching, mining, and farming all provided opportunities for the use of a multiplicity of firearms—from a tiny derringer in the hands of a prostitute to the thunderous Sharp's buffalo rifle used with skill by hunters. Although the basic reasons for owning weapons remained the same, an acceleration in their use resulted because of increased proficiency in firearm design and lack of law enforcement. Thus more people than ever before had access to and use of firearms. Ability with a firearm was of great importance to the frontiersmen: as one wrote, "Straight-shooting are more important than philosophy."[5]

The westward movement also brought changes in the types of weapons available. At the beginning of the century, firearms came in three basic types: a smoothbore musket or shotgun, a Kentucky-style rifle, and a single shot pistol. A hundred years later, the types and styles had multiplied many times. The major changes constituted improvements in firing potential, accuracy, loading ease, killing power, and range.[6] In a battle situation, these changes increased the "tempo . . . and complicated the service and supply."[7] As a result, civilians were better armed than the military, which had become progressively resistant to change. Army ordinance had lagged behind in adopting breechloaders, rifles, or anything that might waste too much ammunition.[8]

Weapons privately owned by army officers and most civilians were the most modern on the frontier. Though the wilderness is in a sense the most backward area of civilization, men who lived on the frontier rapidly adopted the most sophisticated firearms. By 1836, half of the firearms in Texas had a percussion ignition system. This modern weapon apparently gave the Texans a distinct advantage over the Mexicans who carried flintlocks at the Battle of San Jacinto.

Samuel Colt would have had tremendous difficulties marketing his revolver if westerners had not adopted it so rapidly and had not continuously ordered more of his new invention. A case in point is the original Paterson Colt which was only in production a short time after 1836 before the inventor ran out of money. Many of these rare revolvers were purchased for use in Texas by the Republic's navy and some found their way to New Mexico by 1838.[9] The impact of this new weapon is shown by a remark made by Indians who had an encounter with Kit Carson in 1841: "White man shoot one time with rifle and six times with butcher knife [Colt Revolver]. . . ."[10] Several decisive battles occurred in the early 1840s between Indians and Texas Rangers armed with Colts. With the Ranger victories, the fame of the Colt spread. Two Ranger leaders wrote in 1850: "We state, and with entire assurance of the fact, that your sixshooter is the arm which has rendered the name of Texas Ranger a check and terror to bands of our frontier Indians."[11] Walter P. Webb used this quotation to underscore his belief that the evolution of the six-shooter was the "first radical adaption made by the American people" to frontier conditions.[12] More importantly, the use of the Colt revolver shows that the frontiersmen were concerned about being armed with the foremost weapon of the period. So valuable were these pistols that a .44 caliber Colt Hartford Dragoon model worth $25 at the factory sold for $300 in the California gold fields.[13]

The standard Kentucky rifle did not last long in its eighteenth-century form. New percussion locks were fitted to many of these weapons. In addition, as hunters needed to kill bigger, more powerful animals at greater ranges, the bore of the rifle was increased to a larger caliber and shortened for use in dense areas. This was an understandable change since the old Kentucky style rifle did not have the stopping power to halt a charging grizzly and could not be used easily from horseback. The most famous producers of the new mountain rifle were the Hawkens brothers in St. Louis. Before the invention of repeating or breechloading rifles, mountain men employed various odd types of weapons in an attempt to have multiple shots.[14]

As soon as repeating rifles were available, the frontiersmen adopted the new varieties. Josiah Gregg, writing in the late 1830s, recorded: "The repeating arms have lately been brought into use upon the prairies and they are certainly very formidable weapons, particularly when used against an ignorant, savage foe."[15] The Colt Paterson revolving rifle was in use on the frontier at this time. Many of these early revolving rifles were as great a danger to the user as to the intended victim, yet frontiersmen willingly accepted the potential hazard in order to gain the additional firepower.

After the Civil War, when a great number of breechloading and repeating rifles became available, westerners likewise acquired them. The first of this type of rifle to appear were the breechloading Sharp's rifles, or similar types used by hunters. Next to be accepted were the repeaters with their self-contained cartridges, the Henry and the Winchester being the most famous. The enthusiastic reception given the Winchester created a rapidly expanding market for that company. Since Texas lagged behind in providing modern weapons for the Rangers, individual members used their pay to buy the new styles of Winchesters as soon as they were available. In the summer of 1876, the buffalo hunter Wright Mooar traveled to New England where he purchased the new Model 1876 Winchester and was using it on the frontier that fall. Without the westerners' favorable response to the Winchester that company would have had a difficult time surviving. The Winchester became so popular that citizens in Idaho named a town after it.[16]

Moving along with the frontier, of course, was the necessary gunsmith. In the early days of the westward movement, the gunsmiths continued to make individual arms. Fur companies employed skilled gunsmiths to accompany expeditions into the wilderness. Railroad companies also hired gunsmiths and maintained private arsenals at the head of the tracks as they were building across country. The Union Pacific maintained 1,000 rifles and trained its men to use the weapons against Indians. The company also provided its own craftsmen to repair these weapons. But as technological changes developed, the gunsmiths became repairers of the more complex modern weapons produced in eastern factories. They became salesmen for the popular brands and, at the same time, continued to make custom guns for individuals. There seems to have been a fairly quick movement of gunsmiths to the West, keeping pace with the frontier. Milwaukee had twelve gunsmiths in the 1840s, and San Francisco had even more shortly after its founding. Advertisements in the newspapers of the period indicate the volume of business carried on by these men.

Gunsmiths in the West were important members of the society, serving in elected positions in almost every major western town. They staged shooting contests for the community to advertise their commodities. Because of their speciality and involvements, they were among the first skilled craftsmen needed in the community.[17]

With tools in hand, the great westward migration was accelerated by the lure of gold in California. Thousands of settlers and dreamers moved westward. Books and travel pamphlets offered advice for travelers and contained lists of necessities. Chief among the items mentioned was a list of the types of weapons needed. Since many of these early emigrants were in need of more weapons than they had money for, the Congress passed a law in 1849 that persons moving to the territories of Oregon, California, and New Mexico could receive surplus weapons.[18] Although several senators wanted emigrants to pay the government for the weapons, Senator Thomas S. Rusk from Texas argued that "they were to travel over land to that country; and, as it was important that we should have an overland route, it was important to afford facilities and means of defense to emigrants; for, as they traveled through the unsettled parts of the country they would doubtless make valuable discoveries respecting the way thither."[19] The senators must have felt that it was less expensive for the government to provide weapons than to send armed soldiers along with the migrants. This was the first time in our history that the government provided surplus guns for civilians.

Until this time, surplus army guns had usually been presented to the Indians. The action followed the American tradition that the government attempt to arm the civilians rather than use a standing army.

With this movement westward Americans came in greater contact with Indians. Although there had been a string of Indian wars in the early part of the nineteenth century, the hostilities intensified after the Civil War. Until that time, there had been conflicts with the Shawnee Indians under Tecumseh in the War of 1812, with the Creeks in the southern United States, with the Seminoles in Florida, and with Chief Black Hawk in Illinois.

The conflict with Tecumseh demonstrated the esteem with which frontiersmen held a sharpshooter. On September 27, 1813, in Canada during the Battle of the Thames, between the Americans and a combined force of British and Indians, Tecumseh was killed. A Kentuckian named Richard M. Johnson claimed to have shot Tecumseh. Though the battle was raging at the time, making it almost impossible to determine who actually killed the chief, Johnson built a political career on this event. This fame led him to the vice-presidency in 1837, and some of his followers even tried to nominate him for the presidency in 1840.[20]

After the Civil War, the settlers and cavalry fought Indians in almost every western state and territory until the 1890s. Though the eventual subjugation of the American Indians seems now to have been a foregone conclusion, the yearly struggles with the Sioux, Cheyenne, Apache, Commanche, and host of smaller tribes kept the decision hanging in the balance for many years.[21]

The Indians had possessed some type of firearm for

several centuries.²² Until after the Civil War, Indians continued to be armed mostly with the old flintlock style muskets traded to them. The United States government adopted the policy of the other nations that had settled North America, that of trading firearms to the Indians. In the early nineteenth century, the government established the factory system of providing trading posts where Indians could exchange furs for firearms and other necessities. Eventually, twenty-four of these licensed factories were created, although no more than twelve were ever operative at any one time. In addition, the government and private trading companies signed contracts with many gunsmiths to provide an American version of the trade musket. The Indian Intercourse Act of 1834 provided the legal authority for the Indians to acquire rifles. The government also used the handout of rifles to Indians as an inducement for their removal beyond the Mississippi River. By 1840, more than 60,000 Indians had been removed from eastern lands and over half had received rifles. The government also provided gunsmiths to repair the Indians' firearms.²³

Private American merchants, too, continued to sell firearms to the Indians as it was a lucrative business. The American Fur Company sold arms to Indians for several decades of the nineteenth century. By 1818, one common musket cost an Indian ten beaver skins in trade; in current prices, this would be a profit of 500 percent.²⁴

For the first half of the century, the Indians lagged behind the frontiersmen in modern weapons. Some traders purposefully sold outdated and inferior weapons to the Indians. As late as 1875, for example, the Packer-Field Company of Oregon continued to make flintlocks for the Indian trade, even though repeating rifles were then in common use.[25] After the Civil War, however, some Indians became better armed than the soldiers. The army ordnance department provided the soldiers only with Springfield Trapdoor Rifles, the first universal issue army breechloader. This weapon was used against the Indians until the 1890s, when the army finally adopted the Krag, a repeating rifle.

The Indians, through contacts with traders and government agents, came into the possession of a fair number of "Spirit Guns," Winchester lever-action repeaters or other lesser known brands of multi-shot rifles.[26] Custer once caustically remarked that warriors were "supplied with either a breech-loading rifle or revolver, sometimes with both—the latter obtained through the wise foresight and strong love of fair play which prevails in the Indian Department."[27] At Custer's defeat in 1876, while the troops were armed with the single shot Springfield, at least 25 percent of the Indians possessed Winchesters.[28] As the historian for the Winchester Company stated, the Model 73 Winchester "killed more game and more Indians, and more U.S. soldiers when the Indians awoke to its virtues, than any other type rifle."[29]

The running battle between Indians and whites, which had dragged for centuries, reached its wintry conclusion at Wounded Knee, South Dakota, in 1891. This long conflict had resulted in both groups being armed in the frontier area. The Indians had lost much of their independence as they became increasingly dependent on whites for armament. In the end even with some modern firearms, the Indians lost their land, possessions, and families. After this conflict, the American frontiersmen lost one of their chief reasons for being armed. Yet the three centuries-long contest over possession of the

American continent, which resulted in an omnipresent frontier conflict, had an indelible impact on the creation of the armed American.

Another aspect of the movement westward was the great American game hunt. From the time of the original colonists, Americans had shot animals for food and profit. But the movement beyond the Mississippi River brought an acceleration of the great hunt. As Harold Hollingsworth wrote, "Hunting was so necessary a part of living along the frontier that it was studied and practiced almost as a skilled trade."[30]

The American male was, in fact, a skilled hunter. He hunted to augment both the family diet and his finances, or as a career. A traveler in Ohio estimated, in 1807, that a man might kill over 200 deer and eighty bears in one season. The professional hunter might kill 1,500 deer a year to obtain the skins and perhaps the better cuts of meat. To demonstrate prowess with a rifle, hunting contests were often held. East of the Mississippi River these were usually squirrel-hunting contests. In Illinois, in 1820, a writer recorded that eight men shot 300 squirrels in thirty hours. If even a small fraction of the American males killed this number of animals, it is understandable that the supply of American game rapidly decreased in the nineteenth century.[31]

Beyond the Mississippi River, millions of buffalo roamed the prairie in large herds. These magnificent animals attracted both professional hunters and gamesmen. Actually, long before the buffalo hide had become valuable, sportsmen had begun to kill them. It was fashionable for Europeans to come to the Great American West to hunt these and other large animals. Among the many European expeditions, two of the most memorable were the Sir St. George Gore party of 1854-1857 and the hunting party of the Grand Duke Alexis of Russia. The Russian party was escorted by Custer and Buffalo Bill Cody.

The Gore expedition was the more elaborate of the two. Gore spent half a million dollars to cover 7,000 miles of the American West in three years. On this expedition, he carried 100 firearms, including seventy rifles and thirty miscellaneous weapons. He bagged thousands of buffalo and other animals. On one day alone, he killed 1,000 buffalo just to see how many he could shoot. To accomplish this record, he found a buffalo herd; then he set up a tripod to support his rifles. As Gore fired one rifle, his servants handed him another loaded one, and so the killing continued all day. It is reported that the great American frontiersman Jim Bridger became thoroughly disgusted at this wanton killing.[32]

The amount of buffalo killing increased after the Civil War. It is estimated that there were at least 100 million buffalo when the white man first came into contact with them. By 1887, there were only 1,091 left. The slaughter figures are staggering; for example, in one year, 1872, one and one-half million were killed. Passengers shot away at passing herds from railroad cars. Henry Randall reported, in 1862, meeting a hunting party that had killed 1,000 buffalo just for amusement. Buffalo Bill Cody killed 4,200 in eighteen months. Cody, in a contest with Billy Comstock, to determine who was the greatest buffalo hunter, killed sixty-nine in one day and Comstock shot forty-six.[33] As the jingle went,

> Buffalo Bill, Buffalo Bill
> Never Missed and never will
> Always aims and shoots to kill
> And the company pays his buffalo bill.[34]

In the contest between Cody and Comstock, people actually paid to ride a special train to watch the sporting event.

Even after the buffalo was almost wiped out, hunters continued to kill them. Pat T. Tucker wrote in the mid-1880s: "At the first crack of the rifle I dropped the leader of the herd, a magnificent creature that had done well to preserve this last remnant of a once countless herd." Although he must have realized what he was doing, he nevertheless went out to kill one of the last buffalo. By the end of the nineteenth century, this spirit of destruction brought the virtual extermination of the passenger pigeon, trumpeter swan, condor, whooping crane, ivory-billed woodpecker, some species of duck, as well as the buffalo.[35]

The omnipresence of firearms in the nineteenth century was noted by many commentators. The writers of the *Annals of San Francisco for 1854* recorded: "It has always been a practice with a large proportion of the citizens to carry loaded firearms or deadly weapons concealed about their person, this being, as it were, a part of their ordinary dress."[36] A writer for the *Wichita Eagle* remarked in May 1874 that "Pistols are as thick as blackberries."[37] And from El Paso a man wrote, "I would as soon go out into the street without my pants as without my Colt."[38] Cowboys wore pistols to complete their full dress. As Philip A. Rollins wrote, "The gun . . . was to the mind of the cowboy as effective on the female heart, and as compelling an accompaniment of love-making as to the belief of the young soldier has ever been the sword."[39] To many men of the frontier, "God created men; Colonel Colt made them equal."[40] As Washington Irving wrote in *The Adventures of Captain Bonneville,* "With his horse and his rifle, he is independent of the World, and spurns all its restraints."[41]

The tradition of the pistol-packing westerner, prone to shoot first and question later, developed in Texas. In the early days of the Republic, the Texas Rangers were formed to protect the frontier as a mounted military force. For years they had no police power to apprehend law breakers. Because of frontier conditions, these men adopted the tradition of carrying a pistol on almost all occasions.[42] An additional impetus for pistol-carrying came in the gold rushes of the late 1840s and 1850s when men had to be constantly armed to protect themselves and their claims. The exorbitant cost of a Colt in California shows the value that early western settlers placed on that instrument.[43] According to Hinton R. Helper in 1855, "By a calculation, based upon fair estimates, I learn that since California opened her mines to the world, she has invested upwards of six million dollars in bowie-knives and pistols."[44] Although the figures may be exaggerated, this comment does indicate the volume of firearms sold in California. According to another commentator: "The multitude of people from the cotton states have introduced amongst us their views and practices in regard to the use of deadly weapons."[45] It was, however, the cowboy's adherence to the custom which developed the weapons-carrying image of the West. The Civil War, too, had produced a group of men provided with arms and willing to use them.[46]

Mounted cavalry and rangers used revolvers carried in holsters. As cowboys became more accustomed to using revolvers, the holster flaps were cut off for easier use. Many of the cowboys who moved northward with the cattle herds to the railheads after the war were ex-

Confederate soldiers encountering ex-Union soldiers as law enforcement officials. The Civil War was re-enacted on a minute scale in many of these confrontations. Many citizens were not prepared to cope with the pistol-carrying ways of the cowboys. As a result, many western cattle towns were divided into two sections, one for permanent residents and the other for the entertainment of the transient Texans.[47]

A number of individuals became famous for their prowess with a pistol. James Butler Hickok, Doc Holliday, the Earp Brothers, John Wesley Hardin, Ben Thompson, Billy the Kid, Butch Cassidy and the Wild Bunch, among others, developed such a reputation. One famed gunfighter, Clay Allison, summed up his life, when he said, "I am a shootist."[48] David Rosa sees the gunfighter as a central figure in American folklore: "The New World's counterpart of the knights in armor and the Robin Hoods of the Old. His sword was a Colt .45 and his armor the ability to outdraw and outshoot any rival."[49] Such an image has captivated generations of Americans.

In the West, firearms were synonymous with violence. The shooting escapades of Hickok, the classic battle of the O.K. Corral, and a host of lesser conflicts occurred. Despite local ordinances prohibiting the carrying of guns in many town limits, men had access to firearms. Law enforcement was uneven and varied from town to town. Well-meaning town councils hired men who were proficient as gunfighters to be the standard bearers of the law. Often these law enforcement agents scarcely operated within the law that they were, in theory, sworn to uphold.[50]

The gunfighter-sheriff was romanticized. One man described Wild Bill Hickok as "a civilizer, in the sense of a vigilance posse. . . . When Bill drew his pistol there was always one less desperado to harass the law abiding." He continued, "Wild Bill played his part in the reformation of pioneer society more effectively than any character in the annals of American history."[51] To the gunfighter alone, of all the specialists in American history, was given the omnipotent role of judge, jury, and executioner—a novel constitutional concept.[52] The American gunfighter, more fabled than factual, became the representative American of the westward movement. A symbol of complete independence and repression simultaneously, the gunfighter became a unique American hero.

The men employed as peace officers were expected to be able to outdraw and outshoot the opposition. Though glorified in thousands of accounts, the fast shooting sheriff or marshal did in fact exist. Bat Masterson, after a varied career, reminisced in 1907 that it took "courage to step out and fight to the death with a pistol." This he considered "but one of three qualities a man must possess in order to last very long in this hazardous business." He explained that the other two qualities were proficiency and deliberation, both of which dealt with the use of firearms.[53]

The very firearms used to enforce the law were also the agents for breaking that law. In 1837, a ruffian pulled a knife on a judge in a Texas courtroom, claiming that his weapon was the law. The judge in turn drew a pistol, ruling that "if that is the law of Shelby County, this is the constitution that overrules your law."[54] This approach created a situation in the United States where, instead of being governed by law, the people were governed by the force of weapons used by law enforcement agents.

The employment of firearms for legal enforcement, protection, and illegal design became nationwide in the nineteenth century. The statutory laws of the territories and states were subjugated by the most powerful force. The impact of the Colt upon law enforcement was important. Since the pace of settlement proceeded at a faster rate than did the implementation of law, the use of firearms subverted the understanding of the law and its peaceful enforcement.[55]

With opportunities abounding for rapid wealth, many men operated as outlaws. They were not the Robin Hood variety, as some writers have even tried to depict Billy the Kid, but hardened criminals who robbed and murdered.[56] Stage coaches, banks, railroads, mine offices, and individuals all were prey to a variety of outlaws. The get-rich-quick robberies were a hallmark of many of these men. Usually caught and often killed, outlaws still continued their profitable ventures.

Groups of prominent citizens responded to the lack of law enforcement in a variety of ways. On occasion, towns banded together to prevent a robbery. The Dalton brothers' famous attempted holdup of banks in Coffeyville, Kansas, ended in disaster for the brothers, as the result of corporate resistance. Vigilante groups, using lynch law for punishment, appeared across the frontier, in the form of powerful citizens taking the law into their own hands. Frontier citizens united for self-preservation and the protection of their property much as their colonial forebears had done. Members of these vigilante groups operated under the premise that, in view of the limited law enforcement, the people had a right and duty to act.[57] The individual response to law enforcement, as well as the hiring of gunfighting sheriffs, created a situation whereby justice became personal, with the people continuing to rely on their own devices. Violent methods were condoned in order to eventually bring law. Because of this acceptance, firearms and violence have been linked in the history of the frontier. Companies, individual businessmen, and politicians also employed gunfighters to secure their private interests. In the early 1870s, armed bands of men hired by the Santa Fe Railroad fought a small war for the possession of the right-of-way through the Royal Gorge in Colorado. In New Mexico, a bloody range war took place in Lincoln County.[58] Range wars involving roving bands of gunmen became an increasing problem in the 1880s and 1890s, as cattlemen fought for possession of vast quantities of grazing land. In Wyoming, raiders hired by the cattlemen killed 12,000 sheep in one night. As late as 1905, the secretary of the Crook County Sheep Shooters Association bragged that his organization killed 8,000 to 10,000 sheep per season in Oregon.[59] Political battles were also fought with firearms. In the late frontier period, disgruntled politicians joined the Populist movement. In the election of 1892, the Populists won a number of western state governments. In both Kansas and Colorado, Republicans and Populists mustered firearms to prevent the other group from taking over the governmental functions. As is obvious from these examples, as well as from records of family feuds, westerners often resorted to firearms during the developmental period.[60]

The unique position of the shooting specialist in American history has been romanticized in countless books, from the 1860s to the present. Pulp novels of the period, by such writers as Ned Buntline who gave his name to a particular long-barreled variety of Colt, detailed the exploits of many westerners in the last thirty years of the nineteenth century. Buffalo Bill Cody was the subject of more than 1,700 novels between 1869 and

1933. The exploits of such sharpshooters as Kit Carson, Jed Smith, Wild Bill Hickok, the Earps, Bat Masterson, and many more became the ongoing topic of hundreds of novels. The image created was that of good and brave men who were outstanding marksmen with any and all varieties of firearms.[61] In the towns of Abilene, Ellsworth, Wichita, Dodge City, Kansas, and Caldwell, Oklahoma, between the years 1870 and 1885, only forty-five died from gunfire. Nevertheless, the image of constant gunfighting in the West has persisted. Very few of the classic standup gun duels ever took place, yet the popular concept of the western shootout has been a continuing one.[62]

Guns figured in many of the more colorful expressions in western speech. The revolver became known as "Black-eyed Susan." Each term reflected a different use of the revolver. If a group of men barricaded an area, it was known as a "Winchester quarantine." To "lay your guns on the table" meant to be fair, but to say a man was "gun-shy" was to call him a coward. If he was an expert with his pistols, he was a "gun-shark." There is no doubt that the Americans of the frontier developed an affection for firearms unlike any attachment in our history.[63]

The use of firearms in a frontier region is understandable, given the limits of the law and the basic need for food, protection, and survival. The centuries-long struggle for possession of the continent ended with the defeat of the Indians, leaving a legacy of weapons-carrying. However, as Richard Hofstadter wrote, "When the frontier and its ramifications are given their due, they fall far short of explaining the persistence of the American gun culture."[64] When the reasons for the frontier use of firearms were past, those arms remained a fixture in American life.

Punch, 28 June 1856. Reproduced by permission of *Punch*.

Trud, 4 February 1970. Reprinted by permission.

The sign in the Russian cartoon says "unrestricted trade in firearms"; the character on the right is saying, "Let's go hunting in the asphalt jungle, Joe."

Derry, *History of the U.S.*, 1885

Frost, *Pictorial History of the U.S.*, 1846

Frost, *Pioneer Mothers of the West*, 1869

As these illustrations from nineteenth-century history books show, earlier generations accepted the gun as an essential ingredient in the preservation and triumph of American civilization.

Bryant, *Popular History of the U.S.*, 1892

Derry, *History of the U.S.*, 1885

Richardson, *Beyond the Mississippi*, 1867

Competitive shooting on the rifle range became a very popular sport in the last quarter of the nineteenth century. The international matches of 1876, illustrated above, were the object of much national interest.

A *New York World* photographer took this picture seconds after the shooting of Mayor Gaynor of New York City on August 9, 1910. The incident paved the way for the passage of New York's Sullivan Law a few months later.

The Thompson Submachine Gun
The Most Effective Portable Fire Arm In Existence

THE ideal weapon for the protection of large estates, ranches, plantations, etc. A combination machine gun and semi-automatic shoulder rifle in the form of a pistol. A compact, tremendously powerful, yet simply operated machine gun weighing only *seven* pounds and having only *thirty* parts. Full automatic, fired from the hip, 1,500 shots per minute. Semi-automatic, fitted with a stock and fired from the shoulder, 50 shots per minute. Magazines hold 50 and 100 cartridges.

THE Thompson Submachine Gun incorporates the simplicity and infallibility of a hand loaded weapon with the effectiveness of a machine gun. It is simple, safe, sturdy, and sure in action. In addition to its increasingly wide use for protection purposes by banks, industrial plants, railroads, mines, ranches, plantations, etc., it has been adopted by leading Police and Constabulary Forces, throughout the world and is unsurpassed for military purposes.

Information and prices promptly supplied on request

AUTO-ORDNANCE CORPORATION
302 Broadway *Cable address: Autordco* **New York City**

This advertisement for the Thompson Submachine Gun dates from the early 1920s. It reflects the traditional American notion that police and honest citizens could master criminality through firepower.

Courtesy of William J. Helmer

Books Reviewed Next Sunday

The New York Times

Book Review and Magazine Section

The 1920s saw the beginnings of a national anti-gun campaign. This "reward" notice, printed in *The New York Times* in
1921, was one of many circulated in the era.

6 Firearms in the Settled Area of Nineteenth-Century America

The people are arming to protect themselves, because they see from experience that the law is not strong enough to protect them.

—Sidney George Fisher
Philadelphia, 1844

In 1881 the *Los Angeles Daily Times* entertained its readers with an account of a recent criminal trial in Reno. A New Yorker, called to the stand as a witness, mentioned in his testimony that he had never carried a pistol. "A breathless silence," wrote the reporter, "spread over the faces of the spectators, as the lawyers all looked wonderingly at the witness." When the man from New York went on to confess that he had never fired a pistol, "a faint, pitying smile passed over the weather-beaten faces of the

133

audience."[1] The reportage was a humorous effort to express what many westerners must have felt (and perhaps still do)—that their countrymen in the East had sunk into a soft, if not emasculating, way of life in which the gun and other symbols of a more heroic age had no place. Logically, this should have been the case. Armed pioneers cleared the land of hostile Indians and predators. Behind them came farmers and merchants dedicated to more peaceful pursuits. But the gun did not pass with the first frontier; it remained in village and burgeoning city as well as the tranquil countryside.

In part, the nature of the American military establishment ensured its survival, since the nation's armed strength still resided principally in a militia. While its actual military capabilities were very limited, as major wars demonstrated, the institution was enshrined, along with a cult of marksmanship. Generations of school children learned the exploits of the Minute Men; historians like George Bancroft extolled them to a more sophisticated readership. At the beginning of the nineteenth century Americans were convinced that Jackson's riflemen had saved the nation at New Orleans; in 1898 they marched confidently to war against the Spanish, vowing they would "civilize 'em with a Krag." And they marched off to a national valhalla that would later welcome Sergeant Alvin York and Audie Murphy.

Shooting was a manly art useful in war and diverting in peacetime. Hunting remained the chief national sport well into the century. While the first waves of hunters had attacked predators and the more valuable fur-bearing animals, small game remained in boundless numbers, as did wildfowl. With the advent of percussion and cartridge arms, with their more instantaneous ignition, wing shooting became immensely popular. The amateur shared the field with professional hunters, who were taking 15,000 ducks a day from the Chesapeake as late as the 1870s. But the game seemed inexhaustible and the exploitation of this public bounty was little hampered by laws. Iowa's bag limit law, reputedly the nation's first, was not enacted until 1879. Wildfowl was sold in large cities with scarcely any restriction. New York did not ban the practice until the eve of World War I.[2]

Hunting stimulated its companion shooting events as American citizens in the settled areas continued to respond to the need for possession and use of firearms. With the increasing density of the population, some people found vicarious experience in the form of literature, exhibitions, and advertisements. Others seeking experience with firearms could now do so through organized activities. Shooting galleries became a standard business in many cities. For a while, a rifle range even existed under Broadway in downtown New York City. Readers thrilled to the dime novels written about heroes in the far distant West. Others attended one of the Wild West Shows headed by such men as William F. "Buffalo Bill" Cody. These events were orchestrated to show the easterners what the "real" West was like, the standard ingredients being gun fights, shooting exhibitions, Indian attacks, and buffalo hunts. The effect was spectacular. Cody even took his show to Europe.[3]

Large firearms manufacturers responded to the public acceptance of such shows by employing expert shooters to demonstrate their guns to the public. Both Remington and Winchester maintained marksmen to travel the country giving shooting exhibitions. In the 1870s, Captain A. H. Bogardus won fame and fortune as the nation's champion wing shot, holding competitions throughout the country. He once shot 5,500 glass balls in seven hours with a shotgun. Another long forgotten idol of nineteenth-century America was Dr. W. F. Carver, who spent an entire week in 1888 firing his Winchester rifle at wooden balls thrown in the air. He shot 60,000, missing only 670. Both Frank Butler and his wife Annie Oakley toured for Remington arms. Adolph and Elizabeth "Plinky" Topperwein performed the same service for Winchester. Once, Adolph shot eight hours a day for ten days firing a .22 rifle at 2 1/2″ wooden blocks. He missed only 9 out of 72,500 of these targets. Shooting contests of this type were really the first such sporting event where women received equal billing with men.

Other marksmen traveled with the Wild West shows, and still others performed on their own, making phenomenal shots and touting their weapons to the masses. For in this sort of shooting, as well as in hunting, the amateur was always welcome. The industry developed the lowly .22, with ammunition so cheap that it was within the reach of all. In the latter part of the century "youth rifles" were popular items, as was the air rifle, which began to enter the market in quantity in the 1880s.[4]

Firearms companies also used the fame of prominent individuals to endorse their products. Winchester advertised one of their models as "The Rifle That Helped Peary Reach the North Pole." Cody wrote for the same company, "I pronounce your improved Winchester, the Boss." Remington advertised that its rifles were "Fit for the Gods." And a Savage rifle made "Bad Indians Good." The imagery of these advertisements, coupled with distinguished endorsers, contributed to public awareness of the use of firearms.[5]

There was one day in the year when every American metropolis and hamlet rocked to the sound of explosions, and that day was the Fourth of July. The practice of cannon salutes and fireworks displays on occasions for public rejoicings had become popular in seventeenth-century Europe. There it was staged by the public authorities with the masses invited to look on. In America the citizens themselves took an active part in the noisemaking, and characteristically the firecracker and rocket were often replaced by items more immediately at hand. In the countryside, celebrants "shot off anvils," placing a quantity of gunpowder under them and sending them soaring into the air, accompanied by much noise and smoke. Small boys were given firecrackers and "toy" pistols that fired blanks, as adults broke out their shotguns and revolvers for the occasion and used them with a will. On July 4, 1879, Americans probably did more firing than their embattled ancestors had done at Bunker Hill. Nationwide, casualties may have been comparable. In New York City three were killed and seventeen wounded in firearms accidents. At the other end of the country, in San Francisco, the local newspaper reported that "the people celebrated in a mild, submissive, matter-of-fact way."[6] Two were fatally shot, another had his hand shattered by an exploding pistol, and four dwellings, a bakery, and a woodshed were burned down. In the South and parts of the West, Christmas and New Year's Day got the same noisy salute. The practice still lingers in southern towns to this day, police warnings notwithstanding.

By the 1870s, a movement for a more legalized "safe and sane Fourth" began in the larger cities, but at the same time a new burst of enthusiasm for guns was in evidence with the advent of the rifle match. Such contests had existed for years. The turkey shoot had been a favorite at county fairs for generations. A live turkey was staked at a distance and the marksmen would shoot. The first shooter to draw blood from the head or neck won the bird. Eventually, protests arose concerning the brutality of the sport, so targets were substituted for the turkeys.

As humane considerations came to the fore, men turned to the use of targets and trapshooting with clay pigeons. As early as 1831, competitive shooting at clay targets was taking place. Through the decades, trapshooting became more and more fashionable. By 1893, the first Grand American Handicap Trapshooting contest was held at Dexter Park, New York. Yet, even at this late date, occasionally live birds were used.[7] These events, designed in part to replace the vanishing opportunities for live hunting, were very popular.

Rifle matches also became fashionable in the 1870s. These matches originated from challenges offered by the Irish and British rifle teams. Since the Americans had always used rifles for more mundane purposes, Remington Arms undertook to fashion a special target rifle. The range used for these matches was at Creedmoor on Long Island which was developed by the newly formed National Rifle Association. With a Creedmoor-style rifle, the American marksmen successfully defeated the Irish rifle team in the mid-1870s. In 1877, an American team defeated a British team using Sharp's rifles at 1,000 yards. These matches took on a nationalistic fervor as marksmen from various countries vied for the match championship. Another type of match was the Schuetzen which consisted of the marksmen shooting at targets at ranges up to 200 yards.[8]

Parallel with the holding of international competitions was the development of organizations designed to promote shooting. Chief among these groups was the National Rifle Association. This group was formed in

1871 at the instigation of Colonel William C. Church, editor of the *Army and Navy Journal*, and George W. Wingate, an officer in the New York National Guard. This new organization sponsored numerous shooting contests.[9]

Rifle matches sparked an awakening to the challenge of target shooting. In many states, organizations like the Massachusetts Rifle Association were formed. By the 1880s, even as far west as Denver, many such clubs were created. Match shooting, using pistols, shotguns, and rifles, caught on across America. Telegraph matches were even held with contestants shooting in different parts of the country, the results being exchanged by message. Ironically, the National Rifle Association went into eclipse in the mid 1880s because the State of New York withdrew its support and spectator interest in the long range shooting matches declined, now moving toward the more spectacular trap shooting.[10] The continuing local formation of clubs, the holding of exhibition shooting matches, the challenges of target shooting, and the use of National Guard units in the Spanish-American War contributed to the continuing awareness of firearms in American society at the end of the nineteenth century.

In June 1900, Albert S. Jones, an officer in the New Jersey National Guard and secretary of the New Jersey Rifle Association, with the support of governor of New York Theodore Roosevelt and others, sent out an invitation to groups and individuals to form an association to support American marksmen. At the formation meeting in September 1900, Wingate, who had served as the president of the moribund NRA, suggested that his organization become the instrument to implement Jones' ideas. The NRA took a new lease on life.[11] This group was aided considerably in its goal of promoting marksmanship by Congressman Frank Mondell of Wyoming, who introduced a bill in Congress during the 1902 session to create the National Board for the Promotion of Rifle Practice. The act was passed in 1903. At the board's first meeting it recommended that federal facilities be opened to civilians for rifle practice. In 1905, Public Law 149 was passed by Congress, authorizing the sale of surplus arms and ammunition to rifle clubs. The NRA became the chief organ of these sales to its constituent clubs.[12]

In 1908, the NRA moved its headquarters to Washington, D. C. Its national president, James A. Drain, then campaigned to attract public support and create additional rifle clubs. Among the supporters whom he interested in the NRA were President Roosevelt and Secretary of State Elihu Root.[13] Root believed "that the young men of America shall know how to shoot straight is one of the fundamental requirements of our scheme of national defense."[14]

In that same year the NRA organized the first American Olympic team which won the gold medal. Roosevelt continued his support by recommending to Congress that it appropriate money to establish ranges in public schools. With the organizational and public stimulus, target shooting was becoming a year-round sport. International competitions were won by American teams on several continents.

With the coming of war in Europe, preparedness and marksmanship became almost synonymous. Groups formed around the country pressing preparedness for the eventuality of war. Corporations created their own rifle clubs. The National Defense Act of 1916 provided for $300,000 to be used for the promotion of civilian marksmanship. Rifle practice had become an integral part of the preparedness campaign prior to America's entry into World War I.[15]

As the population was urbanized and areas for unrestricted use of rifles became congested, the cult of marksmanship survived. As the United States emerged as a world power, programs for civilian target shooting became part of the national defense system, as was reflected in Root's opinion. Some people, nevertheless, protested federal promotion of marksmanship. Even the National Council of the newly organized Boy Scouts of America split over whether to have a Marksmanship Merit Badge. In the end, it was included, at the cost of losing some long-time supporters.[16] The march to preparedness prior to World War I is important when we consider the influence of firearms.

It was the East rather than the West that showed the greatest interest in the marksmanship programs. And it was also the East that adapted the firearm to another and more sinister use of the gun—the duel. The custom had originated in Europe, having flowered in the Renaissance along with less debatable art forms. By the seventeenth century it had become a fad among the gentility and those who aspired to that state. While it appeared in many parts of this country, it did not thrive in a society of merchants and tradesmen. Its most dedicated practitioners were army and navy officers, by profession followers of a quasi-chivalrous code, and southerners, who embraced it most enthusiastically and clung to it longest. Like most European institutions, dueling suffered something of a sea change in its transfer to the New World.[17] In the Old World it had been a badge of gentility; in America it became an affirmation of manhood. John Hope Franklin has written that in mid-nineteenth-century Mississippi "a man seldom attained high political position if he had not demonstrated his manhood in some bloody affray."[18] Planters and lawyers indulged, as did newspaper editors, saloon-keepers, and boatmen. The punctilious etiquette of the code *duello* gave way to "shoot on sight." The firearm, rather than the aristocratic *arme blanche*, became the preferred weapon. A less sophisticated clientele substituted for the dueling pistol such armaments as Colt's revolvers, army rifles, double barrel shotguns, and "Deringer pistols across the dining room table."

To be sure, dueling was never more than an outlet for a minority of the population. Although a few duels took place in America prior to 1770, most of them came after that date and through the 1880s. It was such an accepted practice that most states did not enact laws prohibiting dueling until the mid-nineteenth century. In fact, dueling was not outlawed in the District of Columbia until 1838.[19] Many of our major political figures fought duels and some died. Sam Houston of Tennessee, future president of the Republic of Texas, engaged in dueling. Alexander Hamilton died at the hands of the vice president of the United States, Aaron Burr. This duel had its origin as a long political battle between the two men.[20] After Hamilton's death the Reverend Lynn Beecher preached: "Dueling is a great national sin. With the exception of a small section of the Union [New England] the whole land is defiled with blood."[21]

In the nineteenth century, dueling did localize, to an extent, in the South. Andrew Jackson personified the dueling politician in the southern United States. Duels and politics became so integrated that many politicians had to fight to be accepted. Once, the loser in a congressional election challenged the winner; the result was repeated with the loser being killed.[22] A political writer noted in 1830: "Many young Democrats, ardent supporters of the administration, were known to be prompt with a pistol, and it was understood that a call to the field would follow any damaging personal attack upon distinguished members of the predominant party."[23]

The cult of dueling became so prevalent that Governor John L. Wilson of South Carolina published a pamphlet on the ritual in 1838. The pamphlet, called the *Code of Honor*, was reprinted many times until 1858.[24] Men purchased specially made firearms to fight duels. Dueling grounds became popular tourist attractions. One such place was "The Oaks" in New Orleans, where dueling masters taught men the fine art of using a dueling pistol.[25] The Bladensburg grounds outside of Washington, D. C., was also the scene for many encounters. As one commentator remarked, "It was the court of last resort, in which weighty points of etiquette, social and political problems and questions of veracity, propriety, and right were expounded by the convincing power of gunpowder." More than 100 men died there.[26] In Charleston, South Carolina, a dueling society was founded, composed of men who had fought successfully on the "field of Honor." The officers were chosen by the number of men they had killed. Ironically, this society existed only until the president died in a duel.[27]

As the number of duels increased, public controversy over the practice developed. Some, like Louis T. Wigfall, a senator from Texas, thought that dueling improved the society. Dueling, he said "engendered courtesy of speech and demeanor—had a most restraining tendency on the errant fancy, and as a preservative of the domestic relations was without an equal."[28] Another writer found "virtue in American duels that they always mean real business, and are not those caricatures of a barbarous custom which, in nine cases out of ten, serve to appease the wounded honor of England."[29] An English writer, in 1841, interpreted American dueling differently. J. G. Milligan wrote:

> Duels in America [are] in general marked with a character of reckless ferocity, that clearly shows the very slow progress of civilization in that rising country. . . .
>
> That duels should be frequent in a new settlement is naturally to be expected, more especially when the settlers are rude and uneducated . . . and the difficulty of having recourse to legal and competent judicial authorities . . . must induce them to take the law into their own hands.[30]

To the Americans, who fervently espoused the cause of the duel, being labeled as rude and uneducated must have been irritating. Yet Milligan correctly expressed the reason for many of these duels. Dueling was a manifestation of a developing society and so it was natural that men resorted to it rather than the legal means of securing a redress of grievance. Moreover, with the prevalence of firearms, there was a ready tool for such an encounter. Legally, dueling became more and more a subject of legislative restraint after the mid-nineteenth century. Most of the states enacted laws against the practice. The New South, striving to adopt the ethic of the industrial age, sought to put such things behind it. Some men continued the practice in spite of the restrictions. When dueling finally died, it was more from natural than legal causes. Social pressure, coupled with cultural change, left dueling without its prior esteem. Yet the cult of dueling for the sake of honor was a unique phase of the impact of firearms on America. In earlier times such personal settlings of accounts had occurred in the absence of law. The *code duello* produced a reversion, offering a socially acceptable alternative to an established framework of civil and criminal justice. If the social utility of the dueling pistol was open to question in nineteenth-century America, that of the gun generically was not. Here most likely lies the basic reason why it lingered in American society. For most Americans it was an instrument for the preservation of order; for the disaffected it was the accepted means for challenging that order. In short, it was a method for the resolution of conflicts, whether those conflicts involved urban mobs, routine criminality, or grave political issues. While it is tempting to trace this attitude to an earlier and more turbulent frontier experience, there is considerable evidence that here, as with dueling, settled America forged its own traditions. In the third and fourth decades of the nineteenth century, for example, American cities experienced a tremendous growth which broke down many of the traditional ties of community association. In place of the small, somewhat cohesive, urban area of the late eighteenth century came the large metropolis divided into different ethnic, racial, economic, social, and political groups. The result was sporadic turbulence that disrupted most of the large cities during the century. Furthermore, with the accumulation of wealth in progressively denser populations, crime became commonplace in the urban centers. In an era of turbulence and crime waves the city discovered the gun.[31] One indicator of this discovery is the escalating armament of the urban mob. At the time of the American Revolution, it had followed the modes of European rioters; by Jacksonian times a change had taken place. While the causes for urban unrest were various, the gun had become a means of its expression.

John Schneider cites numerous cases of urban violence in the decades before the Civil War. In Saint Louis in 1854, the rioting was accompanied by a "run" on gun stores. In the Cincinnati race riots of 1841, both blacks and whites were heavily armed and engaged in a pitched battle. The whites finally put their foes to flight, but only after bringing up a six-pounder cannon.[32] Contemporaries noticed what seemed a new and dangerous phenomenon. A witness to the Philadelphia riot of 1844 noted: "These are strange things for Philadelphia. We have never had anything like it before, but now that firearms have been once used and become familiar to the minds of the mob, we may expect to see them employed on all occasions, and our riots in the future will assume a more dangerous character."[33]

If the mob did not have guns, it now strove to get them. Thus, the New York rioters of 1863 stormed an arsenal, as did the strikers in Pittsburgh in 1877. The Pittsburgh disorders were part of a wave of labor violence in which resort to firearms was a common theme. In Chicago, for example, rioters moved through the streets shouting "we want arms" and sacking hardware and gun stores to fill their needs.[34]

Rioters were not the only element which took to guns in their confrontation with the existing order. In the rising sectional controversy the gun was interjected notably in the struggle over Kansas. Paramilitary groups mustered on both sides.[35] Men such as Henry Ward Beecher, who opposed slavery on both moral and religious grounds, did not balk at using the ultimate weapons to combat it. He once observed that there was more "moral suasion" in a Sharp's rifle than in the

Bible.[36] Far less idealistic was the nation's criminal element, but it was no less well armed. The urban criminal discovered the pistol and adopted it. While there are no reliable statistics available, the criminal use of firearms, particularly revolvers, was increasingly mentioned in newspapers in the two decades before the Civil War. Street gangs made revolvers part of their equipment. New York's infamous "Dead Rabbits" were carrying them by the 1850s.

These various threats were met through the arming of the "honest" citizens, enemies alike to riot, banditry, and radical social reform. In the 1820s armed teamsters were used to preserve order in Boston. Citizen posses patrolled the streets of Philadelphia in the wake of the 1844 disorders.[37] Each outbreak of crime or violence tended to put the friends of order under arms, as society reacted instinctively and directly to threats against it. In the wake of the Chicago riots of 1877, the *Tribune* reported that "every man who could beg, buy, or borrow a revolver carried it," with total disregard to the local ordinance against concealed weapons.[38]

If sudden outbreaks spurred mass arming for the moment, there is evidence of a steady increase in the general tendency to go armed. The phenomenon was noted in Philadelphia in the 1830s. Judge George C. Holt of New York, who was something of an authority on the practice, insisted that in his city the custom appeared with the revolver.[39] The pistol had not been a major item of production in early America but by the 1850s it was making the fortune of a number of enterprising manufacturers. Over the years it was reduced in bulk and became easier to carry concealed. The pocket pistol became a popular item, with none more diminutive and deadly than those of Henry Deringer. On his death in

1868, an obituary notice saluted him for having created a "Lar of Safety" which had carried his name "into every section of this continent and every country of Europe."[40] The derringer and other small pistols were of little use on the most primitive frontier. They lacked both accuracy and power for dealing with such enemies as Indians and wolves. The pocket pistol was essentially the weapon of a more civilized and urban community, where danger came in close quarters and was part of the society itself.

The general tendency to keep arms or carry them on the person may well be linked to what has been called the "urban explosion" that transformed American cities in the period 1820-1860. Its mechanism of everyday law enforcement did not keep pace with its growth, so that the inhabitant felt an increased need to fend for himself in this regard. The sense of personal insecurity in the face of crime probably did more to foster the trend toward personal armament than anything else, with sporadic outbreaks of mass violence accelerating the process from time to time. True to the stern Protestant ethic, most Americans of a century ago regarded the criminal not as a victim of social injustice, but the spawn of idleness, dissolute propensities, and "foreign" antecedents. The thug, the ruffian, was an easily definable and clearly identifiable enemy, who in mid-century cartoons sported vaguely Irish features. The author of a guidebook to New York described the "New York rough" as one might portray the denizen of a zoo: "He is usually of foreign parentage, though born in America, and in personal appearance is as near like a huge English bulldog as it is possible for a human being to resemble a brute."[41]

Thus, by mid-century the battle-lines between society and criminality seemed clearly drawn, with the gun serving the needs of both. Paradoxically, the only forces in this confrontation who were denied arms were the police themselves. The very notion of a large, uniformed, and well-armed police was held to be an affront to the public and an instrument of potential tyranny. This view was shared by many Englishmen in the first half of the nineteenth century; Sir Robert Peel made his police as innocuous as possible for this very reason. It may well be that Americans were slow to perfect police systems for still another reason. It was more economical to leave public order largely to the public, just as it was cheaper to confide the national defense to the militia; in both cases the expense of large professional forces could be avoided. What police there were in the nineteenth century were purely local, and, often, the tool of a political faction or courthouse ring. As such the policeman was more tolerated than venerated.

Most of the concepts of police organization and their eventual arming started during this period. Before that time, the function of the law officer had not evolved into its rather complex role. During the early part of the century, as a holdover from the colonial period, police officials in cities like Boston or New York had only limited functions. Mirroring the English system, there were high constables, constables, marshals, watchmen, and a sheriff. Most of the work was done at night. In Boston the watch was considered a civic responsibility which men of the city performed on a rotating assignment. Their duties ranged from enforcing sanitation laws to serving warrants. At that time the night watch had not yet developed into the investigatory agency designed to capture criminals.[42]

In the 1830s, New York and Boston organized their police forces, as the old concept of a night watch became outdated. A day force was added and administrative departments were developed to manage the police. Still there was no true sense of professionalism. Political shifts in city governments caused disruption in the police departments. In some cities, the chief was elected. The men who served on the force did not wear uniforms, were not trained, and did not carry weapons. Only a badge served to identify their role in society. These early police departments do not seem to have been very efficient, nor did they inspire confidence among the citizenry.[43] As a result, the citizens continued to rely on their own devices for protection.

Police brutality, an old charge in American history, was held to be much less likely if the police were not armed. So it was not until the 1850s that the police began to carry pistols unofficially when some of their members were shot by criminals.[44] Baltimore officials authorized the use of firearms "in emergencies" in 1857. When, in 1858, a New York policeman shot a fleeing suspect, *The New York Times* editor strongly questioned the use of firearms by the police. According to editorial comment, if a policeman needed to defend his life, the use of force was permissible, but if he was chasing a suspect, he had no right to shoot the man. A policeman either had to be swift enough to catch the suspect or justice lost.[45] Because other individuals questioned the advisability of arming the police, they were not armed officially until after the Civil War.

By the Civil War, eight cities had formally organized police departments. The rioting during the war and continued criminal activity stimulated the final arming of the police. After the war, the New Orleans police were authorized to carry Winchesters and revolvers. Nashville supplied its force with official revolvers in 1871. In the

1880s, Philadelphia police were authorized to carry pistols on night duty while at the same time Boston started to purchase weapons for its men. New York finally issued them in the 1890s.[46]

This arming, though questioned for decades, brought significant changes in police procedures in the United States. While the history of the American police is still imperfectly known, three things seem clear. First, the police themselves did not "escalate" the arms race between society and lawbreakers—a fact that should be borne in mind by those who argue that the disarming of the police should be the first step in reducing the tempo of violence. Secondly, for better or worse, law enforcement continued to rely on active citizen participation—to the point that the policeman sometimes seemed the auxiliary in the battle, and the "man in the street" the principal. And finally, the arming of the police stimulated the acceptance in the East of the doctrine that had been developed in the West: law enforcement agencies were to enforce the law with the power of firearms.

To these patterns of weapons use, well set by 1860, must be added the experience of the Civil War. While the northern cities were becoming accustomed to the use of firearms in the urban areas, the South, which was predominantly rural through much of the nineteenth century, continued to be the scene of extensive weaponry. In addition to their use for hunting, another contributing factor was the two-century-old conflict over the use of firearms by blacks and the corresponding fear of slave insurrections which kept southerners constantly armed. Visitors to southern cities like Charleston remarked that at night the town resembled an armed military camp with soldiers mounting guard. Further, police forces in the cities and the patrol in the rural areas were designed to cope with any riotous behavior by blacks.[47] Southern legislatures even passed laws restricting the use of firearms by freed blacks. According to a North Carolina Supreme Court decision in 1844, this type of law did not violate the Second Amendment.[48]

During the antebellum period, across the South militia groups were assembling and drilling. The southern states were always more martial than their northern counterparts, according to John Hope Franklin. The militia groups that assembled in the South had a multiplicity of services. In many areas, they provided much of the social life of the community. They were also responsible for the continuing control of slaves and the capture of runaways. Because of the martial air in the South, southerners through the 1840s had been more expansionistic in terms of acquiring Mexico, and some even participated in filibustering expeditions in Central America. Associated with this feeling came the concepts of southern chivalry and the gallantry of armed conflict.[49] Manifestations of this feeling were found, as we have seen, in the strong adherence by southerners to the forms and principles of dueling. Associated with this martial spirit was, as Augustus Baldwin Longstreet wrote, "the Southerner's attachment to fighting weapons for pleasure and for business."[50]

Firearms, important in the urban centers of the North and the rural sections of the South, played a central role in the struggle that resulted in the American Civil War. This most cataclysmic upheaval of the century did little to alter those patterns; if anything it probably confirmed them. Though the causes of the Civil War were many, the situation was aggravated by the presence of men armed with the force necessary to ignite conflict. It has recently been interpreted as a crisis in law and order. If indeed this was the case, the forces of law and order, i.e., the victors, were confirmed in the view that state and society could be maintained by sheer superiority of firepower. For its part, the South did employ the principles of the federal Second Amendment. Armed citizens of a state, failing all other avenues of redress, resorted to open battle. It is a moot question whether all other solutions had been attempted. The United States embarked on a four-year struggle to determine the nature of the union.[51]

Whatever war-weariness and revulsion against slaughter the conflict engendered, no opprobrium was transferred to the gun itself. The postwar era saw no efforts at personal disarmament, no wave of laws against guns and their use. In practical terms the war had just the opposite effect. It trained millions of men in the use of weapons. The arms production had been voluminous, those same weapons being dumped on the civilian market without a whisper of protest, save from firearms manufacturers. Men were accustomed to the possession and use of firearms. In fact, in the surrender terms given by U. S. Grant to Robert E. Lee, the right of the southerners to keep their sidearms was granted. Actually, there was no general disarming of Confederates after the war.[52]

The conclusion of the Civil War brought other changes: freed black men could now possess firearms. According to contemporary commentators, it became fashionable to carry pistols.[53] Allen Trelease described the situation: "some Negro men began carrying guns. White men did this too, more and more frequently. It became so common that young men of both races felt undressed without a pistol stuck into their belts or hip pocket." The South, he continued, began to resemble the West in terms of the lack of law enforcement, the carrying of firearms, and the roving bands of outlaws.[54] A witness before a Senate investigating committee reported: "It is the greatest place on the face of the earth for pistols. No man is comfortable down there unless he has got his pistols."[55] The use of firearms by blacks took on social and political implications. Some southern legislatures enacting Black Codes prohibited blacks from possessing firearms. Kansas adopted a different viewpoint by trying to forbid ex-Confederate soldiers from possessing them.[56]

With the southern states under presidential reconstruction seeking to impose restrictions on the blacks, the Congress moved in a series of acts to thwart these plans and imposed their own form of reconstruction. One phase of the period of congressional reconstruction is of particular interest in terms of the use of firearms. Under presidential reconstruction, the southerners had restricted militia membership to whites. Therefore, in an Army Appropriation Act passed on March 2, 1867, the Congress disbanded the entire southern militia. Though President Andrew Johnson believed the act unconstitutional since it abolished state militias, he signed it into law. In effect, Congress, virtually unchallenged, succeeded in destroying the state militias in the South. This constituted one of the most unusual events in the history of the Second Amendment.[57]

Late in 1869, as congressional reconstruction progressed, the power was restored to create militias in various southern states. For the next few years, the southern militias were predominantly black and were used to support the Radical Reconstruction governments in the South. As these governments were gradually put back into the hands of southern Democrats, armed conflicts erupted in many states. The black militias supported the Radical governors and bands of armed white men backed the Democratic candidates. In Arkansas, Louisiana, Texas, North Carolina, and South Carolina, armed conflicts occurred as elections were held. For example, in South Carolina, the Democratic Clubs were armed with all types of firearms.[58]

Firearms in the Reconstruction South provided a means of political power for many. They were the symbols of the new freedom for blacks, as well as a tool of suppression for whites seeking to reestablish the old order. In the end, white southerners triumphed and the blacks were effectually disarmed.

In a sense, the Civil War and Reconstruction created the conditions for the next three decades, which probably saw a more widespread dissemination of arms among the populace in general than at any time before or since. Their use was greatly extended through new applications, as a highly efficient industry provided an arm for every need. The briefest glance at catalogues from the era reveals pocket pistols, house pistols, muff pistols for the ladies, and a whole gamut of diminutive weapons for the nation's youth. There was the cane gun, particularly useful against rabid dogs and aggressive tramps. Alarm guns were offered to householders; attached to doors and windows, they fired a warning shot to announce the intrusion of a burglar.[59] Nor did American ingenuity stop here. One inventor designed a firearm concealed in a pocket watch:

> The object of my invention is to provide a pistol that can be carried in the vest pocket like a watch, is as readily accessible, and appears like a watch, whereby

it may be presented and fired at a highwayman while apparently merely obeying his command to "hand over your watch and be quick about it."[60]

The firearm was also adapted to the protection of property, in the form of the set gun or trap gun. This device, marketed into the 1880s, was fired by the tripping of a cord, thus serving as a mechanical sentinel, "protecting orchards and vineyards from the depradations of criminals and thieves."[61] It was even used to protect cemeteries from grave robbers. Though the set gun had been outlawed in England in 1827, it lingered in America long afterward. As late as the 1880s some New York shopkeepers used the device to protect their premises, though journalists condemned the practice as "immoral and inconsistent with the humane principles of the laws."[62]

At about the same time, the advent of the "suicide special" removed the last modest economic restraints to pistol ownership. These cheap pistols, produced in incredible quantities into the 1890s, offered firepower for the price of a man's shirt. Their chief function, according to their historian, was to "provide a gun-toting era with concealable armament at the least possible cost."[63] Small boys won them by selling salves and ointments. They were prizes at carnivals and fairs. "If a man bought a new wagon, he would get a revolver to keep under the seat." In 1879 a religious weekly offered a revolver as a premium to its subscribers. The editors received only four letters of protest. Of the orders that flowed in, five out of seven came from clergymen.[64]

The habit of going armed was now a recognized custom in the civilized East. Tailors supplied men's trousers with a "revolver pocket" placed on the right hip, whether it was to be used for that purpose or not. Americans going to Europe were cautioned about difficulties they might have if they took their pistols with them. It is doubtful if anything more than a small minority of Americans went constantly armed. It was estimated in 1877 that one Chicagoan in ten would be found with a pistol concealed on his person.[65]

But those who declined to carry a pistol acted from choice, for the option was theirs. There was no major outcry against the practice in America's cities until the end of the century. Writing in 1875, the anonymous author of a guide to the purchase and use of pistols hardly dealt with a controversial subject. He called the pistol a superlative instrument for self-defense, since it "renders mere physical strength of no account, and enables the weak and delicate to successfully resist the attacks of the strong and brutal." The author did recommend that such weapons be kept out of the hands of children and imbeciles, and felt they should not be carried by "nervous and excitable persons." As for keeping a pistol handy in the house, "there can be no objections to it on moral or prudential grounds."[66] The sheer utility of guns in the right hands scarcely needed demonstration; they were the best answer to guns in the wrong hands. An authority on New York's underworld, writing in the same decade, complained that day and night "rum crazed ruffians reel through the street heavily armed." Yet he felt that "it may be interfering with personal liberty to a dangerous extent, to make the mere carrying of any deadly weapon a felony."[67]

With the widespread use of firearms in the settled areas during the nineteenth century, some controls were sought. The New Orleans sheriff remarked in 1861 that "the city was a 'perfect hell upon earth, and that nothing would ever put an end to the murders, manslaughters, and deadly assaults, till it was made penal to carry arms.' "[68] As a result of such demands, two major legal controversies developed concerning the use of firearms. These disputes involved the right of self-defense versus limitations upon the carrying and use of firearms. The conflict was stimulated by William Blackstone's commentaries on the right of self-defense endorsed in the popular mind by the Second Amendment, as opposed to a rising tide of state laws and local ordinances prescribing the carrying of weapons concealed on an individual.[69] Laws concerning firearms dealt only with disapproval of concealed weapons that were considered unethical and the use by people considered to be outside the mainstream of society.

Blackstone wrote, "it is lawful for him to repel force by force; and the breach of the peace which happens is chargeable upon him only who began the affray."[70] To countless Americans, this statement became the watchword for a self-defense plea against a murder charge. In fact, Blackstone's comments were embodied theoretically in various American laws. The ordinances of the Northwest Territory contained this clause:

> That nothing herein contained shall be deemed or construed to extend to person lawfully using firearms as offensive or defensive weapons, in annoying, or opposing a common enemy, or defending his or her person or property, or the person or property of any other, against the invasion or depredations of any enemy, or in support of the laws of government; or against the attacks of rebels, highwaymen, robbers, thieves, or others unlawfully assailing him or her, or in any other manner, where

such opposition, defence or resistance is allowed by the law of the land.[71]

What had been a product of popular evolution now found its position in the law. Man by law and Blackstone's commentaries could defend himself. To many, this justified the possession and bearing of arms. In the popular mind this concept became the true meaning of the Second Amendment.

Even as Blackstone was being used in the courts to justify self-defense, states were beginning to write laws prohibiting, in some instances, the carrying of weapons and more often the carrying of concealed weapons. The major writer on this subject is Phillip Jordan who has noted that "Americans developed a strong legal aversion to concealed weapons."[72] To many, it was unsportsmanlike to conceal a pistol. Because of this deep-seated belief, state legislatures responded to the problem.

As Jordan points out, the laws were inconsistent from state to state. Some laws prohibited persons from riding in public with weapons "to the terror of the people" or carrying them "privately." A Louisiana law allowed peace officers to search people "whom they suspected of doing so." By the end of the nineteenth century, Oklahoma prohibited concealment "on a person, on a saddle, or in saddle bags." Further, weapons could not be carried openly unless one was hunting, taking the weapon for repair, or going to or from a militia muster. Firearms could not be given to minors, and peace officers could only wear them while on duty.[73] Many cities and towns passed similar laws, and, of course, there was a difference between laws passed and those enforced. Jordan has stated:

Three dynamic, viable factors thwarted the law. First, men liked weapons, wanted weapons, enjoyed the power that weapons lent them, and insisted on having and using and carrying and handling them as they please. Second, a good many gentlemen of one kind or another—some jurist and some vagrants were disciples of a religion known as the "higher law." Third, personal weapons, upon occasion, were urgently needed for self-defense.[74]

For these reasons laws involving the regulation of concealed weaponry were difficult to enforce. E. Merton Coulter explains: "Carrying concealed weapons which had long been considered a Southerner's privilege, continued to be stoutly defended against legal regulation. A Georgian maintained that more lives were saved than lost by carrying pistols."[75] Despite resistance to such laws, state governments did assert the right to regulate the carrying and use of firearms.

With a developing conflict between the laws governing the carrying and use of weapons and the popular belief that these rights were protected by the Second Amendment and individual state provisions, state court cases were held to determine the meaning of the laws. The earliest case that challenged a concealed weapons law was the unusual situation in Kentucky, *Bliss* v. *Commonwealth.* A Kentuckian was arrested, tried, convicted, and fined for carrying a sword-cane. He appealed the decision as a violation of his rights under the Kentucky constitution. The justices upheld his contention, thus reversing the lower court. They ruled that "if, therefore, the act in question imposes *any* restraint upon the right, immaterial what appellation may be given to the act, whether it be an act regulating the manner of bearing arms of any other, the consequence, in reference to the Constitution, is precisely the same, and its collision with that instrument equally obvious."[76] This is the most striking example of a concealed weapons law being overturned for violating the state constitutional guarantees of the right to bear arms. Kentucky later changed the state constitution to prohibit concealed weapons.

Other state courts took a more modified view by upholding the state police power concept to regulate the carrying and use of firearms. The Georgia Supreme Court in 1846 ruled that a law prohibiting concealed weapons was permissible under state police powers. If the law destroyed the right completely, it was void. The justices wrote: "A law cannot deprive the citizen of his natural right of self-defense or of his constitutional right to keep and bear arms."[77] The Tennessee and Alabama Supreme Courts made similar rulings in the 1830s and 1840s. The Alabama justices commented:

A Statute, which, under pretence of *regulating* the manner of bearing arms, amounts to a destruction of the right, or which requires arms to be so borne as to render them wholly useless for the purpose of defence, would be clearly unconstitutional. But a law which is intended merely to promote personal security, and to put down lawless aggression and violence, and to that end inhibits the wearing of certain weapons in such a manner as is calculated to exert an unhappy influence upon the moral feelings of the wearer, by making him less regardfull of the personal security of others, does not come in collision with the constitution.[78]

Later court rulings of the nineteenth century dealt

more precisely with the military aspects of the right to bear arms. In the early 1870s, William English, a Texan, was arrested, tried, and convicted of carrying a concealed broken, unloaded pistol. The Texas Supreme Court ruled that the only protection of the right to keep and bear arms was in a military sense. This decision was later supported by the West Virginia Supreme Court in 1891.[79] The courts usually walked the tightrope between outright restraints on the possession of guns and the interpreted constitutional limitations on such restrictions. Yet the precedents were inconclusive, and the laws and local ordinances on carrying concealed weapons tended to have only sporadic enforcement. By the end of the nineteenth century, legal control of the mass use of firearms had never been employed in a consistent manner.[80]

As the nineteenth century drew to a close, American firearms legislation was still confined to state and local enactments chiefly directed at the carrying of concealed weapons—enactments that for the most part seem to have been indifferently enforced. These modest beginnings may be compared to a renewed interest in firearms legislation that was developing in Europe at about the same time. In the 1880s there was considerable talk in England of the need for new legislation on the carrying of deadly weapons. In 1889 the British government solicited from its diplomatic representatives information on the practices of various other governments. These reports are a valuable index to the European approaches to the question. They indicate a considerable range of attitudes. In Scandinavia, for example, there were scarcely any laws on the use of firearms. In Montenegro every male carried a large revolver in his belt. Not surprisingly, in many countries the right to bear arms was still linked to the right to hunt. But in many cases there was already a clear effort to discourage the use of weapons by vagrants, minors, mental defectives, and habitual criminals. In the more industrially advanced nations, serious social antagonisms dictated still further regulations. In Bismarckian Germany the threat of socialist movements led to a considerable extension of police power in 1879. The authorities were empowered to ban even the possession of firearms for a period of up to a year in areas of unrest and civil strife. The Belgian government had added restrictions on weapons use after a series of labor disorders in the mining industry. The Dutch government was studying similar proposals. In England important new restrictions were added in the Pistol Act of 1903. These laws, national in scope and for the most part resting on solid precedent, were the work of governments of differing ideologies. More than anything else, they represent a common approach to the problems of crime, violence, and sedition in the increasingly complex society of the industrial age.[81]

Yet, the American reaction to these problems was more an individual approach. An armed society was the nineteenth century's legacy to the twentieth. Before the nineteenth century, Americans had armed themselves as a protection against common enemies and for food. But in the development of American society the enemy became internal. Society felt threatened by criminals, ethnic groups, racial groups, rioters, and malcontents. Political faction was pitted against political faction, race against race, the law versus the outlaw—and so the pairing continued. Violence became more closely associated with the use of firearms. Pistols were used to uphold the law or to break it. Politicians waved guns on the floor of congress, the police shot fleeing suspects, grandmothers rigged trap guns, and criminals shot their victims. With the use of firearms so varied, the Americans of the nineteenth century became armed individuals as a reaction to the increasing diversity and complexity of their society.

7 The Beginnings of Controversy: The Sullivan Law

This is a bill against murder.

—Timothy D. Sullivan in the New York State Senate, 1911

The gun came to America with the Pilgrims but the "gun problem," as anything more than a minor social irritant, appeared only with the twentieth century. The burgeoning concern over firearms and their role in American life which began around 1900 was undoubtedly part of the new national consciousness of the Progressive Era. Novelists, social critics, and a new generation of political leaders brought the nation to take a fresh and often unflattering look at its way of life. Cities discovered their slums, and with them a new understanding of the "dangerous classes." Muckraking journalists flayed trusts, lobbies, and courthouse rings. The corner saloon and the neighborhood brothel found themselves the objects of swelling indignation. Much that had been unthinkingly accepted now became intolerable—and the object of legislation unprecedented in its social thrust.

Laws barred children from work in mills and factories and threatened the drayman who abused his horse.

The new awareness of old problems made inroads on many American habits, among them the use of firearms. Much of the early agitation touched the practice only tangentially. This was the case with the humane movement, led by Henry Bergh and his Society for the Prevention of Cruelty to Animals, founded in 1866. This group mounted a lively and eventually successful campaign against the competitive sport of live pigeon shooting; as states banned the practice the clay pigeon came to take the place of the live one. Similarly, conservationists brought hunting under stricter control. By 1900 state legislation on this subject was so extensive that the Department of Agriculture began the publication of an annual bulletin on state game laws.

But inherent in the new approach was a more direct confrontation with the traditional right to bear arms. With new laws came new methods of enforcement; criminology and police science developed. As law enforcement became a more professional and specialized function, the need for the armed citizen became less obvious. Law and its enforcement increasingly impinged on sociological considerations. Contributors to legal journals, who had long ignored the legal problems inherent in the right to bear arms, now turned to the social implications. "Is the Pistol Responsible for Crime?" The new *Journal of the American Institute of Criminal Law and Criminology* asked its readers this question in its first volume.[1] Lucilius Emery, writing in the *Harvard Law Review*, took another look at the Second Amendment in light of contemporary social problems. His conclusions would be cited for a decade: "Women, young boys, the blind, tramps, persons non compos mentis or dissolute in habits, may be prohibited from carrying weapons."[2] A few journalists with advanced notions suggested that guns, like other objectionable features in society, be brought under control by legislation that would make them "the costliest type of luxury."[3]

Added to this rising concern was a disturbing and alien element. The public had always been sensitive to the dangers of armed minorities such as blacks and Indians, but this concern took on new dimensions as cities filled with unassimilated masses of immigrants from Southern and Eastern Europe, packed into restless and teeming enclaves. With the foreigner came alien ideas that altered the traditional pattern of violence. The second major case on the Second Amendment—the Presser case —had been sparked by the activities of a radical paramilitary organization of German-Americans. Marxism crossed the Atlantic; anarchism came too, producing a series of violent incidents that culminated in the assassination of President William McKinley. The swarthy, hirsute, and wild-eyed anarchist became the new shibboleth.

From these preoccupations came a period of firearms agitation and legislation that would continue until World War I. The debate scarcely reached national proportions in this period, and seldom concerned anything but the concealable firearm, the pistol. But in this restricted area it had some significant results. A few state legislatures went beyond the traditional prohibition or regulation of carrying concealed weapons. Alabama attacked the pistol obliquely in 1892 by imposing an expensive business license on those who sold handguns.[4] In 1907 Texas levied on these merchants a stiff tax of "fifty percent of gross receipts from all such sales."[5] Oregon adopted a more direct approach with a 1913 statute that required a license to purchase handguns.[6] Most of these laws were difficult to enforce and not well supplied with machinery for that purpose. In the case of Alabama and Texas they were probably "propitiatory," designed to satisfy a momentary outcry that something be done, while at the same time doing no real violence to the old ways. The Texas law was massively evaded; the more scrupulous merchants avoided the tax through the fiction of "leasing" pistols to their customers rather than making outright sales.[7] Innovative state legislation of this sort was generally ineffective and of short duration, but these laws were straws in the wind.

Where the problem seemed most acute was in the cities. Then, as now, the issue was preeminently one of urban life. The experience of New York in this period is worth tracing for several reasons. It demonstrated, in microcosm, many of the forces and arguments still in contention. The path of debate can be followed in detail, thanks to extensive press coverage. Finally, it culminated in the Sullivan Law, which stood as the high water mark of firearms legislation for half a century.

New York City emerged from the Civil War still bearing visible scars of the massive draft riots of 1863, the most recent evidence of the city's turbulent past. Though the causes and substance of that turbulence varied during the century, the firearm was already one of its hallmarks. The city's street gangs had discovered the revolver before the Civil War, and so had its professional criminals. Officer Eugene Anderson, the first New York policeman admitted to the force's roll of honor, had been killed in a gun battle with a burglar in 1857. The authorities had replied in kind, permitting policemen to carry revolvers of their own. They committed armed police to pitched battles with the rioters of 1863.[8] Respectable New Yorkers approved of this strong stand in the face of rioting mobs. "This mob is not the people," thundered one of the newspapers in 1863, "give them grape and plenty of it."[9]

Though pistols were plentiful among what were then called the "criminal classes," the city fathers gave no thought to disarming them as a part of everyday law enforcement. They seem to have been content to maintain a superiority of armament in the hands of police, militia, and honest citizens, should the latter be needed. The state's concealed weapons law of 1866 forbade the carrying of such exotic weapons as "sling shot, billy, sand-club or metal knuckles and any dirk or dagger, or sword cane or air gun," but omitted pistols from the list.[10] This was not an oversight: the carrying of pistols did not attract the attention of the legislators until a decade and a half later. Even then it was made a misdemeanor, rather than a felony, as was the case with the weapons enumerated earlier.[11] New York City was scarcely provided with more stringent regulations of its own. A provision in the city code of 1866 made it a misdemeanor to discharge firearms within its corporate limits.[12]

In the 1870s several proposals to regulate the carrying of concealed handguns by a permit system failed to gain the approval of the Board of Aldermen, on the grounds that only respectable citizens would be affected. Moreover, the lawabiding members of society would be less able to defend themselves against lawbreakers, who would flout a pistol law as they flouted all other regulations. It was not until 1877 that the Aldermen were won over. Mild in itself (it allowed permits to carry pistols to virtually anyone who asked), the ordinance was not well enforced, despite occasional newspaper editorials on the subject.[13] In 1881 the *Tribune* found that, though authorities were liberal in issuing permits, many New Yorkers did not take the trouble to procure them. The Twenty-Sixth Precinct had issued about 4,500, but its captain estimated that at least 1,000 men in his jurisdiction went armed without them. The maximum fine for noncompliance was ten dollars, and the police had considerable discretion in making cases. Officials had little interest in tightening regulations. There was no ordinance prohibiting the sale of firearms to minors. Though the district attorney felt guns should not be put in the hands of children under the age of "twelve or thirteen," he did not think it practical to regulate sales. Recorder Hackett was loath to maintain the existing ordinance, being in the habit of carrying a pair of derringers himself.[14] Nor were civic groups interested in the matter. Reverend Howard Crosby's Society for the Prevention of Crime, active in the 1880s, directed its efforts at closing saloons and racetracks and redeeming falling women.

The town's newspapers returned to the theme periodically, arguing that those who went armed were looking for trouble, while citizens who kept revolvers at home would still find themselves at a tragic disadvantage when confronted with local burglars, who also went armed and were better shots. But this journalistic threnody had none of the earnestness of a crusade. After all, New Yorkers were less addicted to the pistol habit than Americans in other parts of the country. The South rather than the West, was held to be most afflicted, particularly Kentucky. And there was, after all, less need for the citizen to own a pistol, much less carry one, in "older and better-established communities" such as New York.[15]

Until the end of the century, the press tended to treat

pistol-carrying in quasi-humorous fashion, as though it were more a whimsy than a serious menace. In 1892 the *Tribune* published such an essay on "that pleasing American custom of carrying deadly weapons," which it held to be the practice of "a very fair percentage" of New Yorkers: "Let a mad dog, for instance, take a turn around Times Square, and the spectator is astonished to see the number of men who will produce firearms from some of that multitude of pockets with which man, as constructed by the tailor, is endowed." Of one hundred men who fired at the dog, the *Tribune* continued, ninety-nine would miss, and one in ten would put a bullet through a bystander's leg, for "the average New Yorker who carries a pistol cannot hit anything with it." The town's inhabitants were discriminating in their taste for pistols, with the .22 caliber a heavy favorite among suicides. "But generally speaking, the twenty-two calibre may be said to lack emphasis; it cannot command the respect accorded to the thirty-two calibre, nor rivet the attention like the thirty-eight calibre, nor depopulate the neighborhood as can the forty-four and forty-five calibre."[16]

With the turn of the century there was a distinct change: the outmoded habit of going armed had become an increasingly intolerable practice. Newspaper editors once again supplied most of the leadership for what had become a serious crusade. They were now joined by an increasing number of public officials—judges, magistrates, and police officials. The movement acquired a valuable ally in William T. Jerome, the city's hard-driving district attorney. At his urging the Board of Aldermen adopted a new concealed weapons ordinance in February 1905. The new measure continued the permit system but greatly increased the penalty for violation, which became a maximum fine of $250 and a prison term of up to six months.[17] Not content with this, Jerome sought to buttress the measure by a state statute along the same lines. He went to Albany to confer with the governor and arranged to have his bill introduced in the legislature.

Jerome's bill died in the session of 1905, but he and others continued their efforts at Albany. Assemblyman Mark Goldberg introduced a bill in 1909 that would require sellers of pistols to make sales only to customers with permits. This bill, too, died in committee.[18] The movement was gathering momentum, however. Judge Foster of the General Sessions Court came out strongly for a state pistol law in 1906, pointing out that there was no reference to the right to bear arms in the state constitution.[19] He was joined by George C. Holt, U.S. District Court Judge. Holt told the Wisconsin State Bar Association in 1910 that his service on the bench in New York had convinced him that "the repeating pistol is the greatest nuisance in modern life."[20] His speech was reprinted in *The Independent* and editorialized in *The Nation*.[21] The advocates of tough new legislation on concealed weapons planned to renew their efforts when the legislature convened in 1911 but none could have guessed how drastically events would improve its chances of passage.

In 1910 William J. Gaynor was the mayor of New York. On August 9 of that year he went aboard a liner moored at one of the city's piers. The liner was crowded with celebrities, including President Montt of Chile. The mayor was accompanied by a large party. Unnoticed among them was James Gallagher, an embittered former employee of the city Dock Department. In a scene of wild confusion Gallagher opened fire with a pistol, wounding

Mayor Gaynor in the neck. Though the mayor recovered, his convalescence was a long painful one, fully chronicled in the press. Understandably, the assassination attempt led immediately to a renewed onslaught against the pistol and its users. Assemblyman Goldberg, now a veteran in the battle, urged the city's newspapers to "keep the present agitation afloat."[22]

The press responded with a will, publishing letters from indignant citizens. One letter recommended that New York copy the law of Japan, "where intending purchasers of revolvers must first obtain police permits, and sales must always be reported to the police." The writer urged other readers to clip the letter out and send it to their legislators—perhaps the first instance of the mail campaigns that would become a feature of the firearms controversy in later years.[23] The press drew from the police blotter in its efforts to keep the issue in the public eye. News items that had simply been isolated instances of pathos and tragedy now seemed to be part of a sinister pattern: "Cleans Pistol, Shoots Wife;" "Father Shot by Son, Dies Clasping Child." In truth, the turbulent city provided ample fare of this kind throughout the summer and fall of 1910. The members of a fraternal organization called "The Forty Thieves" engaged in a revolver battle on an excursion boat.[24] A passerby was set upon by a group of factory workers who mistook him for a scab; the terrified man emptied his revolver into the crowd around him.[25] A bloody tong war broke out among the city's Chinese population. A series of shootings, stabbings, and bombings, attributed to the Black Hand, erupted in the Italian community. The city seemed in the grip of a crime wave of unprecedented proportions.

By the end of the year, a "Citizens' Committee" made up of prominent business and professional figures was pressing for stringent legislation. Aspiring politicians had been drawn to the issue, foremost among them Timothy D. "Big Tim" Sullivan. Big Tim had powerful connections with Tammany, holding the Bowery as his fief.[26] Now bound for the State Senate, he pledged to introduce a bill for the statewide regulation of the purchase, possession, and carrying of concealed weapons. By the time the legislature got down to work in January 1911, another series of spectacular happenings had fanned the issue to white heat. There was the Houndsditch affair, in which a band of anarchists, holed up in one of the quarters of London, had withstood repeated assaults of British police and soldiers. There was even talk of making revolvers a part of the Bobbies' equipment. Then, on January 23, the well-known novelist David Graham Phillips was shot to death on a New York sidewalk. His assailant, a demented violinist, then turned his pistol on himself, with equally fatal results. The exact motivation for the attack was never clear, but the press pointed out that the assassin had been enrolled in the Rand School for Social Science, "an institution for the dissemination of socialist propaganda."[27] A few days later the Coroner's Office issued figures showing that the number of homicides with firearms had increased by almost 50 percent in 1910. Coroner's Clerk George P. Lebrun called for "severe measures for the regulation of the indiscriminate sale and carrying of firearms."[28]

Hearings on the Sullivan Bill began before the State Senate's Codes Committee on February 1, 1911. The only testimony hostile to the bill came from New York hardware merchants and spokesmen for small arms manufacturers.[29] The merchants protested that the measure would simply drive their pistol customers to New Jersey and Connecticut. Representatives of the industry warned that the bill worked a greater hardship on legitimate purchasers than anyone else. Though their arguments were well presented, their appearance was probably counterproductive. The public mood regarding business interests was then one of deep suspicion (the Supreme Court ordered the breakup of the Standard Oil empire that spring). There was much talk of the "Bathtub Trust," the "Potash Monopoly," and other collusive organizations. The "Gun Trust" was added to the list. Senator Sullivan inferred that those who voted against his bill were in its pocket.[30]

A stream of witnesses appeared on behalf of the bill, many of them public officials with long experience in law enforcement. The Manhattan Coroner's Clerk came with his statistics. Other witnesses told of revolvers being sold from pushcarts on New York's East Side. Impressed by these revelations and spurred by Big Tim, the committee reported the bill out favorably. It was approved by the Senate by a vote of 37 to 5, its way prepared by Sullivan's oratory: "If this bill passes, it will do more to carry out the commandment thou shalt not kill and save more souls than all the talk of all the ministers and priests in the state for the next ten years."[31] Two days later the bill cleared the Assembly by a vote of 123 to 7. Governor John A. Dix signed it into law on May 29, 1911.

The Sullivan Law was a statute without precedent in the United States, since it subjected to strict regulation not only the carrying of deadly weapons, but also their sale and simple possession. Though its provisions had application throughout the state, it was tailored to the interests and needs of the great city on the Hudson. There it received the impetus that helped get it through the legislature with remarkably little opposition.[32] In the city it was supported by a phalanx of interests so impressive that few dissenting voices were heard. There was first of all the massive support of the press, then the chief medium for the expression and formation of public opinion. The law enjoyed the endorsement of the "experts" of the day—all of the city's judges, its magistrates, and its police officials. Equally valuable was the support of the city's notables, whether members of the Merchants' Association, the City Club, or other groups. Social and cultural leaders pleaded for its adoption—men like Bishop Greer, John Wanamaker, Hudson Maxim (himself a firearms inventor), and John D. Rockefeller, Jr., whom Big Tim Sullivan described to the awed Senate as "a social acquaintance of mine."[33] Such men spoke for a sophisticated and cosmopolitan society in which the pocket pistol had no place, where men of culture were in agreement that "good morals and the public welfare require all possible discouragement of the pistol habit."[34] New York, with its Wall Street, Broadway, 376,000 telephones, and other monuments to modern culture, should lead the nation in breaking a habit that had become "a reproach and a byword among other nations."[35]

An appeal of this sort was all the more understandable since it was but one of many efforts then being made to reform and refine the city's life. Simultaneously, the Anti-Profanity League was working to remove offensive language from the theatres, and the Society for the Suppression of Unnecessary Noise was endeavoring to make the Fourth of July less noisy and dangerous. The nation's largest fireworks firm went into bankruptcy that year, partly through the Society's efforts.[36] Even the recently organized Boy Scouts came under close local scrutiny by those who felt the organization subjected the nation's youth to brutalizing militarism. Remington unwittingly added to these suspicions by designing a "Boy Scout

Rifle" complete with bayonet.[37] All of these movements were altruistic in inspiration and they all shared the belief that legislation was as important to their goals as moral suasion. Legislators were surprisingly receptive to their proposals, producing enactments whose subject matter was sometimes novel at the very least. While the New York Legislature was considering the Sullivan Bill, neighboring New Jersey enacted a sterilization law designed to curtail the procreative capacities of the "hopelessly defective and criminal classes."[38] At the same time the lower house of the Colorado Legislature approved a measure outlawing cigarettes, and a Massachusetts legislator introduced a bill that would prohibit women from wearing any skirt "which does not come six inches below the kneecap."[39]

It would be wrong to consider the Sullivan Law as the work of a few organized groups with political leverage in an era that some have called "law-happy." It had strong arguments in its favor that won it wide support and neutralized much of the potential opposition. Its advocates spoke of it as directed at clearly definable criminal elements that were all too active in the metropolis —long-forgotten denizens like "Eat'em up" Jack McManus, "Mushy" Miller, and the notorious Car Barn Gang. As if to underline this intent, the police staged an impressive series of "shakedown" raids in the spring of 1911, concentrating on the haunts of known criminals. A well-publicized raid on French Max's Place in February yielded a bushel basket full of knives and revolvers.[40] Even more appealing was the clear inference that the new measure would strike hardest at the foreign-born element, seemingly responsible for most of the violence in the city. It had long been held that pistols were found "chiefly in the pockets of ignorant and quarrelsome im-

migrants of lawbreaking propensities."[41] The Italian
population seemed particularly addicted to criminality
(the *Tribune*'s annual index frequently crosslisted the
entries "Crime" and "Italians"). As early as 1903 the
authorities had begun to cancel pistol permits in the
Italian sections of the city.[42] This was followed by a state
law of 1905 which made it illegal for aliens to possess
firearms "in any public place."[43] This provision was retained in the Sullivan law.

With such impressive endorsements and such compelling arguments for its adoption, it is not surprising that
opponents of the Sullivan proposal had an uphill fight.
There is no evidence of any organized opposition of any
consequence. Those who spoke against the proposal
openly were few. Only a small percentage of letters to the
newspapers, at least those which saw print, were hostile.
Even these few seemed to realize that their position was,
for the moment at least, hardly the popular one; many
declined to sign their names. Their arguments have a
familiar ring to those who have followed the controversy
in recent years. "J.W.E." felt that the laws already on the
books were quite adequate if properly enforced.[44] A
more outspoken correspondent who signed himself "38
Colt" asked what consideration a hardened criminal
could be expected to give to the proposed law. "Even if he
obeyed the law, which is unlikely, he could still choose an
ice pick, a reaping hook, or a butcher's cleaver." He
concluded with the graphic observation: "If Mayor
Gaynor had been hit in the neck with a sharp cleaver he
would not be recovering."[45]

It is probable that many did not understand the importance of the new law, or the drastic change it promised to
work. Previous enactments, both state and municipal,

had had little practical effect, so it was logical to assume that the Sullivan Law would have a similar fate. Since the new enactment elevated the carrying of pistols without permit to the status of a felony, all cases would have to pass before grand and petit juries. It was well known that in the past jurors had "quite uniformly" declined to convict those charged under the old statutes.[46]

Certainly, there was a sizable element of latent opposition in the thousands of New Yorkers who habitually went armed and in the infinitely greater number who kept revolvers at home. How extensive the practice of pistol-carrying was cannot be determined with any precision. In 1903 a *Tribune* feature article contained a police estimate that 20,000 people regularly carried handguns on their persons, about 600 of them with the requisite permit.[47] But this was a ball park guess and may have been well on the conservative side, judging from the large numbers of weapons that came into the hands of the police. In the four-year period 1907-1910 inclusive, they seized 10,567 revolvers, an average of more than seven a day—and this was not the result of a concerted drive against pistol-carrying, but rather incidental to routine arrests.[48] Existing laws notwithstanding, it was an unexceptional thing to see a revolver in the city, and of this we have vivid evidence. Several persons saw Mayor Gaynor's assailant brandishing a pistol before the shooting, and even twirling it around his finger. Yet "nobody made any move to apprehend him, nobody suspected him."[49] Of the number of firearms kept in homes, there was not even an estimate, but the number must have run to the many thousands. There were more than a few instances in 1910 and 1911 in which residents summoned police and firemen to their neighborhood by the simple expedient of firing pistols out of their windows. This was apparently quicker than going to an alarm box or telephone.

The *Tribune*'s survey of 1903 also indicates quite clearly that honest citizens often went armed. Those who traveled at night or with sums of money felt much safer with revolvers in their pockets. Many carried them in Manhattan but fewer in Brooklyn. Physicians often followed the practice but not musicians. Most felt they needed them for self-defense, holding that the public guardians of the peace could not always be relied upon to protect life and property. Less clearly voiced was the sentiment that a gun was a handy thing to have if public peace and order were distributed by a rabid dog or other menace.[50]

This last point is intriguing, since it links the habit of going armed with a vague obligation many residents felt to "pitch in" when peace and order were threatened. Whether this could be traced to a frontier experience now far in the city's past or to an even more remote heritage from the Old World is difficult to say. It is more likely that the massive and unthinking spontaneity with which citizens sometimes intervened in cases of real or supposed wrongdoing suggests the ancient "hue and cry" rather than anything else. Whatever its cause, the impulse was emphatically present in that sophisticated metropolis of five million and it surfaced a number of times while the Sullivan Law was under consideration. In January 1911, a woman discovered a thief in her home. He fled into the street, pursued by her screams. Though he brandished a revolver as he ran, a "small army of citizens" chased him through the streets until they eventually lost him.[51] One day in March two men were shot down in the street in a section of the city known as "the

Gap." Their assailant, still armed, took to his heels. A crowd of boys playing ball nearby were the only witnesses; they immediately set off in pursuit. The chase was a long one and the gunman's steps began to flag. His pursuers overtook him and tripped him, sending him sprawling to the pavement. Then they knocked him senseless with baseball bats and sat on him until the police arrived.[52] On March 19 an apartment dweller noticed a "suspicious Negro" who entered the building several times. The intruder was challenged and manhandled by a crowd that had grown to considerable proportions by the time the police arrived. The suspect turned out to be Booker T. Washington, who had been trying to locate the address of an acquaintance in the neighborhood. Washington had to be hospitalized.[53]

This phenomenon of "popular involvement" was thus Janus-faced. At its best it revealed a concerned citizenry that would warm the heart of any magistrate. At its worst it came chillingly close to a lynching party. For better or worse it would eventually disappear from the city, as would the armed citizen. In banning the one, the Sullivan Law probably conveyed a message of modernity that hastened the demise of the other.[54]

The Sullivan Law went into effect on September 1, 1911. Despite the delay in its implementation and the press coverage that attended its passage, the act was not well understood. It was in fact a mixture of old and new. It reiterated with minor changes the earlier legislation touching deadly weapons other than firearms—sling shot and the like—and likewise preserved the earlier measures on the possession and carrying of weapons by aliens and minors under sixteen. There were three new provisions of major importance. (1) Section 1897 of the Criminal Code was altered so that the unlicensed carrying of a concealable firearm by residents of cities, villages, and towns became a felony; thus the pistol joined sling shot and brass knuckles in this regard. (2) Section 1897 also now required urban residents to secure permits to possess concealable firearms, with failure to do so a misdemeanor. (3) Section 1914 required those who sold pistols to make sales only to persons who presented "a permit for possessing or carrying the same as required by law." Sellers were required to maintain records of all sales which clearly identified both customer and firearm.[55]

The advent of the law prompted a spate of inquiries from New Yorkers who wanted to know how it would apply to them. Collectors wondered how it would affect their antique weapons. One gentleman wanted to know if he could keep the brass cannon that adorned his residence. An official assured him: "He can keep a Krupp gun in his parlor if he wants to."[56] But sometimes the authorities themselves were confused. A spokesman for the State Conservation Commission warned that his reading of the law would bar boys under sixteen from hunting.[57] District Attorney Charles S. Whitman ruled that permits to possess pistols were required only for those purchased after September 1. Police Commissioner Rhinelander Waldo, however, held the provision to be retroactive, so that the police would have a record of all handguns in private possession for use in solving crimes.[58] Waldo's view prevailed, and myriad New Yorkers had to decide whether it was worth paying ten dollars a year to possess legally a five dollar revolver. The authorities announced that while they would be chary about issuing permits to carry, those to possess would be as easy to obtain as dog licenses.[59] Through an oversight these permits were not available from the printer until several days after the law went into effect. Pawnbrokers wanted to know what to do with pistols left as pledges; this question was referred to the courts.

Whatever the confusion over the new statute, the police set out to enforce it vigorously. They made five arrests on September 1 and more in the following days. They too were not always sure how to apply the law but when in doubt they apparently preferred charges. For example, they arrested a gentleman from Seattle passing through town with a cased shotgun in his baggage and booked several pawnbrokers for displaying pistols in their windows. The cases made were vigorously prosecuted. Juries, perhaps influenced by the attitude of police, judges, and prosecutors, took the new law seriously. The first man convicted under the new law, an Italian immigrant arrested with a pistol in his pocket, was arraigned, indicted, convicted, and sent on his way to a year's stay in Sing Sing within thirty days. The judge handed down a somewhat xenophobic lecture with the sentence: "It is unfortunate that this is the custom with you and your kind, and that fact, combined with your irascible nature, furnishes much of the criminal business in this country."[60]

The new law continued to trouble the city's inhabitants, some of them in a humorous way, others tragically. A Harlem householder, armed with his pistol, apprehended a burglar in his home one night. The burglar inquired whether his captor had a permit for his revolver and the householder admitted that he did not. After an awkward moment burglar and householder each agreed to go his way and say nothing.[61] A South African engineer sought a permit for a pistol because he had been threatened by one of his workers. The permit was denied because the engineer was an alien. He went to New

Jersey, bought a pistol, and when the worker attacked him with a shovel he shot him to death.[62]

Serious protests arose as the law took hold. For the first time its constitutionality was widely questioned (it was to be confirmed in 1913). The Sullivan Law was denounced as "asinine," "vicious", "despotic," and "an outrage against the rights of all American citizens."[63] Newspapers received denunciatory letters from people as far away as Ohio and Vermont. One of the city's judges who had given several stiff sentences under the act received a crudely scrawled letter from "the Gangs of 19th Street," daring him to "come up Tenth Avenue between 19th and 20th Street."[64]

Yet, the new law seemed to be having an effect on the gun-bearing habits of the city's criminals. Raids on their haunts, conducted by the recently organized "Strong Arm Squad" of the city police, produced a shower of weapons at first, but the yield soon dropped off. A search of 3,000 men toward the end of 1911 produced one stiletto and three razors.[65] Rumor had it that hoodlums now rented pistols when they needed them, for a fee of twenty-five cents a night, rather than carry them constantly.[66] The police had long argued that such a law would enable them to deal sternly with armed criminals before they committed crimes, and here the Sullivan Law brought spectacular results early in September. The first person indicted under the act was Giuseppe Costabile, an Italian mobster of some notoriety, whom police had been watching for some time. Though he was reputedly a chief of the Black Hand, the police had been unable to make any charges against him. Now he was searched and found to have a bomb concealed under his coat.[67] Obviously pleased officials announced that thanks to the Sullivan Law they could send him to prison for as long as seven years.

The supporters of the new law felt it would show immediate results so impressive that all criticism would be silenced. Big Tim Sullivan had argued that it would reduce homicides drastically. Charles E. Van Loan, writing in 1912, the first full year under the Sullivan Law, was equally optimistic: "New York State is the pioneer in a movement to make the pistol a dangerous thing to have in one's pocket. The result of this campaign will begin to appear when the Coroner issues his statistics for 1912, and the result will be worth watching."[68]

The Coroner's Report for 1912 was issued on January 26, 1913. Coroner's Clerk Lebrun, who had played a major role in the drafting of the Sullivan Law, pointed out that the number of suicides by firearms had dropped 40 percent over the previous year. He credited the new law with this decline.[69] Lebrun did not comment on the number of homicides by firearms, but opponents of the Sullivan Law were quick to do so. In the last pre-Sullivan Law year, 1910, there had been 108 such homicides; in 1912 there were 113.[70] The quarrel over statistics made its debut as part of the firearms controversy.

Though the *Times* was discouraged and found criminals "as well armed as ever,"[71] the Sullivan Law's backers persisted in believing they were on the right track. The measure would show more positive results in the long run, especially if it were strengthened. Too many permits had been issued and there were too many unlicensed revolver sales. Most of the city's suicides by firearms were people who had gone out and bought pistols expressly for that purpose—and without permits. Coroner's Clerk Lebrun and Chief Magistrate William

McAdoo, two of the measure's most outspoken supporters, called for similar legislation in New Jersey and Connecticut, the chief sources of illegal handguns in the city.
McAdoo went further, urging a federal law on concealed
weapons.[72]

Sixty years later the Sullivan Law remains on the
books, having survived numerous efforts to repeal it. It
has been amended scores of times, but its basic thrust
remains the same. The arguments it engendered would
not change either. Within a decade they would be resumed on a national scale.

8 The Interwar Period

The pistol is the curse of America, and they are as common as lead pencils.

—William McAdoo, 1924

The proponents of the Sullivan Law hoped that it would serve as a model statute for other states, but the New York experiment was hardly under way before other preoccupations monopolized the national attention. World War I broke out in 1914; by 1916 the United States had begun its preparedness effort and the following year it entered the conflict. The war effectively stilled the debate over firearms for it was incongruous at a time when the entire nation was taking up arms. If anything, the national predilection for firearms became a virtue, symbolized by figures like Sergeant York.

If the war stopped the talk of firearms regulation, the postwar period brought it back on a truly national scale. While social historians are still probing the significance of that frenetic era called the "Roaring Twenties," it seems clear that one of its themes was an obsession with threats to law and order and traditional American values.

187

The decade took on a xenophobic cast, with new laws curbing immigration.[1] Then there was the "Red Scare," a menace that seemed so real that Kansas made it a crime to display a red flag.[2] Even more important to the present study, the entire nation seemed to be in the grip of an unprecedented crime wave. In reaction to these threats, real or imagined, came a significant extension of state police power, which even made inroads on the traditional right to bear arms. In this connection a California court ruled in 1924: "It is clear that, in the exercise of the police power of the state, that is, for public safety or the public welfare generally, such right may be either regulated or, in proper cases, entirely destroyed."[3] Similarly, an Illinois tribunal found that "the sale of deadly weapons may be absolutely prohibited."[4]

Along with these new directions in legislation there were new patterns in lawbreaking. Contemporaries may have exaggerated the crime wave of the 1920s, but it was spectacularly innovative. Newspapers reported in 1924 that poachers had taken to the air, sweeping up great flocks of wildfowl with nets suspended below airplanes. Game wardens with high-powered rifles were dispatched to shoot down the offending planes.[5] The criminal made an even more important discovery in the automobile, which enabled him to give up furtiveness and the cover of night. (The Ford Motor Company would receive testimonial letters from John Dillinger and Clyde Barrow.) The eastern metropolis came to resemble the western cowtown, with its daylight holdups, gun battles in the streets, and cross-country pursuits. To the roar of racing motors would soon be added the blast of sawed-off shotguns and the chatter of automatic weapons.

The crime wave was an affront to peace and order and

it was costly to the business community. In 1921 the National Surety Company made an appeal to law enforcement officials all over the country to do something about bank robberies that had already cost it a million dollars in the first eight months of that year.[6] Insurance rates went up; hard-hit jewelers formed their own National Crime Committee, as did business and professional figures in many large cities.[7]

As had been the case in New York a decade before, these groups goaded officials to act against criminals and the weapons that made them so formidable. Typical was the case of Chicago, which was acquiring the unenviable reputation of being the crime capital of the nation. The city had experienced its first daylight payroll robbery in 1917, in the course of which two men had been killed. Public indignation eventually led to the creation of the Chicago Crime Commission early in 1919. In their drive against gunmen the city police began rigorous enforcement of the ban on carrying concealed weapons and by 1921 they were making three arrests a day on this charge.[8] But those arrested were soon out on bail, replacing their confiscated pistols from a seemingly inexhaustible supply. Though sales were regulated in the city itself, it was a simple matter to buy guns in surrounding towns or order them from mail-order houses. This prompted an outraged Chicago businessman named John R. Thompson to embark on a one-man crusade against the handgun in the summer of 1921. He placed notices in newspapers throughout the country offering $1,000 "To anyone who would give one good reason why the revolver manufacturing industry should be allowed to exist and enjoy the facilities of the mails."[9] Thompson's efforts were applauded by the other businessmen in the city, especially after they learned that premiums on their robbery and theft policies would go up 50 percent.[10]

Chicago had a particularly bad day of criminal violence late in January 1922: two kidnappings, two burglaries, twenty-eight street robberies, and the attempted murder of the president of the Chicago Music College.[11] This brought the city's most outspoken journal, the *Daily Tribune*, into the anti-pistol crusade. Though the newspaper had itself run advertisements for mail-order pistols a few months before, it now attacked the handgun and what it called "the Crime Camorra" with the flamboyance that had made it famous. Beginning late in January 1922, it ran daily articles and editorials on the subject for a month. The *Tribune*, like Mr. Thompson, wanted to suppress the pistol industry and ban sales of its products. Each day's crime statistics seemed to underline its argument: "Big guns and little guns, blue steel and nickel steel, continued to plunder Chicagoans yesterday at the behest of the Crime Camorra."[12] The newspaper made news of its own by ordering pistols under assumed names. Its staff fashioned dumdum bullets and fired them at telephone books. One of its reporters put a large automatic pistol in each pocket of his overcoat and "slunk slowly and furtively past three uniformed policemen and half a dozen traffic cops in the Loop."[13] The *Tribune* vigorously supported public protest meetings and solicited from the head of the Illinois State Bar a pledge to "rid the state of concealable weapons."[14]

Though few cities had newspapers as aggressive as the *Tribune*, many of them saw the same agitation develop. The chief of police of Detroit estimated that mail-order firms alone supplied 5,000 pistols a year to inhabitants of his city, most of them to "dope addicts, feeble minded citizens, beer-runners, stick-up men, and gentlemen full of moonshine."[15] A group of concerned citizens calling themselves the American Reclamation Society made a standing offer of $5,000 for "one good reason for the existence of revolvers."[16] Even traditionally conservative southern cities like Memphis, Chattanooga, and Atlanta were stirred. Atlanta had operated since her founding with a single firearms ordinance that made it illegal to discharge them in the city. Her 1924 Code contained an elaborate set of regulations on handguns.[17]

By the mid-1920s the "pistol problem" was getting national coverage in *The Spectator, Literary Digest, World's Work*, and other magazines.[18] Nationally recognized experts on the problem were beginning to appear, one of whom was William McAdoo, chief magistrate of New York City. An early backer of the Sullivan Law, he wrote extensively in the 1920s and was in great demand as a speaker. In his view, "the curse of the pistol" went far beyond its misuse by hardened criminals: "I would as soon place a full-venomed cobra snake in my house as a loaded revolver. Look at the tragedies in the morning newspapers; where husband shoots wife, man shoots mistress, one child shoots the other, frenzied head of family kills the whole family and himself, until all over the country it is bang! bang! bang! every hour of the day and night."[19] Another authority on the question was Frederick L. Hoffman, a consulting statistician. For years Hoffman had helped insurance companies prepare their actuarial tables, and in the course of this work he had become an expert on homicide statistics. According to his calculations, firearms figured in three-fourths of such deaths. These and other findings convinced him that new laws were absolutely necessary.[20]

The most radical solution was to close the pistol factories. This had been suggested as a remedy for Chicago's problems and was widely discussed. It received an impressive endorsement from the American Bar Association in 1922: "We recommend that the manufacture and sale of pistols and of cartridges designed to be used in them, shall be absolutely prohibited, save as such manufacture shall be necessary for governmental and official use under legal regulation and control."[21] Some felt this measure would produce a 90-percent drop in crime, while others felt that if just pistol manufacture were stopped, the nation's insurance companies would reap such savings that they could afford to purchase all existing handguns and dump them into the Gulf of Mexico. (The number of these was generally placed at ten million.)[22] A New York judge suggested that this general disarmament be extended even to the police. (Concerned Americans were already drawing an unflattering comparison with England, with its low crime rates and unarmed police.)[23] Proponents of this idea even formulated a slogan: "If nobody had a gun, nobody would need a gun."

Aside from this solution, admittedly revolutionary, another possibility was to find a formula that discriminated not against guns themselves, but against certain categories of users. A proposal along these lines came from the United States Revolver Association, an organization of competitive handgun shooters founded in 1900, and which by the 1920s had some 3,000 members. One of its officers, Karl T. Frederick, had been an Olympic pistol champion in 1920. Frederick and others in his group put together a model law that came to be known as the Uniform Firearms Act, though it dealt essentially with pistols. A person desiring to purchase a handgun would identify himself to a licensed dealer and fill out a form. The actual purchase could only be made forty-eight hours later. This delay had two purposes: first, it made it impossible for a man to dash into a store for a revolver and then rush back to shoot his wife while still in the grip of anger. Second, the police would examine his application to determine if he belonged to a category of persons forbidden to make purchase: chronic alcoholics, certain types of criminals, drug addicts, minors, etc. The police could also issue permits to carry guns to respectable citizens who had reasons to do so. Several other provisions were designed to make it hazardous for lawbreakers to have concealed weapons.[24]

The Uniform Firearms Act was only one of several schemes examined by state legislatures in the 1920s.[25] There was a considerable amount of legislation in the period: a recent survey shows that seventeen states enacted "major legislation" during the course of the decade.[26] For all this activity, the general result seems to have been unsatisfactory. In the first place, there was no consistent pattern in state enactments. Perhaps a half dozen followed the Uniform Firearms Act, generally with modifications to meet their own needs. Others were inspired by the Sullivan Law. Arkansas voted statewide registration of all handguns in 1923,[27] as did Michigan in 1925.[28] South Carolina held to a bizarre law which made it illegal to sell or manufacture any pistol that did not measure twenty inches in length and weigh at least three pounds.[29] A handgun that met these qualifications would have been virtually impossible to conceal—or to obtain. Lack of uniformity in state laws made for problems in interstate relations. New York urged New Jersey to enact a Sullivan Law, but *The New York Times* complained in 1922 that the recent New Jersey legislation actually made it easier for criminals to carry weapons than before.[30] City sometimes clashed with state. Chicago, which issued no permits to carry pistols, found itself obliged by court order to honor those obtained outside its limits.[31] Subsequently, a state court ruled its strict pistol ordinance invalid because it conflicted with state law.[32] The same thing happened to Chattanooga, whose ban on the carrying of weapons was more severe than the state statute.[33]

Even more irksome to advocates of strict regulation was the influx of arms from mail-order houses. Under popular pressure, advertisements for cheap mail-order pistols began to disappear from newspapers and magazines. The American Legion and the American Medical Association were denounced for carrying them in their publications; the *Saturday Evening Post* was regarded as one of the last holdouts by the mid-1920s.[34] The larger mail-order houses felt the pressure too and eventually bowed to it. Sears Roebuck began in 1922 to require that prospective purchasers of pistols send in their permits in places where they were required.[35] A spokesman for the company confessed "that little notice has cost us easily $150,000 a year."[36] Two years later Sears dropped all handguns from its catalog. But not all mail-order firms gave up the market voluntarily, for it was a lucrative one.[37] There was increasing talk of seeking federal legislation since the Post Office was the chief accomplice in mail-order sales.

Countercurrents existed, though hardly what could be called a well-organized opposition. Small arms manufacturers, at least the older and well-established companies, were feeling severe competition from cheap, imported pistols and thus could not be expected to come to the defense of mail-order firms that distributed them. In 1925 the National Rifle Association was a modest organi-

zation of a few thousand members, and was just beginning to take an active interest in the controversy. The
most outspoken opponents of firearms legislation were
the sporting magazines of the day, whose arguments did
not go far beyond their own readership. Horace
Kephart, writing in *Outing* and speaking for the "seven
million sportsmen" in the country, warned that their
legitimate interests could be harmed. He also cited the
Second Amendment, but significantly enough he argued
most forcefully for the notion that armed citizens were
"the best protection we have against robbery and arson,
murder and rape."[38]

The most telling opposition did not come from organized groups protecting their special interests. When
both houses of the Arizona Legislature passed a firearms
bill modeled on the Uniform Firearms Act, the governor
vetoed it as "a serious invasion of personal liberties."[39] A
United States Representative from Texas proclaimed on
the floor of the House that the Sullivan Law was patently
unconstitutional, whatever the courts of New York had
said.[40] But here too, the chief argument was not a constitutional one. More frequent and more strident was the
assertion that arms in the hands of reputable citizens
would help check the crime wave. The police, it seemed,
needed all the help it could get. Philadelphia authorities
announced in 1924 that they were issuing pistols to their
1,600 firemen.[41] Armed bands of citizens organized in
small towns to defend their local banks from robbers.
New York City rearmed to meet the crime wave; women
bought pistols there in record numbers, as did those who
worked on Wall Street. Armed guards were appointed to
protect the fines collected in traffic courts. A *New York
Times* canvass of gun stores in 1922 revealed that "never
before has there been such demand for sidearms of every

kind in the entire history of the city."[42] The city fathers
bowed to the pressure. They opened police pistol ranges
to bank messengers and private security guards, and they
eased the Sullivan Law restrictions. In 1916 city authorities had issued 8,000 permits to carry pistols; in the
first three months of 1922 they issued 35,000.[43]

The armed citizen might be better equipped to resist
thieves and robbers, but should he try to resist at all?
William McAdoo, who had been robbed himself, insisted
that it was better to submit, and thus avoid giving up
one's life along with his wallet. But this kind of reasoning
was repugnant to a great many. Even *The New York Times*
took issue with McAdoo: "The deterrent effect of resistance is, in the long run, considerable."[44] Would the
criminal really think twice if he suspected his intended
victim had a pistol within easy reach? The attorney general of Florida was convinced he would.[45] So apparently
was the superintendent of the Pennsylvania State Police,
who thus broke ranks with many of his colleagues. Speaking of crimes of violence he reasoned: "The outlawing of
pistols and revolvers is not likely to decrease crimes of
this character; in fact, it might tend to increase them, as
thugs would no longer have any cause to feel that their
victims might be armed."[46] Such arguments figured in
the repeal of gun registration acts in Arkansas and
Michigan and played a role in the turnabout of the
American Bar Association. Abandoning its earlier position against pistol manufacture, it endorsed the Uniform
Firearms Act in 1926.[47] The National Conference of
Commissioners on Uniform State Laws had given its
support the year before.[48] Most surprising of all, both
houses of the New York Legislature passed the Hanley-
Fake Bill, which would have replaced the Sullivan Law
with regulations inspired by the Uniform Firearms Act.

Only the veto of Governor Franklin Delano Roosevelt prevented its enactment.[49]

While the agitation over firearms legislation was producing these confusing results in various state legislatures, it was also penetrating for the first time to Capitol Hill. With the "pistol menace" now debated across the land, it was inevitable that a national solution would be sought. Congressmen with big city constituencies were most sensitive to the issue. The federal postal service, chief transporter of cheap, mail-order handguns, was the object of mounting criticism. A great number of bills concerning firearms were introduced in the course of the decade—some thirteen in the House of Representatives alone in 1924. Almost without exception they vanished into committee, never to be heard from again.

There were three proposals, however, that deserve some attention. The Capper Bill, named for Senator Arthur Capper of Kansas, had no direct national import since it was designed to regulate firearms in the District of Columbia. The bill did get nationwide attention briefly in 1924 when Senator Frank Greene of Vermont was seriously wounded on a street in downtown Washington, having been caught in the crossfire between police and armed bootleggers. The bill was noteworthy chiefly because it represented a victory for congressional partisans of the Uniform Firearms Act, on which it was modeled. After lengthy hearings it was signed into law in 1932.[50]

The Shields Bill, sponsored by Senator John K. Shields of Tennessee, attracted great attention in the early 1920s, and was the main hope of those who looked to Washington to banish the pistol from American life. Few of its partisans knew that Shields had introduced it as early as 1915, and several times thereafter. Its rein-

troduction in 1921 was acclaimed in the now aroused
urban press, which in many cases mistakenly saw in it an
absolute ban on handguns. Senator Shields' home state
was one of several that had long prohibited the carrying
of any handgun other than the "army" and "navy" pistols, which had to be carried "openly in the hand."
Senator Shields adopted this distinction in his bill, which
would prohibit the interstate shipment of any handguns
except the service models. With manufacture highly concentrated, this prohibition would soon stop production
of all other types. To the senator's way of thinking, the
service models were "big pistols," which were suitable to
keep in the home. Commercial types were "little pistols,"
suitable for concealment and therefore preferred by
criminals.[51]

The Shields Bill got one brief hearing in June 1921.
Though the proceedings do not appear to have been
published, it is clear from newspaper accounts that most
of the testimony was hostile. A representative of the
United States Revolver Association spoke against it, and
spokesmen for the railroads were worried about unwittingly violating such a law. Pistol manufacturers were
represented by S. M. Stone of Colt, who thought firearms
laws were more properly a matter for state legislatures.
He warned that such an enactment might hamper the
work of inventors in a field vital to national defense.[52]
But the chief obstacle to the bill's progress was the Senate
Judiciary Committee, to which it was invariably referred.
Senator Frank Brandegee of Connecticut was unaltera-
bly opposed to any measure which would adversely affect
one of his state's most important industries. Though
repeatedly introduced, the bill never came out of
committee.[53] An official of the Illinois State Bar who
inquired about its chances was told that it would never

become law so long as "the United States Senator from Connecticut" was on the Judiciary Committee.[54] Shields persisted until 1924, when his constituents voted him out of office.

A different fate was reserved for the Miller Bill, the most successful of several attempts to ban pistols from the mails. Representative John F. Miller of Washington had introduced the measure at the urging of citizens and officials in Seattle, who were concerned about mail-order sales in their city. Miller's proposal soon attracted much wider support, some of it carefully organized. At the House Committee hearings in 1926, testimony revealed that President Coolidge had received a large number of letters telling him in identical terms that because of mail-order pistols "young boys are being lured into crime."[55] A spokesman for the United National Association of Post Office Clerks presented a resolution supporting the proposal. Small arms manufacturers sent no representative to these hearings, though Representative Frank Foss of Massachusetts appeared to say that one pistol manufacturer in his state was opposed. The most voluble witness was J. W. Hull, who spoke on behalf of the American Reclamation Society of Detroit. He told the committee that England's low crime rate resulted from a general absence of firearms. The English policeman, he said, carried "a little billy, only 4 1/2 or 5 inches long," and seldom used it.[56]

The Miller Bill was reported out favorably and gave Congress its first chance to discuss firearms legislation at length. The House debates, which were extensive, revealed no opposition from Congressmen from Massachusetts and Connecticut, the so-called Munitions Belt. Congressman Miller and other supporters of the measure made it clear that the demand for it came from the cities, and stressed that it was aimed at the criminal element. Opposition there was, but it came from southern and western congressmen who frequently cited the Second Amendment in their arguments. To some of them, any federal legislation in this sphere was an infringement on the prerogatives of the states, sure to bring in its wake a horde of meddlesome functionaries. Congressman Otis Wingo of Arkansas felt there were already more than enough of these: "I tell you that right now in the state of Arkansas there are more Federal agents camped on its soil nosing into the private affairs of individuals than we have State, county, township, and municipal officers."[57]

The most vehement opponent of the Miller Bill was Congressman Thomas Blanton of Texas. It would not work, he insisted, since the criminal would get a gun in spite of any law. This proposal he held to be of doubtful constitutionality. The Sullivan Law, which inevitably came up in the debate, he considered "not worth the paper it was written on."[58] Most of all, Blanton argued that firearms in the proper hands were the best defense against aggression, foreign or domestic, military or criminal:

> I want to say this: I hope that every American boy, whether he is from Texas, New York, or Washington, will know how to use a six-shooter. I hope he will learn from his hip to hit a dime twenty paces off. It would be their only means of defense in combating that deadly art of jiu jitsu in close quarters should war ever face them with such danger. It is not brave men who know how to shoot straight that violate laws or carry concealed weapons.

I hope every woman in America will learn how to use a revolver. I hope she will not use it but I hope she will know how. It will be for her safety; it will safeguard her rights and it will prevent her rights from being jeopardized. That is what the framers of this Constitution had in mind when they said the Congress should never infringe upon the right to keep firearms in the home.[59]

The Miller Bill cleared the House several times, only to be crowded out of the Senate calendar. It was eventually passed by the Senate and signed into law in 1927. With a few minor exceptions, it effectively closed the mails to the pistol.[60]

Federal firearms legislation in the 1920s was modest at best. There is little doubt that the Shields Bill and others of the same cast could not surmount the opposition of congressmen from the Munitions Belt, who were also successful in getting high tariff protection for small arms in the Fordney-McCumber Tariff of 1922 and the Hawley-Smoot Tariff of 1930.[61] Yet, other factors were probably as important. There was, first of all, no real leadership from the White House on the issue. Indeed, President Coolidge said publicly that he did not think federal legislation would help much.[62] The concept of federal police power was still new and any talk of its extension stirred states' rights advocates. Nor was there any promise that federal authorities would be more successful than the states, their record in Prohibition enforcement hardly being encouraging. As the *Saturday Evening Post* pointed out: "If the Federal government cannot prevent the landing and distribution of shiploads of rum, how can it stop the criminal from getting the most easily concealed and vital tool of his trade?"[63]

Yet within a few years the drive for federal action became so intense that the government did enter the field decisively. With the onset of the Depression criminal activity became even more rampant. Desperadoes such as John Dillinger, Clyde Barrow and his consort Bonnie Parker, the Barker-Karpis Gang, and others made the worst excesses of the 1920s pale in comparison. To the repertory of crime was added kidnapping on grand scale. The criminal added new and formidable weapons to his arsenal, weapons that in most cases were not covered by existing state laws. As early as 1922, Chicago police made the disquieting discovery that the city's lawbreakers were ordering sales catalogues from the Maxim Silencer Company.[64] New York hoodlums developed an interest shortly thereafter.[65] The term *silencer* was something of a misnomer since at best the device only muffled the report of a gun rather than rendering it inaudible. Even so, press and public began to talk of the sinister apparatus that made death "a ghostly visitation."[66]

Then too, there was the sawed-off shotgun, a weapon of devastating effect at close range. In itself the arm was hardly new. As early as 1898 Winchester had introduced a shotgun with a barrel shortened to twenty inches, advertising it as a police weapon useful in riot control.[67] This riot gun, as it was known, had been adopted by the American Expeditionary Force as a "trench gun," useful in close combat. The weapon got considerable publicity when the Germans officially protested its use as contrary to the laws of war.[68] By the mid-1920s the sawed-off shotgun began to find favor in criminal circles. Compact and effective even without careful aiming, it could be used from moving vehicles—though Clyde Barrow perfected a "quick draw" with one concealed in a special holster sewn into his trousers.[69]

But nothing quite symbolized the crime of the era as did the "Tommy Gun." This weapon was a product of World War I, having been devised by Colonel John M. Thompson of the United States Army. It too was designed for trench warfare; indeed, its inventor used the colorful term "trench broom" in describing its function.[70] It came too late to be used in the war, but Thompson and his associates formed a company called Auto Ordnance to market it commercially. Colt agreed to do the actual manufacture, and several thousand were made. Thompson called his weapon a submachine gun, to distinguish it from the bulkier and less portable machine guns that had been used in the war. It was a fully automatic arm, and would fire a stream of .45 caliber bullets until the trigger was released or the magazine exhausted.

After the war, military interest in the new weapon was not great. Thompson offered it to police departments —it was demonstrated to the Chicago Police in 1922[71]—but once again few sales were forthcoming. The United States government was also a poor prospect. Even as late as 1926, the Treasury Department had only four machine guns on its inventory. (Inexplicably, the Department of Agriculture had one.)[72] The original price of $225 was dropped by $50, but business scarcely improved. By 1925 Auto Ordnance had sold only 3,000 of the initial lot of 15,000 manufactured by Colt.[73] The company took what orders it could. Salesmen became, as a Colt official put it "a bit careless in their merchandising."[74] The first large order, subsequently seized, turned out to have been placed by the Irish Republican Army.[75]

Chicago gangsters were the first to discover the submachine gun's formidable attributes in the winter of 1925-1926. It appeared in Philadelphia in 1927 and in New York in 1928.[76] By the early 1930s the Tommy Gun had become a household word, winning the endorsement of Mad Dog Coll, Ma Barker, and Pretty Boy Floyd. More than anything else, the submachine gun opened the doors to federal legislation. Like the silencer and the sawed-off shotgun, it seemed something no reputable person would want or need, and no criminal should be allowed to have. Here, at least, was a category of deadly weapons eminently deserving of the strictest regulation at the national level.

The clamor for federal action coincided with the advent of the New Deal, an administration resolved to mobilize the full power of the national government and direct it at a whole range of besetting problems. Along with revolutionary economic programs, the New Deal intended a major assault on crime. A strengthened Federal Bureau of Investigation would be one part of the plan and Federal firearms legislation another. Even before he was elected, Franklin D. Roosevelt had raised the possibility of a federal law on weapons.[77] His newly appointed attorney general, Homer Cummings, announced in the summer of 1933 that existing laws on pistols were woefully deficient.[78] He and his staff began the preparation of a dozen anti-crime bills, including a proposed National Firearms Act.

The attorney general had every hope of success. The nation had the most forceful chief executive it had seen in decades, and Congress had accepted his leadership rather consistently. With newspapers daily placarding the latest exploits of the country's major criminals, the time seemed at hand for decisive federal intervention.

The prospect for strict firearms controls was particularly promising. Gangster activity had given weaponry a sinister connotation. So probably would the Nye Committee investigations into excessive profits and illicit practices in the munitions industry.[79] This would limit the effectiveness of whatever opposition the small arms industry might put up.

Yet Cummings probably underestimated the forces opposing him. Small arms manufacturers, already wrestling with the problem of survival in the Depression era, would present a solid front.[80] There was also potential opposition in the nation's several million hunters and in its lesser numbers of gun collectors and target shooters, who had found a common spokesman in the National Rifle Association. The organization had changed considerably since its founding in 1871, with most of the change coming after World War I. The transformation was largely due to an enterprising NRA executive named C. B. Lister, who had joined the organization's staff in 1921 with the title promotion manager. At that time the NRA was still small; of the 3,500 individual members in 1921 the great majority were connected with the Army or National Guard.[81] Their concern and that of the organization was essentially military markmanship, particularly with the service rifle.

Lister directed a membership drive that brought thousands of sportsmen into the NRA. By 1934 its membership had increased tenfold and it had as affiliates over 2,000 local sportsmen's and shooters' clubs.[82] Government sales of surplus arms were a vital element in the organization's growth, especially after 1924, when the War Department channeled all sales through it. NRA membership and club affiliation enabled thousands to purchase surplus arms at nominal cost. Some 200,000 were sold from government arsenals in the interwar period, the great bulk of them service rifles.[83] Though military figures remained prominent in its directorate, the NRA broadened its interests as its membership grew. In 1925 it took over a youth marksmanship program previously sponsored by Winchester.[84] It began to take an interest in firearms legislation generally, and played a role in the framing of the Capper Bill. By 1934 it was the largest association of firearms users in the country and the best organized. During the hearings on the National Firearms Act, a United States senator would describe its executive vice-president as "the most influential man in this country in opposition to firearms legislation."[85]

Hearings on the National Firearms Act began before a House Committee in April 1934. Senate hearings got under way the following month. The Senate hearings were the more interesting because of the presence of Senator Royal S. Copeland of New York, an outspoken advocate of strict firearms control with ideas of his own on what should be done. Cumming's proposal (S. 3680) had to share the spotlight with two bills (S. 885 and S. 2258) which incorporated Copeland's views.

Cummings proposed to use the federal tax power to secure the nationwide registration of several categories of firearms and devices to which the criminal was addicted. These included pistols of greater than .22 caliber, shotguns and rifles with barrels less than eighteen inches long, machine guns and other fully automatic weapons, silencers, and certain types of "freak" weapons (firearms concealed in canes, etc.). His plan would require a federal license for anyone who manufactured, imported, or dealt in such weapons. Each time one of these changed hands, a transfer tax would be imposed—one dollar for pistols, two hundred dollars for machine guns. The transfer would be made on forms provided by the Internal Revenue Service, and would require fingerprinting of the purchaser. With each gun would go one or more forms, with tax stamps attached. These would be something in the nature of a title to an automobile. Each time an arm was sold another form would accompany it, with a copy preserved by the IRS. An additional provision (absent from the House version) called on Americans already possessing pistols to register them with the IRS within four months of the time the bill became law. No penalty was attached to the violation of this provision. Cummings apparently hoped for voluntary compliance. (He had earlier expressed doubts about its constitutionality if enforced.)[86]

Senator Copeland's approach was different, being based on the federal power to regulate interstate commerce. Only manufacturers would be able to ship concealable firearms across state lines. Such shipments had to be carefully marked and certified and could not be made to anyone other than licensed dealers in states like New York, whose laws might thus be violated. Interstate shipment of machine guns was flatly banned. Copeland and his colleagues added two provisions which they felt would greatly assist in criminal investigations. One of these required manufacturers to keep on file at least one bullet fired from each weapon they produced, for purposes of ballistic comparison. This procedure had figured in the Sacco-Vanzetti Case. The other provision called for bullets to be marked on their bases with a code number or letter corresponding to an IRS district in which they were sold.[87]

Among the witnesses who appeared before the com-

mittee were a number of veterans in the debate over
firearms legislation. Karl T. Frederick of the United
States Revolver Association and the NRA spoke against
the bills. Frederick L. Hoffman provided the committee
with several sets of statistics. His estimate was that,
through homicides, suicides, and accidents, firearms had
taken 250,000 lives in the preceding two decades.[88] Colt
representatives spoke for the small arms producers.
They were worried that high federal license fees for
dealers in firearms would destroy their distribution
chain. Colt President Frank C. Nichols felt obliged to
defend his company in light of adverse publicity (Colt
was at the time the only manufacturer of machine guns):
"We have been in business nearly a hundred years, an
honorable business and a legitimate business. We have
used the utmost care in the distribution and sales of our
product."[89]

The star witness in the hearings was General M. A.
Reckord, executive vice-president of the NRA. By wire
and by mail the organization had alerted its members to
the hearings. In its opposition to the National Firearms
Act of Attorney General Cummings the NRA conjured
up the spectre of compulsory registration of *all* firearms:
"Within a year of the passage of H.R. 9066, every rifle
and shotgun owner in the country will find himself paying a special revenue tax and having himself finger-
printed and photographed for the Federal 'rogue's gal-
lery' every time he buys or sells a gun of any
description."[90] Though Cummings may well have had
such a scheme in the back of his mind, it did not figure in
any of the bills being examined. Both committees were
visibly angry at the flood of letters and telegrams they
received, and for this they blamed the NRA. General

Reckord was closely questioned by Representative John W. McCormack of Massachusetts:

Representative McCormack: You have contacted such as you could and wired the members of the Association?
General Reckord: In each state, or practically every state, we have a state rifle association, and we advised a number of those people that the hearing would be held today. Nothing was said about Mr. [Karl T.] Frederick or any particular individual being present.
McCormack: Did you ask them to wire here?
Reckord: I do not recall the exact language of the telegram; I would say yes, probably we did. . . .
McCormack: Did you wire the people telling them what the recommendations were going to be to the Committee?
Reckord: No, except that the legislation was bad.
McCormack: And they blindly followed it?
Reckord: I would not say blindly.[91]

Senator Copeland was even more incensed: "The impression has been sent all over the country we are trying to embarrass the farmer so that he cannot use a revolver or shotgun, or leave one with his wife, or take a pistol along in his automobile."[92] He asked General Reckord to submit copies of NRA releases and mailouts, and quizzed him closely on NRA finances. The general maintained stoutly that the association had no financial ties with arms manufacturers, though he did acknowledge that on one occasion the NRA had served as agent for the transfer of $300 of industry money to the New Jersey Rifle Association.[93] The motive for this transfer was not given.

Copeland was no doubt chagrined that his own bills got

short shrift; the House committee had already reported out an amended version of Cummings' bill. It was demonstrated in the hearings that the schemes for preserving sample fired slugs and marking bullets would be of little practical use in solving crimes. The NRA had described the bullet marking plan as "one of the outstanding bits of asininity in the proposed law." Reckord and others conversant with firearms were able to point out several inaccuracies in phrasing. Much of the nomenclature and many of the definitions were rewritten in light of their criticism.

General Reckord had no objection to strict legislation covering machine guns and other "gangster type" weapons: "You can be just as severe with machine guns and sawed-off shotguns as you desire, and we will go along with you."[94] On the matter of handguns, Reckord thought the Uniform Firearms Act provided the best solution. At one point in the House hearings, a congressman tried to pin the general down on the value of registering all the guns in the country: "I ask you if you do not think it would be really a fine thing for every firearm which could be used to take human life and in the committing of robberies and other crimes, to be registered so we could know where they are in the United States?" The general replied: "I do not think it would do a bit of good."[95] In an apparent effort to get the Cummings Bill through unaltered, the attorney general's office suggested a compromise that was also proposed in the House hearings: ownership of pistols would be regulated, but with special consideration being given to members of organized groups such as the NRA. General Reckord was not receptive to the idea.[96]

Both committees eventually reported out amended versions of the Cummings Bill which omitted pistols from the list of weapons to be taxed and registered. Cummings tried to rescue his bill by drumming up public support. Assistant Attorney General Joseph Keenan told a meeting of the General Confederation of Women's Clubs that the NRA had emasculated the proposal, thus showing itself more powerful than the Justice Department. The clubwomen took up the gauntlet. One of their speakers assured Keenan that "two million American club-women are strong enough to lick them into a frazzle and make them put back into that measure the pistols and revolvers they deleted from it."[97] Another wave of letters and telegrams arrived in Washington.

Though the amended bill was approved by both House and Senate with little debate, there were congressional misgivings. At one point the entire anti-crime package was stalled in the House Judiciary Committee. Its chairman, Congressman Hatton Summers of Texas, felt the measures violated states' rights. President Roosevelt had to call Summers to the White House and make a special appeal for the legislation.[98] A few weeks later Roosevelt signed the National Firearms Act into law.[99]

In the aftermath of the 1934 hearings, Senator Copeland was still anxious to secure some sort of federal regulation on firearms generally. Exploratory talks with NRA representatives and others established enough common ground to serve as the basis for the Federal Firearms Act. When hearings were held in 1937, they were brief and unmarred by the acrimony that had attended the earlier proceedings.[100] The new act established a general licensing and recordkeeping procedure for those who made or sold firearms in interstate commerce. The license fees were low—only one dollar for dealers. No arms could be shipped across state lines to individuals unless they could establish that the purchase was not contrary to state laws by showing permits where required, etc. From Copeland's point of view, this was the chief value of the proposal, since it buttressed the restrictive legislation of New York and other states. Several provisions were probably inspired by the Uniform Firearms Act, notably those barring convicted felons from receiving interstate arms shipments and curbing the movement of stolen arms and those with serial numbers altered.[101]

The Federal Firearms Act of 1938 was the last major piece of federal legislation before World War II. It did not completely still the discussion on the subject. Attorney General Cummings, for example, continued to talk about further efforts. He still felt that a comprehensive system of national registration was a worthwhile goal. Addressing the International Association of Chiefs of Police in 1937, he said it would be no more onerous than registering one's automobile. "No honest man can object to it. Show me the man who does not want his gun registered and I will show you a man who should not have a gun."[102]

Opponents of federal legislation thought they detected a new and ominous note in the administration's efforts. The attack on the pistol and the machine gun, said one of the hunting magazines, was "believed by many people to be part of an avowed effort to eventually deny all citizens the right to possess firearms of any kind and for whatever purpose."[103] Cummings himself encouraged this view: "I am convinced of this—any practical measure for the control of firearms must at least contain provision for the registration of *all* firearms."[104] The idea cropped up again on the eve of World War II in the guise of a "census" of all arms in civilian hands. The purpose was twofold: to determine the ability of the home front to resist aggression, and to detect arms stockpiling by subversives. These proposals produced little except strong condemnations in hunting and sporting periodicals.[105] In Europe, by contrast, the threat of war and subversion produced a wave of significant firearms legislation of a generally restrictive nature. This was the case in Great Britain (1937), Germany (1938), and France (1939). These laws remained in effect after the war, and later were further strengthened. By the middle of the twentieth century, Europe and America were as far apart on the issue as they had been at the end of the eighteenth.

Confusing though it was in terms of its legislative results, the firearms controversy of the interwar years does seem to have shaken the traditional attitude of unthinking acceptance. The pistol remained, in the popular eye, the chief object of concern. A 1938 Gallup poll revealed that 79 percent of those responding felt "all owners of pistols and revolvers should be required to register with the government."[106] Though there are no earlier statistics for comparison, the handgun had probably acquired a more sinister connotation than before. There is also clear evidence for the first time of a tendency to attach moral taint to *all* firearms, including the hunter's shotgun and the marksman's rifle. The movement to register all arms, modest though it was, reflects this change.

In part, this new attitude may have been inspired by international developments. Advocates of rigid gun control often spoke of personal disarmament as a logical corollary of international disarmament. Then too, pacifism developed a certain vogue in the 1930s. Perhaps more influential than any other element was the Nye Committee and its marathon investigation of the munitions industry. It has been said that the committee's slant was both anti-business and anti-war; whatever its purpose, it cast a cloud of suspicion over the arms maker and his wares. The small arms industry was only one of the committee's concerns, for it also spent a great deal of time investigating the du Pont empire, the Electric Boat Company, which made submarines, various aircraft manufacturers, and others. But it did bring to light some troubling revelations about small arms sales to warring nations. The letter of a Remington sales representative was much quoted: "We certainly are in a hell of a business when a fellow has to wish for trouble so as to make a living, the only consolation being, however, if we don't get the business, someone else will. It would be a terrible state of affairs if my conscience started to bother me now."[107] The hearings also produced a climate favorable to rumor. Colt, it was said, had started tooling up for World War I as early as 1908 and J. P. Morgan was reputed to have gotten his start selling defective weapons that shattered the thumbs of Union soldiers.[108]

Nor was this all. The Depression and the New Deal had the effect of directing public attention at social problems and the environment that bred them. If the pistol had been attacked as the instrument of the gangster, the gun generically was now for the first time challenged for the moral dangers it posed to unsuspecting users, especially the young. Women's organizations, which were active in the controversy, were impelled primarily by maternal concern. The subject of guns came up at a White House Conference on Child Health early in 1932. At the conclusion of the conference, one of its spokesmen delivered a radio address sponsored by the National Anti-Weapons Society. "Pistols and guns," he argued, "do not fit into the pattern of a safe, healthy, and happy environment. They belong to an environment which breeds delinquency, accidents, and crimes in sudden anger."[109] Senator Capper also went on the air, sponsored by the same organization. Parents, he observed, thought it "cute" to have their children play with toy guns. "I do not think this is 'cute.' I think it is the real American tragedy."[110]

In 1934, *Parents' Magazine* offered its readers a symposium of views on a question that would have been unthinkable two decades before: "Should a Boy Have a Gun?" Bob Nichols, writer for *Field and Stream*, thought that with proper supervision it was an excellent idea. The .22 caliber rifle was a "character builder;" it taught responsibility in the best American tradition. Indeed, he thought the question might never have been raised but for women, who "as a rule instinctively fear and mistrust guns."[111] But Mr. and Mrs. Robert E. Simon of the United Parents' Association of New York City were of a different mind. To them any gun was harmful, even a toy one, since it symbolized "gangsterism and war."[112] Thus, the firearms controversy of the interwar period, which began with a crime wave, ended on a note of concern for American youth. It would resume on that same note, but not before two decades had passed.

9   The Crisis of
      the Sixties

He is a citizen who has kept his nationalistic youth in a society that is becoming sophisticated and jaded.

—Definition of the American hunter, American Rifleman, 1967

The onset of World War II effectively stilled all talk of firearms legislation, just as had been the case in World War I. Once again the gun became a symbol of the nation's strength, proficiency in its use an important asset to the war effort.[1] The war also enabled the small arms industry to close the books on what had been a troubled era in more ways than one. There had been the opprobrium attending the Nye Committee investigations. Pacifists had picketed the plants of several manufacturers. There had also been much talk of nationalizing the munitions industry, though it had not produced much more than government controls over exports.

216

In strictly business terms the interwar period was far from prosperous. Following World War I came inevitable problems of conversion. Labor difficulties further clouded the picture. The inside contract system gave way to unionization and collective bargaining. The transformation was not always smooth. Many of the companies resisted—Smith & Wesson to the point of turning their plant over to the government in 1918 rather than accept a strike settlement proposed by the National War Labor Board.[2] Colt subsequently collided with the National Recovery Administration over the labor issue and lost its "Blue Eagle."[3] The Depression dealt the industry a severe blow. Smith & Wesson's president later recalled his company had operated "ten years in the red."[4] A Nye Committee investigator reported that at the Winchester plant in 1934 "every department has been cut to the bone and the whole place seems to be wheezing along on one cylinder."[5] In 1919 there had been twenty-six manufacturers; by 1933, as a result of mergers and failures, there were only twenty-two. In the same period the value of the industry's products had dropped from $30 million to $9 million.[6]

The war changed all of this. Remington expanded 2,000 percent to fulfill its war contracts.[7] In the 1940s Smith & Wesson manufactured more arms than they had produced in the preceding ninety years. In the process, the firm developed a manufacturing capacity "larger than that of the combined revolver manufacturers of the world."[8] Well before the war's end, small arms firms laid plans for conversion to peacetime manufacture, developing new lines in anticipation of a lucrative civilian market.

They were not to be disappointed. This time war production had absorbed virtually all their manufacturing capacity. By 1945 there was considerable pent-up demand in a civilian market that had been neglected for nearly half a decade. The demand was further spurred by returning veterans. Some twelve million men had received military training and some familiarity with firearms, and many of them returned to civilian life with a continuing interest in weaponry. (It has been shown that the incidence of firearms ownership among veterans is significantly higher than among nonveterans[9].) There was an expanded interest in shooting sports generally, as is evidenced by the increase in clubs and associations. Before the war the NRA had had some 3,500 affiliated local clubs. By 1948 the number had climbed to 6,500, and by 1963 it stood at 11,000. Hunting, too, became increasingly popular after the war. In 1937 hunters had purchased seven million licenses; the number had doubled by 1961.[10]

In the postwar period, film producers rediscovered the frontier and western themes in American history and exploited them thoroughly. The new medium of television served up similar fare to its enthralled viewers. It made Davy Crockett into a major folk hero and it popularized his Kentucky rifle, the "all-American weapon" to which the *Saturday Evening Post* and other magazines dedicated feature articles.[11] The cowboy and his weaponry got even greater attention. In 1956 *Life* magazine examined the western film genre, noting that "in Hollywood eight films with 'gun' in the title have been completed and actors are learning how to shoot and be shot."[12] And each evening, a television critic in *The Nation* reported, "twenty to thirty million American homes rock with the sound of sudden gunfire."[13]

The cult had its effect on American youth. In 1962 toy guns were the largest category of toys for boys, with sales exceeding $100 million annually.[14] Fathers caught the contagion along with their sons, though the six-shooters they sought were real ones. The most famous of these had been Colt's Model 1873 Single Action Army Revolver. Colt had produced a third of a million of them before dropping them from their line in 1947. Demand for the pistols became so great that the company resumed production in 1955. The fad for things western added a new dimension to shooting with the emergence of the quick-draw or fast-draw fraternity. By 1960 there were hundreds of clubs whose members were busy reviving such lost arts as "up-twist fanning," "the border shift," and "the road agent's spin."[15]

Interest in historical firearms had its greatest effect on the hobby of gun collecting. Before the war it had been the pastime of relatively few: in 1939 the number of collectors was placed at only 50,000.[16] While many of the collectors of that era were persons of modest means, the gun collection was still thought of as something a gentleman displayed on the walls of his oak-paneled study. Charles Edward Chapel, who wrote the gun collector's first handbook in 1939, clearly described a hobby that was in its infancy. He suggested looking in attics, barns, and junk shops. Extremely rare and valuable specimens, he wrote, could be purchased "for a few cents."[17] That was not to be the case in the postwar era. The demand for antique weapons skyrocketed as an army of novice collectors appeared—and prices skyrocketed too. One expert has estimated that from 1938 to 1958 the price of Kentucky rifles increased 430 percent, and that of antique Colt arms 800 percent. Collectible arms of foreign origin had only doubled in value in the same period.[18] By 1958 the number of gun collectors was placed at 650,000.[19]

As interest continued to grow, the traditional lines of demarcation separating hunter, target shooter, and col-

lector became increasingly blurred. The handgun, usually associated with the pistol range and self-defense,
became a hunting weapon. There was also a "black powder" boom—shooting and hunting with antique arms or
modern replicas of them. The Civil War centennial inspired a number of these replicas. But perhaps the most
intriguing phenomenon of the era was the self-styled
"gun buff" or "gun nut." While he might not have the
expert's knowledge of internal ballistics or skeet range
decorum, he made up for this lack in his enthusiasm and
catholicity of taste for anything that would shoot, from
antique derringer to anti-tank gun. Part-time collector,
spare-time shooter, he avidly read the popular shooting
magazines and he attended the gun shows held in countless armories and exhibition halls all over the country. He
and hundreds of thousands like him acquired firearms in
staggering numbers. In the twenty-two year period from
1946 until the Gun Control Act of 1968, American industry sold some 45 million small arms into the domestic
civilian market, as many as it had sold in the preceding
half century. During the same period about 10 million
imported arms were sold.[20] In addition, untold
thousands of souvenir firearms were brought home by
returning veterans. There were also large sales of U.S.
government surplus, though there are no complete figures for the number sold in the period.

Enterprises associated with firearms could not help
but prosper. A 1955 survey by *Business Week* projected a
booming market of $200 million in sales of rifles, shot-
guns, and ammunition for them, with Winchester's business alone nearly half of that amount.[21] A thriving press
sprang up to serve the shooting fraternity. In the 1940s
the NRA's *American Rifleman* and the annual *Gun Digest*
had been the chief literary fare for firearms en-

thusiasts, supplemented by articles in hunting publications and a column for gun collectors in *Hobbies* magazine. Then came *Gun Report* and *Guns* in 1955, *Guns and Ammo* and *Guns and Hunting* in 1958, followed by *Shooting Times* and *Gun World* in 1960. The number would continue to grow. Books on firearms, rare before the war, became profitable to publish. A 1963 bibliography listed over 200 titles.[22]

The National Rifle Association thrived too. Before the war its membership had reached 50,000; by 1963 it had exceeded half a million.[23] Though part of this phenomenal growth can be traced to government surplus arms sold in large numbers to those who joined, the increase in membership was also a reflection of rising interest in all that had to do with firearms. With growth came inevitable adjustments. The Association's governing body, a sixty-member Board of Directors (today seventy-five), had customarily been elected at its annual convention by the "life" members (life membership costs $100). At the 1952 convention, the governing body for the quarter-million member organization was elected by ninety-eight life members in attendance. Beginning the following year mail ballots were sent to all life members.[24] The military continued to figure prominently in its directorate; in 1949 its thirteen-member Executive Council included five generals and a colonel. But here too there were signs of change: the first woman was elected to the Board of Directors in that same year.[25]

The NRA's chief organ of expression was its monthly *American Rifleman*, which now competed with a host of other publications. The publication was somewhat hampered by its distribution system, for it was seldom sold on news stands. Its editorial policy made it less attractive than its competitors to the casual reader. It was (and is) of high technical quality, but its treatises on sectional density and pressure curves did not always make exhilarating reading to the "gun buff." The *Rifleman* took a dim view of what it called "the quick-draw craze."[26] It remained equally reserved in its advertising policy, refusing to take ads for products it considered dangerous or shoddy in quality. It ran no ads for bazookas, anti-tank guns, and other such lethal items. Its authoritative if sober tone seemed suited to the *doyen* of firearms publications. It also projected the self-image of a long-established and respectable organization which by 1961 numbered among its life members Dwight Eisenhower, Richard Nixon, and John F. Kennedy.

The gun culture, then, flowered spectacularly in the years following World War II. The war itself had only served to stimulate a predilection for firearms long characteristic of American society. A conjunction of circumstances in the postwar era allowed that predilection to flourish unhampered. For all its problems, the era was one of prosperity and leisure, permitting an unprecedented indulgence in popular tastes. At the same time there was no simple return to "normalcy" as in 1918. The cold war kept the nation on the *qui vive* for more than a decade. As had been the case before, concern over military preparedness lent to the gun a certain respectability and acceptance. Domestic preoccupations—such problems as crime, civil disorder, and social unrest which customarily sparked anti-gun sentiment—were pushed into the background. Tragic incidents there were involving firearms, some of which attracted great public attention: the 1949 shooting rampage of a mentally disturbed veteran in New Jersey which left thirteen dead, the abortive attempt on President Truman's life, and the fusillade that Puerto Rican nationalists unleashed in the U.S.

House of Representatives. But none of these events sparked an anti-gun crusade.

In this climate there was no drive for gun control in Congress.[27] State legislatures were more active, but even here there were few radical departures. The NRA's legislative service screened the proposed bills, several hundred of which each year dealt in some way with firearms. Of these, it would find perhaps fifty "objectionable" and so notify its members. Well into the late 1950s its annual roundup of legislative activity would conclude with the statement: "No unduly restrictive legislation was passed." There was little acrimony even over objectionable proposals. Most of them were sponsored by conservationist groups which themselves had ties with the shooting fraternity.[28] An *American Rifleman* editorial of 1955 held that the greatest danger to the right to bear arms came from people who were "sincere," "conscientious," but "misguided."[29]

It is customary to consider that this climate changed abruptly with the tragedy in Dallas on November 22, 1963. Something of the gun's charisma did die that day with John Kennedy, but already there had been tremors of concern. Initially that concern had been over accidents with firearms rather than the morality of their use. With a record number of Americans using guns, and often ill-trained in their use, shooting accidents became all too common. The quick-draw fad began to draw adverse comment; some of its devotees persisted in using live ammunition, and this produced a number of tragedies. They shot themselves so frequently that by 1960 a medical journal published an article on a new national malady: "Gunshot Wounds of Lower Extremity: Fast Draw Syndrome."[30] In shooting circles it was feared that the craze would give all shooting sports a bad name.

This concern was even more pronounced in hunting, where millions of novices were taking the field. There were periodic complaints about the hunter's destructiveness and recklessness.[31] And there were tragedies here too: Colorado's 1948 big game season cost seventeen hunters their lives.[32] Hunting magazines sounded warnings. The NRA became so concerned that it launched its own effort to compile statistics on hunting accidents. In 1950 it introduced a hunter safety course.[33] But the problem persisted and grew. The *Saturday Evening Post* and other magazines devoted feature articles to it.[34] In 1959 it received national attention when a retired General Motors vice-president was accidentally killed on a duck hunt. *Life* magazine found this tragedy "a grimly dramatic illustration of the toll among today's mushrooming multitude of hunters."[35]

Even more significant, and more ominous from the hunter's standpoint, was the questioning of the "ethical aspects" of the sport—a term devised by the *Reader's Guide to Periodical Literature* to cover articles that began to appear in the late 1950s. The author of an article in *Holiday* magazine defended the sport as necessary to hold down the game population but felt people hunted because they "like to kill."[36] Another wrote of his experience on an antelope hunt. After it was over he resolved it would be his last: "I will never again interfere with the lives of my fellow creatures."[37] The nation also discovered ecology, which for many was yet another reason to dislike the hunter. By 1963 *Field and Stream* could detect a swelling aversion to man's oldest sport.[38]

With the late 1950s also came a rise in public concern over certain internal problems that did or could involve the gun. *The New Republic* warned as early as 1956 that the growing civil rights controversy was causing tremendous sales of firearms in southern communities.[39] Crime, too, called for increasing public attention, and particularly juvenile delinquency. It was linked to comic books, television violence, and the easy availability of firearms to minors. A *Saturday Evening Post* editor ordered a "deactivated" machine gun in his infant daughter's name and made it operative with a few minutes' work.[40] The possibility of such traffic indicated to him "a yawning loophole in the National Firearms Act."[41] By 1959 mail-order peddling of deadly weapons to minors had drawn the attention of a Senate subcommittee. In the summer of that same year *McCall's* carried a long article by Carl Bakal. He too dwelt on the tragic consequences of guns in the hands of teenagers. He went on to launch an attack against the gun itself, which he held responsible for a grim saturnalia that brought death to some 14,000 Americans each year.[42] At the time Bakal's article was the only frontal assault on the gun, but he began gathering materials for a book on the subject.

By the late 1950s the hunting and shooting fraternity was becoming alarmed. In August 1959 the American Institute of Public Opinion (Gallup Poll) asked Americans a series of questions about guns—the first such inquiry in twenty years. It revealed that though there were firearms in half the homes in the nation, three out of four who were questioned felt a police permit should be required for anyone wishing to purchase a gun. Fifty-nine percent agreed that handguns should be outlawed except for police use. The results were furnished to a hundred newspapers, though many editors did not feel the poll was sufficiently newsworthy to publish. But the sporting press did not dismiss it so lightly.[43] Already, in September 1958 an *American Rifleman* editorial had urged "let's take the offensive." It counseled vigilance against a heightened effort to obtain rigid gun control legislation, supported in some instances by "those who would like to see America a disarmed nation."[44] At the end of the year the *Rifleman* introduced a new column, "The Armed Citizen." Here were listed instances in which law-abiding citizens with guns had thwarted criminals. *Field and Stream* sponsored a conference in 1961 that led to the creation of the National Shooting Sports Foundation (NSSF). Its contributing members, nearly a hundred firms dealing in firearms and accessories, sporting publications, etc., underwrote a campaign to emphasize the positive aspects of the various shooting sports.[45]

Out of the public eye another controversy was developing within the world of guns itself. Domestic small arms producers were unhappy over the government's sale of surplus weapons to NRA members at a fraction of the cost of commercial arms. What concerned them even more was the enormous quantity of foreign surplus arms that began to enter the American market in the mid-1950s. The largest import, and the most troubling one from the industry's point of view, was the surplus military rifle. With a customs valuation of under five dollars it easily surmounted the tariff barrier, to be sold to the gun enthusiast at a fraction of the price of center-fire rifles manufactured by American firms. By 1958 an enterprising businessman named Samuel Cummings, president of International Armament Corporation, had erected an empire in military surplus.[46] As the chief importer of surplus small arms, he believed he was the main target of SAAMI, the manufacturers' trade organization. In 1965 he told a Senate subcommittee that SAAMI and its various members had made no fewer than eleven efforts to throttle the import business through legislation.[47]

The industry found considerable sympathy for its efforts in the congressional delegations of Connecticut and Massachusetts, the two states in which small arms production was centered.[48] The Massachusetts Senate sent a memorial to Congress asking a curb on imports, and the Department of Commerce was induced to undertake a study of the industry's economic difficulties.[49] The problem was also discussed in Congress. In April 1958 Congressman Albert P. Morano of Connecticut introduced a measure designed to bar imports of foreign surplus arms. A few days later Senator John F. Kennedy introduced a similar proposal in the upper house. Many of the foreign arms were dangerous, said Morano, particularly the Italian Mannlicher-Carcano rifle, which had "a tendency to blow up in the shooter's face." (A rifle of this type, imported a few months later, was used by President Kennedy's assassin.) Morano called on Congress to stop "a practice which not only jeopardizes life and limb of American citizens, but also is a contributing cause to unemployment and economic decline in our domestic arms industry."[50] As had been the case numerous times before when the industry sought protection, its role in national defense was emphasized.

These efforts came to nought, the chief obstacle being congressional inertia. The importers were of course opposed, but lacked political leverage. Sportsmen and hunters, who stood to lose a considerable windfall, remained silent, perhaps because the issue received relatively little publicity. Opponents of the ban found a strange ally in the State Department, which felt that it was better for foreign military hardware to be absorbed by the American market than to flow to various foreign trouble spots.[51] The shooting press took no public stand on the issue and gave it little publicity. Advertising revenues from domestic manufacturers were an important item in their budgets. On the other hand, the deluge of inexpensive weapons from abroad was fueling the boom in shooting sports. The NRA also stood to lose if sales of U.S. government surplus arms to its members were suspended. The *American Rifleman* prudently limited itself to reporting the various maneuvers in Washington.[52]

Senator Thomas J. Dodd of Connecticut had also spoken in favor of curbing imports of surplus arms that were damaging the economy of his state. In his capacity as chairman of the Senate's Subcommittee on Juvenile Delinquency, he was encountering another aspect of the problem: the mail-order sale of cheap, imported weapons to teenagers. He was particularly concerned about the importation of cheap pistols, the so-called "Saturday night specials." These were entering the country labeled as parts, and sometimes as junk, to be assembled and sold through pulp magazine advertisements at ten dollars or so to anyone who could fill out an order form. In 1961 Dodd and his staff began discussions with representatives of the domestic industry, the NRA, and other interested groups, with a view to framing a bill that would curb these practices. Their response was cautiously favorable. A few importers were creating a problem that could hurt the shooting world generally. (The Subcommittee's investigations were beginning to be picked up by the press and brought to public attention.)[53] These considerations apparently overrode any fears that the Dodd Committee might be opening a Pandora's box from which other gun control laws might spring.

The Dodd Committee began public hearings on mail-order firearms in January 1963. A series of police officials reviewed the problems that their cities had encountered through the sale of pistols and other weapons to juveniles. It soon became apparent that the Department of State, which licensed arms imports, could not or would not do much to curb the flow.[54] The Treasury Department, which had been charged with enforcement of the 1934 and 1938 firearms statutes, similarly professed itself helpless. The Federal Firearms Act of 1938 had been designed to aid states in their own control efforts. In states where the law required a permit to purchase, interstate dealers could send weapons to individuals only if they could establish they had the requisite permit. Only seven states, however, required purchase permits. Even in these states arms could be shipped to federally licensed dealers and anyone (felons and fugitives excepted) who filled out a form and paid a dollar could secure a dealer's license. The Treasury Department's Alcohol and Tobacco Tax Division, which was charged with enforcement of the federal firearms statutes, estimated that only half of the 60,000 persons with licenses were bona fide dealers. The license fee was not sufficient to defray the costs of processing applications, much less screening them.[55]

There were only five days of hearings, in January, March, and May 1963. A total of fourteen witnessess were heard, most of them law enforcement officials. The shooter's interests were represented by Robert S. Carr of the Ohio Gun Collectors' Association, Howard Carter, Jr., of the NSSF, and Franklin L. Orth, executive vice-president of the NRA. Orth told Senator Dodd: "I do not deny you have a problem with mail-order guns, Senator. We want to do everything we can to help you. We will support any reasonable type of legislation to beat that type of business because it is unconscionable."[56] Orth's chief concern was to block any legislation that would place a burden or odium on the legitimate user of firearms: "We do not think the proper use of firearms in recreation, law enforcement, and national preparedness should be overshadowed or tainted by the same black brush that is being wielded against a small minority of lawless individuals."[57] The NSSF spokesman voiced the same fears and went to some lengths to distinguish between good quality arms of "reputable manufacturers" and the cheap, mail-order import which would appeal to "a purchaser with criminal intentions, or to a juvenile about to acquire a firearm without parental consent."[58] "Mail-order guns have not helped our industry," he told the committee, "but have really hurt us."[59] The discussions were cordial and unmarked by rancor. At their conclusion Dodd thanked both the NRA and the NSSF for their constructive attitudes.

Senator Dodd introduced his bill, S. 1975, on August 2, 1963. It had been drafted so as to meet the objections raised in the hearings and private discussions with the NRA, and that organization had assured Dodd of its support. Though the *Rifleman* did not echo that support, its August issue pointed the finger at a few unscrupulous mail-order dealers.[60] S. 1975, offered as an amendment to the National Firearms Act, was clearly tailored to strike at those dealers. It would have tightened the dealer licensing system, raising the fee to ten dollars and requiring that dealers be at least twenty-one years old. It singled out the mail-order pistol for special attention. Dealers could not make shipments of these across state lines unless they notified carriers of the nature of their merchandise. Carriers, in turn, were prohibited from delivering pistols to customers whom they had reason to believe were under eighteen years of age. Finally, a person ordering a pistol through interstate commerce had to accompany his order with a notarized statement that he was eighteen years of age or older, and not barred by any law from making the purchase.[61]

The Dodd Bill was referred to the Senate Committee on Commerce, chaired by Senator Warren Magnuson of Washington. The measure was not given high priority. Hearings still had not been scheduled three and a half months later when President Kennedy made his trip to Dallas. The tragedy which occurred there hardly needs be recalled to a generation that carries an indelible and painful memory of it a decade later. The reverberations were profound: shock, disbelief, confusion, and swelling anger. And much of that anger became fixed on a tangible object: a mail-order Italian rifle ordered under a fictitious name. The ubiquitous gun had already become the object of a vague concern in the public mind. The tinder, accumulated over the preceding years, had begun to smoulder. Now John F. Kennedy's death fanned it into a fierce blaze.

Within a week of President Kennedy's death a dozen firearms bills had been placed in the congressional hoppers. Senator Dodd, who had been first in the field, amended his S. 1975 to give it more teeth. The new version applied to all mail-order firearms, not just pistols. Anyone who ordered a firearm had to send along the name of his local law enforcement chief. The mail-order firm was required to notify that official of the purchase before it made shipment.[62] The NRA's vice-president, Orth, told Dodd he would back this measure too, though there was apparently some hesitation about it at NRA headquarters.[63] The whole gun world was shaken. The January 1964 issue of the *Rifleman* acknowledged: "never before has there been such a wave of anti-firearm feeling, or such vocal and almost universal demand for tighter controls over the mail-order sales of guns."[64]

Gone was the leisurely and amicable atmosphere of the earlier hearings. The American public had injected its own voice into the issue. A Niagara of mail descended upon Congress, most of it initially calling for strong gun controls. Most congressmen conceded that they had never received such an outpouring as the gun controversy produced. By the time the Senate Commerce Committee began hearings on the Dodd Bill in December, the pro-gun forces had also begun to stir. (The terms pro- and anti-gun are admittedly oversimplified, since each persuasion masked a variety of opinions. Generally, the dividing line was over rigorous controls which would be felt by legitimate users as well as minors, criminals, etc.). Pro-gun witnesses went to great lengths to make their voices heard: a North Carolina engineer named Darrel Peeler drove most of the night to defend his hobby before the committee;[65] four residents of Bagdad, Arizona, drove 2,500 miles in fifty-four hours to plead for what one of them called their "God-given right" to keep and bear arms.[66]

So began four years of voluminous debate over the gun and its place in American life, fully documented in 4,000 pages of congressional hearings and hundreds of magazine and newspaper articles.[67] It was to be a tedious and repetitive dialogue of the deaf, which can only be summarized here. The arguments presented on both sides contained little that was new, most of them having been used in the Sullivan Law debate half a century before. The atmosphere of acrimony reappeared too. Representative John Lindsay of New York showed up at the hearings brandishing a Carcano rifle. Senator Ralph

Yarborough of Texas, a member of the Commerce Committee—and of the NRA—told him: "You will observe all of the National Rifle Association rules of safe gun handling in the demonstration, please." Lindsay replied "I can't help but do that, because they run the show." Lindsay went on to epitomize the anti-gun position:[68]

> Today the Nation no longer depends on the citizen's weapon, nor does the citizen himself. And, most significant, the population is now densely packed into urban areas, and it is diverse and mobile. In our changed and complicated society, guns have become more dangerous, and they demand more careful use. The Constitution must be interpreted in the light of the times; protection today means the reasonable regulation of firearms—not the absence of regulation.[69]

There were few in the debate who did not quote the Second Amendment and then construe it. Statistics on crime, gun ownership, and the correlation between them were variously interpreted. The FBI's Uniform Crime Reports provided an inexhaustible fund of arguments. Pro-gun groups also cited in this connection a study made by Professor Marvin E. Wolfgang, which tended to show there was no direct correlation between homicides and the availability of firearms.[70] So frequently was Wolfgang's name invoked that Senator Dodd put through a telephone call to him, and then interrupted a witness who had just cited the professor to announce: "He wants to be on record as supporting the strongest possible Federal legislation restricting the use and distribution of firearms."[71] Inevitably, there were comparisons with other countries. Advocates of strong gun laws pointed to England's severe restrictions and low crime rate. Those opposing preferred to attribute her near catastrophe in 1940 to the disarmed state of her population.[72]

Yet the debate did move, in the sense that opponents became more bitter and divided. The NRA and its allies professed themselves in favor of legislation that struck at certain categories of gun users rather than at guns themselves. The Casey Bill, sponsored by Representative Bob Casey of Texas, reflected this approach. It would have made it a felony under federal law to use a firearm that had been in interstate commerce in the commission of certain crimes; the penalty was a draconian twenty-five years' imprisonment.[73] But such proposals did not get very far, being eclipsed by Dodd's bills and those of the Johnson administration. Pro-gun forces felt their solutions were being ignored, and that they themselves were being pictured as opposing any new measures. Anti-gun groups were charged with "upping the ante" with increasingly severe proposals; they in turn accused the "gun lobby" of unethical and devious opposition to the manifest will of the American people. A gulf widened between what the one side would concede and what the other demanded—not as a solution, but as a "step toward sanity,"[74] presumably to be followed by others. The gun, rather than the mail-order pistol, became the issue and positions tended to polarize. A witness told the Senate Commerce Committee with utter candor that whenever people have guns "somebody is going to get shot." But to him it was "part of the price of freedom that we are going to have to pay in order to have freedom."[75] There were equally categorical statements at the other end of the spectrum: "Put simply, private citizens should be disarmed."[76]

The tone of invective increased. Gun control was a Communist conspiracy, opposition to it "all too illustrative of the paradoxical right-wing anarchy which infects some segments of our national consciousness."[77] Freud entered the debates, albeit posthumously: people who liked guns had doubtful virility; so did those who disliked them. The NRA's building in downtown Washington became a marble and glass den of conspirators. *The New York Times* was called "perhaps the best journalistic friend that Castro's Cuba and Ho's North Viet Nam ever had."[78] The same tone appeared in congressional mail, though the NRA counseled its members not to write abusively. A Maryland assemblyman named Angelo Palmisano, who favored stricter gun laws in his state, received a letter which began: "You dirty wop."[79] Not even the dead were spared: Theodore Roosevelt, NRA member and gun enthusiast, was portrayed as a lifelong adolescent; the Sullivan Law was said to be "sired by crazy old Tim Sullivan."[80] The appearance of Carl Bakal's *The Right to Bear Arms* added more fuel to the fire in 1966. The book was the first ever dedicated to the problem of the gun and it was the work of a thoroughly angry man. It flayed the gun world without mercy, from the NRA ("Vigilante on the Potomac") to the sinister psychological impulses of the hunter.[81]

As each side sought to land more damaging blows on the other, distortion and misrepresentation appeared; part of this was intentional, part was the inevitable consequence of a deepening suspicion of the enemy's motives. Senator Dodd accused the NRA of giving lip service to his bills and then painting them in the darkest colors to its

members. He led Orth through a series of the organization's communications, pointing out errors and
misinterpretations in the analysis of his bills. He gave the
same treatment to a gun magazine editor who appeared
under subpoena, and who defended himself by saying
that he had been "editorializing." "Some people call it
lying," said Dodd, "and I am one of them."[82] *The New
York Times* printed an inaccurate front-page story on the
NRA and made corrections nine days later on page 28.[83]
A news magazine writer claimed that the Defense Department furnished the NRA with "machine guns, aerial
bombs, and flamethrowers."[84] These instances and
numerous others make it difficult to quarrel with the
assessment of Roger Caras: "Any careful observer of the
battle must be distressed at the ignorance, ill will, and
dishonesty apparent on both sides."[85]

The violent episodes of the 1960s played a part in
stoking the fires of controversy. The public was now
"sensitized" to the presence of the gun. For many it
seemed the common thread in the tragedies of the
decade: the murders of Lemuel Penn in Georgia and
three civil rights workers in Mississippi (1964); the kil-
lings of Mrs. Viola Liuzzo and Malcolm X (1965); the
fatal shooting of George Lincoln Rockwell (1967); and
the paroxysm of assassination which brought death to
Martin Luther King and Robert Kennedy in the spring
of 1968. Such highly publicized tragedies provided fresh
ammunition to the anti-gun forces. It was pointed out
that the man charged with the 1963 slaying of Medgar
Evers was a gun collector who acknowledged "anything
that shoots I like." Following the death of Martin Luther
King, an editorial in *The Nation* assailed the pro-gun
slogan "guns don't kill people, people kill people." "This

is a truism," said *The Nation*, "but it is also a fact that at 200 yards a rifle is a big help."[86]

Urban riots, beginning with Watts in 1965, gave the gun a new notoriety in the hands of the rooftop sniper. So did the activities of right-wing paramilitary groups such as the Minutemen and the Paul Revere Associated Yeomen. Even more ominous was the emergence of armed and militant groups among blacks and in the radical left. The radical left's views on firearms were a curious parody of those held on the other end of the political spectrum: "Guns, especially to middle-class people, are tools we have been taught to be afraid of or reject. This, combined with heavy anti-weapon propaganda and legislation, may land us in a situation where 'when guns are outlawed, only pigs will have guns.' The time to buy a gun is now, while it is still possible."[87]

As the lines of battle were extended, each side drew further recruits. Pro-gun forces received expressions of support from the Izaak Walton League, wildlife and conservation groups, and organizations such as the Liberty Lobby, American Legion, and Disabled American Veterans. Against them were arrayed the American Bar Association, the International Association of Chiefs of Police, the American Civil Liberties Union, three-quarters of the nation's newspapers, and most of the periodical press. The Minutemen organization urged its members to join the NRA, while the Communist *Worker* jumped into the fray with a vigorous condemnation of the gun cult. The NRA welcomed the *Worker*'s attack while formally disassociating itself from the Minutemen.

Pro-gun forces were by their own admission an embattled minority, an assertion borne out by frequent polls which indicated three Americans out of four favored rigid gun control.[88] A sizable majority of the American people wanted something done—as did the Johnson administration and the insistent voice of the national media. How is it then that the congressional mills ground so long without producing anything? The blame is usually placed on the NRA, spokesman of the "gun lobby," whose oratory "mysteriously mesmerized" the Congress.[89] The NRA was certainly effective in marshalling the sentiments of those who took its side. It was frequently said that it could provoke half a million letters to Congress in the space of a few days. Through its membership, which reached a million in 1968, it could coordinate the efforts of pro-gun forces.[90] It was their central nervous system, though hardly their brain.

The very nature of the American governmental system lent itself to defensive strategems. It has always been easier for special interest groups to preserve the status quo when it favors them than to change it when it does not. In the latter case they must win over all the branches of the federal government and in the former they need only make their view prevail in one. For all its numbers, the anti-gun camp was not well led. There was no orchestration such as that provided by the NRA.[91] It has also been said that Senator Dodd, for all his determination, was not the best standard bearer—especially after his own political career came under a cloud.[92] And, too, though President Johnson could be counted as an ally, his support was sporadic, and the proposals of his administration competed with those of Dodd and others.[93] The very plethora of proposed measures tended to dissipate efforts on their behalf.

Congress probably stood somewhat to the right of the country in its attitudes toward gun control. The Senate had the larger proportion of members from the South and West—areas unsympathetic to innovative gun laws—and these same senators occupied key posts on committees such as the Commerce and Judiciary Committees, where most of the bills became lodged. Though the House had greater representation from large urban areas where the impulse for action was strongest, caution was the watchword here. The prime political consideration in both houses was essentially this: inaction would be more readily forgiven by voters who wanted something done than would new laws, particularly stringent ones, by constituents in the pro-gun camp. Sentiment for gun control proceeded from the general feeling that something should be done, that something being directed at others. Pro-gun people saw the issue as intensely personal, directed specifically at them and their guns. They would be more inclined to take their feelings with them when they went into the polling booth. Even presidential aspirants of a liberal stripe went out of their way to avoid offending the pro-gun minority.[94] Such political realities have often decided the day against the big battalions.

If the pro-gun forces had a political advantage in their defensive position, it was nonetheless unsettling. There were numerous calls to take the offensive and though the will was there the means were lacking. As we have seen, the media were mostly unsympathetic. Television reportage was considered "balanced" by people like Carl Bakal and outrageously biased by the gun world.[95] Large urban dailies with mass circulation—*The New York Times, Washington Post, Los Angeles Times*, and *Christian Science Monitor*—issued continual calls for new and tougher laws.[96] With few exceptions the popular magazines followed suit.[97] Though the NRA took out full-page ads with its journalistic enemies and even entered a float in the Rose Bowl parade, the overall effort to get out its side of the argument was doomed to failure.[98] Most of its preachments were of necessity confined to those already converted, a fact that sometimes provoked explosions of frustration, as when a witness told the Dodd committee: "We are becoming sick and tired of being pictured by supporters of this measure as wild-eyed gun nuts, extremists, militants, and so forth."[99] Richard Starnes, writing in *Field and Stream*, lamented: "No bloc of equal size takes the chronic cuffing that is the lot of hunters and target shooters."[100]

The continual need for self-justification, the stigma of what has been called "societal disapprobation," was a weakness keenly felt by the pro-gun forces. This explains in part the vehemence that often characterized the letters hunters and shooters sent to Congress—virtually their only access to the forum of debate. Yet, paradoxically, this weakness was a source of strength. Every tragic incident provoked first a flood of demands for tough gun laws. The assault on the gun was then followed by a wave of letters in its defense, as the pro-gun forces reacted to provocation. Anger and frustration made that reaction all the more massive and vehement.

The periodic deluges of pro-gun letters that have descended on congressmen are usually attributed to the prompting of the NRA. Yet in many cases they have been utterly spontaneous.[101] This self-propulsive tendency at the grass-roots level is perhaps the hallmark of the "gun lobby" and a good indication that the term *lobby* is a misleading one. If anti-gun leaders had difficulty in marshalling their effectives, those on the other side had no less difficulty keeping theirs well in hand. Indeed, they sometimes give the impression of generals trying to stay in front of their soldiers.

No one was quite so aware of this phenomenon as the

directors of the NRA. Had they held the powers of command that their enemies attributed to them, they would probably have adopted a fairly moderate and conciliatory approach to the whole problem. This assertion will no doubt raise some eyebrows, but it seems nonetheless clear that by inclination and interest the NRA would have preferred this course. It saw itself as a reputable organization which over the years had enjoyed a mutually beneficial relationship with the federal government. Through the National Board for the Promotion of Rifle Practice it had close ties with the Pentagon. Franklin L. Orth had served as deputy assistant secretary of the Army. The organization also had a working relationship with the Treasury Department, which enforced the federal firearms laws. It was in a sense the unofficial adviser to the government on matters dealing with firearms. Attuned to the world of Washington, it knew the give-and-take, the bargaining which was the political reality of that world, and which militated against blind and obstreperous intransigence. At the same time the NRA was virtually a quasi-governmental organism itself. The civilian marksmanship program and the distribution of surplus government arms had been important elements in the NRA's success—and they could all be lost.

Yet the NRA aspired to leadership of the untold thousands of gun enthusiasts who insisted that every trench be defended. This perhaps explains why the organization did not placard its support of Dodd's original bill, and why it supported the amended version in the hearings after President Kennedy's assassination, while giving it hostile treatment in its communications to its members. Even so, the news seems to have gotten out. According to some accounts, there were disturbing numbers of resignations from the NRA. In any event,

spokesmen of other gun groups did not hesitate to criti-
cize its stand in the hearings.[102]

In the end, the generals followed their troops and
though there were occasional cries from the ranks that
the NRA was "selling out" the interests of the shooter, the
organization did establish its leadership.[103] Its membership roles swelled rapidly: 160,000 joined in 1968, the
greatest annual increase the NRA had ever enjoyed. As
the argument grew more clamorous the NRA raised its
voice. The *Rifleman* got a new editor late in 1966 and
immediately took a more combative, hard-hitting line.
But the cost of leadership was high. The NRA became a
prime target for the opposition: its headquarters was
picketed, its finances dissected, its tax-exempt status
challenged, and its public image generally battered.
There were demands that it register as a lobby. The
civilian marksmanship program was so bitterly assailed
that the Defense Department ordered a study of its effectiveness. The flow of surplus arms from government
arsenals to NRA members dwindled.[104] In 1967 the Defense Department withdrew its support of the national
matches, ostensibly for budgetary reasons. One year
later still another budget cut left the civilian marksmanship program little more than a vestige.[105]

The NRA's difficulties were symptomatic of the generally angry mood that pervaded the whole firearms
controversy. Pro-gun forces argued that the climate of
vindictiveness and "hysteria" was not one in which
worthwhile laws could be framed. But this very climate
had goaded legislators to action. Between 1965 and 1968
anti-gun sentiment secured new laws in several states,
including major legislation in Connecticut, Illinois, New
Jersey, and New York. Tough new ordinances were

adopted by such cities as Chicago, Philadelphia, and New York.[106] Then the deaths of Martin Luther King and Robert Kennedy in the spring of 1968 gave even greater impetus. By September of that year the *Rifleman* reported: "Registration grips 5 cities."[107] And the shock wave of 1968 broke the congressional log-jam. A bill from Senator Dodd, strikingly similar to his S. 1975 of five years earlier, was signed into law as Title IV of the Omnibus Crime Control and Safe Streets Act (19 June 1968).[108] It in turn was incorporated into the more sweeping Gun Control Act of 1968, signed by President Johnson on 22 October 1968.[109] The Gun Control Act replaced the Federal Firearms Act of 1938 with more comprehensive measures resting on the power to regulate interstate commerce. It tightened the federal firearms licensing system, so as to limit foreign and interstate traffic to bona fide importers, manufacturers, and dealers, with a few minor exceptions. This drastically reduced the mail-order business in modern types of weapons. The federal dealer's license fee was raised to ten dollars and could not be issued to minors. These dealers could not sell rifles or shotguns and ammunition for them to anyone under eighteen years of age (twenty-one in the case of pistols and their ammunition). Further provisions closed the door to imports of foreign military surplus, and extended the registration and transfer tax provisions of the National Firearms Act to "destructive devices"—bazookas, anti-tank guns, mortars, etc. Finally, a series of provisions were aimed at criminal use of firearms. Certain types of criminals, drug addicts, and mental defectives were barred from sending or receiving arms in interstate commerce. Federally licensed dealers could not knowingly sell arms to such persons. Anyone who used a firearm in the commission of a federal felony risked a separate penalty for such use, a minimum of a year's imprisonment.

The Gun Control Act was the result of a great deal of maneuvering and debate in that hectic summer. It was grudgingly accepted by those who feared even more stringent measures, and unenthusiastically endorsed by those who would have preferred stiffer provisions.[110] The manufacturers announced their support in June.[111] Some of the press felt its title was its most imposing feature, while the NRA called it "the most sweeping Federal legislation ever imposed on U.S. firearms owners."[112]

When it came up for a vote in the House on July 24, it got the support of all the anti-gun element. A number of those who had been prominent in the pro-gun camp, men like Representative Bob Casey of Texas, also voted for it. But an irreconcilable minority of 118 congressmen found it too severe. The analysis of this negative vote is revealing. In the entire northeast quarter of the country—the fourteen states north of the Mason-Dixon Line and the Ohio River and east of the Mississippi—the opposition picked up only ten votes. Southern delegations generally voted with the nays, those of Mississippi, South Carolina, and Alabama to a man. What defectors there were usually represented large urban constituencies—Memphis, Atlanta, New Orleans, etc. A second center of opposition lay in the states west of the Mississippi and east of California. The delegations of Idaho, Montana, Nevada, New Mexico, Oklahoma, Utah, and Wyoming all voted in the opposition; so did fifteen of Texas' twenty-one congressmen.[113]

The House vote was probably an accurate reflection of the thinking in various parts of the country: 1968 was an election year, and the Representatives would be facing their constituents in less than four months. The western congressman acted for ranchers and farmers who refused to be inconvenienced in purchasing cartridges simply because people in eastern cities had a penchant for shooting each other. And no doubt the vote reflects the repugnance that a southerner might feel at the prospect of the federal government concerning itself with his pistol or any other fixture of his life. What the congressional alignment does not show, and what must next be considered, is the survival to the present day of a basic set of popular attitudes about firearms that color the thinking of Americans generally. For it is these attitudes, rather than any sectional vagaries, that lie at the heart of the gun controversy. They are of more than historical interest. If other preoccupations have driven the controversy from the headlines, a spectacular crime will serve to bring it back—the attempts on the lives of George Wallace and John Stennis are cases in point. In city halls and state legislatures it flares up repeatedly. The "Saturday night special," against which the 1968 legislation erected no effective bar, is the subject of frequent editorials and an annual legislative drive in Congress. The controversy simmers; on occasion it boils over on a national scale; but it shows no sign of going away. Like the gun itself, it has become a constant in American life.

Conclusion

To say that these weapons have helped establish the American way of life is actually too modest a judgement: they are a part of America's life, and we respond to and with guns in a very American way.

—Robert Sherrill, The Saturday Night Special

In the tumultuous summer of 1968 President Johnson named a National Commission on the Causes and Prevention of Violence. That commission, like others that have preceded and followed it, called for restrictions on the ownership and use of firearms. Its recommendations were accompanied by a staff report, *Firearms and Violence in American Life*. The work of jurists, law enforcement specialists, and figures from the academic world, it is a sort of *summa* of expert opinion on the gun problem. Its findings, buttressed by charts and tables, make sobering reading. The gun emerges as the common ingredient in suicide, crime, and collective violence. Rows of figures

247

indicate that the gun is of doubtful utility to potential victims of crimes and point to a sinister equation: more firearms—more firearms violence. The study considers the gun, because of its lethal efficiency and easy availability, an essential part of the broader problem of American violence. Books on this larger subject have appeared in great numbers, and invariably the gun reappears as agent and instrument. Some who have studied human violence generally suggest that the weapon may be more than an incidental ingredient. Robert Ardrey, for example, has offered the disturbing proposition that "man is a predator whose natural instinct is to kill with a weapon."[1] Psychologists have lately been pursuing the theory that the weapon itself provokes its use, that, as someone put it, "the trigger pulls the finger." But the exact role of the gun in this connection, as agent, accomplice, or author, has yet to be fixed. While violence itself is not our subject, nor even the peculiarly American strain of that virus, it does lie at the heart of the modern gun controversy. As groups and as individuals, Americans come into collision all too frequently; we are notorious in this regard, though hardly unique. But the American is unique in that when such collisions occur, he is prone to reach for a gun.

In human confrontations, violence, like argument, is a form of dialogue. Words and weapons both serve as means of expression and convey messages. And in both cases the "vocabulary" is extensive, the range of options considerable. Choice of weapons in the dialogue of violence, like the choice of expletives in argument, may reflect the depth of antagonism. It is quite possibly for this reason that the essentially apolitical urban rioters of eighteenth-century Europe did not resort to firearms, while the revolutionaries did. But distinctive cultural patterns may also dictate the choice. Thus between Bobby and criminal in England, the dialogue of violence does not rise beyond the level of the nightstick. French rioters and police have traditionally "conversed" with paving stones and tear gas. In the United States the gun has been a feature of that dialogue.

Some argue that Americans use guns on one another because the guns are there. To be sure guns have always been abundant. A survey made at Jamestown in 1624 reveals that there was a firearm for each colonist. It is estimated that today there are about 200 million guns in the United States; the ratio of people to guns is thus about what it was 350 years ago. Yet the sheer number of weapons at hand does not always translate itself into violence along the American pattern. Israel, which has survived by becoming an armed camp, is a case in point. Switzerland, whose military constitution requires that able-bodied men keep weapons in their homes, is another. More important than the number of weapons is their perceived role, which determines how they will be used.

In American history the gun has been more than just present—it has been prominent. The country is uniquely "gun-minded." Colt and Winchester have been universally understood synonyms for pistol and rifle for a century. Fiction writers are periodically reminded that a discriminating readership will instantly object if pulp novel cowboys are armed with .45 automatics. The gun has always figured in American folklore, from "Old Betsy," to the .44 with which Frankie shot Johnnie, to the ivory-handled revolver of George S. Patton. The linguistic impact of the gun has been enormous, and its terminology has been extended in countless ways. Thus, "son of a goniff" (Jewish thief) has become the familiar if less meaningful "son of a gun." The American receives a shot from a hypodermic syringe, takes one with a camera, or imbibes one from a whiskey tumbler (this last usage derived from the much more colorful term "a shot in the neck"). The heritage is as old as it is pervasive; the expression "flash in the pan," for example, goes back to flintlock days. The gun has made major contributions to American folklore. And this has been possible not only because the gun was present in American society, but familiar and accepted as well. This acceptance, in turn, derived from the role Americans assigned it in their lives.

There seems to be universal agreement that the gun has always been preeminently a "man-thing" in American society. Those who lean to psychiatric approaches to social problems see in it a phallic symbol, an interpretation which never fails to outrage the gun world. To others, it symbolizes the protective function of the male. Certainly the gun helped fix the status of the American man in his protective role. In early America arms and service in the militia were required of all able-bodied males. Well into the nineteenth century the gun was a more widely held badge of membership in the body politic than the ballot. For whatever reason, the gun is linked to manhood. Probably in no other language can the whole gamut of male virtues and weaknesses be expressed as in the terminology of firearms. The forthright man is a straight shooter, while the methodical man makes every shot count. The impulsive shoot from the hip, the impatient go off halfcocked, and the prudent keep their powder dry. A boy's first .22 is virtually an American puberty rite and so is his first hunt. This has found frequent expression in literature—in William Faulkner's story *The Bear*, for example.

Hunting also helped make the gun a "people-thing."

An economic necessity for the first Americans, it became a diversion for succeeding generations and the nation's most popular sport well into the nineteenth century. But from the beginning it was a right of all; the country's wildlife was a bounty that could be harvested or looted by any man with a gun. The private game preserve and the poacher who trespassed on it were never salient features of the American field. Many other shooting sports, skeet, for example, are in a sense modern surrogates for the hunt. The enduring popularity of the shooting sports tends to be overlooked, perhaps because they are not spectator sports with media coverage. Hunting, by its very nature, demands a degree of privacy. The popularity of gun sports may help explain why, after the gun had conquered the continent, it was not relegated to the museum along with the Conestoga wagon. But it is only a small part of the explanation.

An armed population was long held to be a necessary prop to the American way of life. No amount of historical evidence has ever shaken the popular notion that individual Americans and their guns preserved the nation from foreign dangers, whether they were the Minutemen at Lexington, Davy Crockett at the Alamo, or Sergeant York in the trenches of France. Even more pervasive was the idea that the gun helped preserve the social fabric of the nation, "the establishment." Those who were not in that establishment, notably slaves and Indians, were the only people who had no business being armed. Even if they were, their cause was hopeless, for they would be outgunned. The problems which Tecumseh, Nat Turner, and John Brown presented to American society were resolved through superiority of fire. Perhaps this was not the best solution, but it was a distinctly American one, incorporating the idea that the gun is its own antidote. This view was popular, and it was official as well. Colonial governments thrust arms in the hands of their populations in the seventeenth and eighteenth centuries; government in the nineteenth century left them there, virtually untouched by legal restrictions. It is only with the present century that that policy has been reversed. Elsewhere the armed masses remained a vision of revolutionaries. In America, by a curious inversion, they became a symbol of order and a conservative totem.

This same notion of the gun's utility extended to the matter of crime. Lawbreakers were seen as a clearly defined minority whose propensities kept them in a perpetual state of war not only with the authorities, but also with the citizenry generally. This minority, too, could be outgunned. With the police slower to develop than in Europe, so that they scarcely existed above the purely local level until the present century, it is easy to see where the next line of defense lay. Here again the gun was its own antidote; more than that, it was argued, it shifted the balance in favor of the victim, it "equalized." Even the most frail of women could exert four pounds of pressure on the trigger of a revolver, and with its awesome assistance fell the most muscular of attackers. For better or worse—probably both—the gun came to symbolize popular participation in the processes of justice and whoever carried one regarded himself as an auxiliary in the struggle to preserve society. The man who rode in the sheriff's posse conceived of himself as a volunteer in that struggle. So, too, no doubt, did those who rode with vigilantes or wore the white robes of the Ku Klux Klan. The attorney general of New Jersey recently expressed amazement that the very people who fought gun laws were the same who rallied around the slogan "support your local police." Historically, there is no contradiction.

But if the armed citizen is an ally of the authorities, why does he so violently object to obtaining a license for his arms or registering them with those self-same authorities? The usual objection is that these steps may be a prelude to confiscation. The fear may be groundless, but it is no less real. Though Americans own more firearms than ever before, they are increasingly unwilling to reveal that ownership to pollsters or others. It has been suggested that this fear is linked historically to the negative and distrustful attitudes toward government common when the Union was formed. Thus the gun owner fears the government will take away his gun and leave him defenseless against further inroads on his rights. Perhaps the fear of government itself does make all talk of registration like the touching of a raw nerve, but there may be an even more deeply rooted attitude about firearms that goes beyond considerations of society and government and touches the individual directly.

Some years ago there was considerable discussion in the shooting press about the best "survival gun." This was not the weapon a man would choose if he were lost in the Rockies, but the one he would have with him when he crawled out of the rubble after a thermonuclear holocaust. With government, police, and courts gone, with social bonds dissolved, each man's survival would presumably depend on his wits, his strength, and his weapons. Such a spectacle may seem frightening or fanciful, but it reflects the persistent view that the ultimate defense of the individual American, his final, back-to-the-wall recourse, is his gun. It is a sentiment that was felt in frontier log cabins and in isolated farmhouses and lingers today in city and suburb. The ultimate fear is not that government will tyrannize, but that it will fail to protect. That fear persists; it causes lines to form in front of gun stores after every major riot or atrocity. To many Americans, probably to most, the gun remains the hedge instinctively sought against that ultimate fear. Nowhere is this feeling better expressed than in James Jones' short novel, *The Pistol*: "The world was rocketing to hell in a bucket, but if he could only hold on to his pistol, remain in possession of the promise of salvation its beautiful blued-steel bullet-charged weight offered him, he would be saved."[2]

The gun, then, is part of a whole series of traditional attitudes about government, society, and the individual. They run, like so many threads, through the whole tapestry of the national past. In its essence, the gun controversy is a struggle between these attitudes and new ones. The city has spawned the new and negative view of the gun; rural and small town America tends to hold to the older, more positive view. There is also evidence of cleavage along class lines. For Herman Kahn, well-known propounder of unsettling theories, the crusade against the gun is the work of an upper middle class minority, whose views are at variance from the rest of the nation. Kahn told a correspondent of the *Washington Post*, which has been active in the crusade: "You had no idea what you were doing. You were hitting America in the teeth, right in the center of the culture."[3]

Along similar lines, a writer in the *Wall Street Journal* has seen the gun controversy as a skirmish in the larger battle over the nation's cultural values, a battle in which "cosmopolitan America" is pitted against "bedrock America."[4] The terms are apt; they could be used to describe the protagonists when the Sullivan Law was debated fifty years ago. Pro-gun spokesmen have long been addicted to those assaults on the liberal establishment in which Spiro Agnew excelled, and those in the other camp have not always concealed their contempt for the "shirtsleeve crowd." Cosmopolitan America foresees a new age when guns and the need for them will disappear; bedrock America conceives of it as 1984. Cosmopolitan America has always been concerned about its international image; bedrock America has always been nativist. Shortly after Robert Kennedy's assassination, Gunnar Myrdal reportedly said that if the Constitution allowed such indiscriminate ownership of guns, "then to hell with the Constitution." Cosmopolitan America would have found this food for sober reflection; bedrock America, without reflection, would have said: "To hell with Gunnar Myrdal."

But not even these cultural battle lines are rigidly fixed. Sophisticated America and shirtsleeve America war in all of us. We abhor the gun in the hands of the assassin but find it a comfort in our bureau drawer. A majority of Americans, the polls tell us, would subject their right to bear arms to police control and a majority of Americans would not hesitate to use those arms if threatened by urban rioters. In the face of certain crises the old attitudes will re-emerge with great force. In crime-plagued Washington, the secretary of labor reportedly keeps a gun close at hand. The chief justice of the United States Supreme Court recently opened his door to a late night visitor pistol in hand.

But in the long run, time works against the gun. Increased social consciousness finds its excesses intolerable, whereas they were once accepted without thought. The era of thermonuclear war has made the citizen-soldier harder to defend. The war against crime has mobilized the computer and other sophisticated techniques. Moreover, the police have come to regard the armed citizen more as a hazard than an ally. The city is the enemy of the gun, and the city is growing. This year's dove field or skeet range is tomorrow's subdivision. In megalopolis the gun as necessity seems doomed; what can be salvaged of it as sport and diversion remains to be seen. In some attenuated form it will no doubt linger, the distinctive heritage of a nation that began with a shot heard 'round the world.

Notes

Chapter 1

[1]J.-C.-L. Simonde de Sismondi, *Histoire des républiques italiennes du moyen age* (Paris: Furne et cie., 1840), IV, 85.

[2]Niccolò Machiavelli, *The Art of War*, revised edition of the Ellis Farnsworth translation, with an introduction by Neal Wood (New York: Bobbs-Merrill Co., 1965), p. 30.

[3]G. Liebe, "Das Recht des Waffentragens in Deutschland," *Zeitschrift für historische Waffenkunde* 2, no. 9 (1900-1901): 341.

[4]V. G. Kiernan, "Foreign Mercenaries and Absolute Monarchy," in *Crisis in Europe, 1560-1660*, edited by Trevor Aston, with an introduction by Christopher Hill (New York: Anchor Books, 1967), p. 136.

[5]Bayard himself is said to have ordered such executions; this would add a final irony to the manner of his death. Several other instances of this practice are cited by Sir Charles Oman in his *A History of the Art of War in the Middle Ages*, 2d ed., revised and enlarged (London: Methuen & Co. Ltd., 1924), II, 309; and in his *A History of the Art of War in the Sixteenth Century* (London: Methuen & Co. Ltd., 1937), p. 44.

[6]Michel de Montaigne, *Les essais* (Paris: Librairie Garnier frères, n.d.), I, 323.

[7]Chevalier Bail, *Essais historiques et critiques sur l'organisation des armées et sur l'administration militaire en France* (Paris: Le-´vêque, 1817), p. 44.

[8]John U. Nef, *War and Human Progress: An Essay on the Rise of Industrial Civilization* (New York: W. W. Norton and Co., 1968), p. 42. But for a different view, see Roy S. Wolper, "The

Rhetoric of Gunpowder and the Idea of Progress," *Journal of the History of Ideas* 21, no. 4 (October-December 1970): 589-598.

[9]A. Gaibi, *Le Armi da Fuoco Portàtili Italiane dalle Origini al Risorgimento* (Milan: Bramante Editrice, 1968), p. 13.

[10]*Notes and Queries*, 7th series, VIII (9 November 1889), 365.

[11]The British charged the American Revolutionary hero Joshua Barney with violation of the laws of war when he fired a crowbar into the rigging of an English warship. Hulbert Footner, *Sailor of Furtune: The Life and Adventures of Joshua Barney, U.S.N.* (New York: Harper and Brothers, 1940), p. 62.

[12]It should be noted that technically the air gun is not a firearm since it does not require the ignition of an explosive substance. For various instances of prejudice against this weapon, see *passim* Eldon G. Wolf, *Air Guns, Publication No. 1* of the Milwaukee Public Museum *Publications in History* (Milwaukee, 1958).

[13]*Répertoire de droit pénal et de procédure pénale (Dalloz encyclopédie juridique)*, published under the direction of Maurice Aydalot (Paris: Jurisprudence générale Dalloz, 1967), I, 190.

[14]Letter of Marshal de Créqui, cited in Camille Rousset, *Histoire de Louvois et de son administration politique et militaire* (Paris: Didier et cie., 1864), II, 101.

[15]Jacques Gebelin, *Histoire des milices provinciales (1688-1791),* (Paris: Librairie Hachette et cie., 1881), pp. 179-182.

[16]Jean Bodin, *Les six livres de la république* (Geneva: E. Gamonet, 1629), p. 755.

[17]Ibid., p. 781.

[18]Report of the Venetian Ambassador Giustiano, 1537, as cited in L.-M.-M. Chassignet, *Essai historique sur les institutions militaires, ou la formation, l'organisation, et l'administration des armées en France depuis les temps les plus reculés jusqu'en 1789* (Paris: Victor Rozier, libraire-éditeur, 1869), p. 219.

[19]Gebelin, *Histoire des milices*, p. 224.

[20]Ibid., Note 1.

[21]The Fronde occurred during the minority of Louis XIV, lasting from 1648 to 1653. It is generally regarded as a protest against the rising power of the monarchy.

[22]Edit qui défend le port d'armes à toutes personnes, gentilshommes ou autres, sous peine de mort, 11 July 1546, as found in Isambert, *et al.*, *Recueil des anciennes lois francaises depuis l'an 420 jusqu'à la Révolution de 1789* (Paris: Isambert, Jourdan, Decrussy, 1822-1833), XII, 910.

[23]Robert Baldick, *The Duel, A History of Duelling* (London: Spring Books, 1970), p. 52. Other authorities place the number as high as 8,000.

[24]Marcelle Thiébaux, "The Medieval Chase," *Speculum* 42, no. 2 (April 1967): 261.

[25]Gabriel Hanotaux, *Tableau de la France en 1614* (Paris: Firmin-Didot, 1898), p. 109.

[26]Letter of the Count de Guiche to Jean-Baptiste Colbert, 18 February 1671, as found in G. P. Depping, ed., *Correspondance administrative sous le règne de Louis XIV entre le cabinet du roi, les secrétaires d'état, les présidents, procureurs et avocats généraux des parlements, et autres cours de justice, le gouverneur de la Bastille, les évèques, les corps municipaux, etc., etc.* (Paris: Imprimerie nationale, 1850), I, 825.

[27]Roland Mousnier, *Fureurs paysannes: les paysans dans les révoltes du XVII siècle (France, Russie, Chine)*, (Paris: Calmann-Levy, 1967), p. 71.

[28]Jacques Saint Germain, *La Reynie et la police au grand siècle, d'après de nombreux documents inédits* (Paris: Hachette, 1962), p. 97.

[29]Letter of M. Arnoul to Colbert, 15 January 1667, as found in Depping, *Correspondance*, I, 779.

[30]Edit sur le port d'armes à feu, la vente de ces armes et les formalités à suivre par les fabricans, 21 October 1561; Isambert, *Recueil*, XIV, 123.

[31]For the government's attempts to regulate the arms industry in Saint Etienne, see L.-J. Gras, *Historique de l'armurerie stéphanoise* (Saint Etienne: Société de l'imprimerie Théolier, 1905), pp. 25-103 *passim*.

[32]Andrew Phelan, "Men and Arms," *Law Journal* 110 (26 February 1960): 131.

[33]Geoffrey Cousins, *The Defenders: A History of the British Volunteer* (London: Frederick Muller, 1968), p. 19.

[34]C. H. Firth, *Cromwell's Army: A History of the English Soldier During the Civil Wars, the Commonwealth and the Protectorate*, 4th ed., with a new introduction by P. H. Hardacre (London: Methuen & Co. Ltd., 1962), p. 67.

[35]T. A. Critchley, *The Conquest of Violence: Order and Liberty in Britain* (London: Constable & Co. Ltd., 1970), p. 61.

[36]Lindsay Boynton, *The Elizabethan Militia, 1558-1638* (Toronto: University of Toronto Press, 1967), p. 57.

[37]Critchley, *Violence*, p. 100.

[38]Writing of the situation after the Revolution of 1688, Max Beloff noted: "The confiscation of weapons held by supposed adherents of the Catholic religion or the legitimist cause, which was . . . soon to become a regular part of the machinery of order, was now carried on locally by adherents of the new regime, and in some places occasioned further disorder." Max Beloff, *Public Order and Popular Disturbances, 1660-1714* (London: Humphrey Milford, 1938), pp. 43-44.

[39]English officers stationed there refused to teach marksmanship to Irish soldiers on the grounds that if they did so "within a week there would not be one living landlord left in Ireland." James R. Newman, *The Tools of War* (Garden City, N.Y.: Doubleday, Doran & Co., 1943), pp. 40-41.

[40]1695, 7 William and Mary, Ch. 5 (Ireland).

[41]An Act to explain, amend, and make more effectual an Act passed in the seventh Year of the Reign of his late Majesty King William the Third of Glorious Memory, intituled, An Act for the better securing the Government by disarming Papists, 1739, 13 George II, Ch. 6 (Ireland).

[42]An Act for preventing Tumults and riotous Assemblies, and for the more speedy and effectual punishing the Rioters, 1714, I George I, stat. 2, Ch. 5.

[43]An Act for the more effectual securing the Peace in the Highlands in Scotland, 1715, I George I, stat. 2, Ch. 54.

[44] An Act for the more effectual disarming the Highlands in Scotland; and for the more effectually securing the Peace of the said Highlands; and for restraining the Use of the Highland Dress; and for further indemnifying such Persons as have acted in Defence of his Majesty's Person and Government, during the unnatural Rebellion; and for indemnifying the Judges and other Officers of the Court of Justiciary in Scotland, for not performing the Northern Circuit in May one thousand seven hundred and forty-six; and for obliging the Masters and Teachers of Private Schools in Scotland, and Chaplains, Tutors, and Governors of Children or Youth, to take the Oaths to his Majesty, his Heirs and Successors, and to register the same, 1746, 19 George II, Ch. 39.

[45] 1503, 19 Henry VII, Ch. 4.

[46] The Bill for Cross-bows and Hand-guns, 1541, 33 Henry VIII, Ch. 6.

[47] H. N. Brailsford, *The Levellers and the English Revolution*, edited and prepared for publication by Christopher Hill (Stanford: Stanford University Press, 1961), p. 149.

[48] These stern measures lend further proof to recent research indicating that following the wars of the 1640s "the people at large were still in possession of arms." J. R. Western, *The English Militia in the Eighteenth Century: The Story of a Political Issue, 1660-1802* (London: Routledge and Kegan Paul, 1965), p. 3.

[49] An Act for Householders to Give an Account of Lodgers, Horses, Arms and Ammunition, 22 July 1659, *Acts and Ordinances of the Interregnum, 1642-1660*, collected and edited by C. H. Firth and R. S. Rait (London: His Majesty's Stationery Office, 1911), II, 1317-1319.

[50] An Act for the better Preservation of the Game, and for securing Warrens not inclosed, and the several Fishings of the Realm, 1670, 22 and 23 Charles II, Ch. 25.

[51] An Act declaring the Rights of the Subjects, and settling the Succession of the Crown, 1689, I William and Mary, stat. 2, Ch. 2.

[52] It is significant that efforts in Parliament to carry out the

arming of the people in general failed. Western, *The English Militia*, pp. 82-86, 102.

[53]*Some Considerations on the Game Laws, and the Present Practice in Executing them; with a Hint to non-Subscribers* (London: A. Dodd, 1753), pp. 14-15.

[54]Sir William Blackstone, *Commentaries on the Laws of England in Four Books,* edited by William Draper Lewis (Philadelphia: Rees Welsh & Co., 1902), II, 412.

[55]William Nelson, *The Office and Authority of a Justice of the Peace; Collected out of all the Books, whether of Common or Statute Law, hitherto Written on that Subject*, 10th ed. (London: E & R. Nutt and R. Goshing, 1729), *passim*.

[56]Ibid., p. 53.

[57]This policy has also been explained in economic terms: "From the mechanistic view of society came the notion that arms and property ought to be in the same hands." Western, *The English Militia*, p. 92.

[58]There is a general dearth of monographic material on this subject; see, however, Charles Buttin, *Les armes prohibées en Savoie sous les royales constitutions* (Annecy, France: Imprimerie de Abry, 1896); and chapter six of Gras, *Historique*. Some notion of policy trends in other countries may be gleaned from legal compilations. Thus, a Prussian code of 1794 required that those entitled to own firearms unload them before entering houses and keep them out of reach of children. Gunpowder was to be sold only to persons "above suspicion;" it fell under the same regime as poisons and dangerous drugs. *Allgemeines Landrecht für die Preussischen Staaten von 1794*, with an introduction by Hans Hattenhauer (Frankfurt am Main: Alfred Metzner Verlag, 1970), pp. 694, 696.

[59]C. G. Cruickshank, *Elizabeth's Army*, 2d ed. (Oxford: Clarendon Press, 1966), p. 115.

[60]Federico Negri, *Il Fucile da Caccia: Armi-Munizioni-Tiro*, 4th ed. (Florence: Editoriale Olimpia, 1964), p. 10. The price of the wheel lock did later drop to a level that made its military use practical.

[61]Carl P. Russell, *Guns on the Early Frontiers: A History of*

Firearms from Colonial Times Through the Years of the Western Fur Trade (New York: Bonanza Books, 1957), p. 23.

[62]Carl Bridenbaugh, *Vexed and Troubled Englishmen, 1590-1642* (New York: Oxford University Press, 1970), pp. 36-37.

[63]P[atrick] Colquhoun, *A Treatise on the Police of the Metropolis; containing a Detail of the Various Crimes and Misdemeanors by which Public and Private Property and Security are, at Present, Injured and Endangered: and Suggesting Remedies for their Prevention*, 6th ed., corrected and considerably enlarged (London: For Joseph Mawman, 1800), pp. 540-541.

[64]Jacques Delperrie de Bayac, *Du sang dans la montagne: vrais et faux mystères de la bête du Gévaudan* (Paris: Fayard, 1970), pp. 36-37.

[65]V. V. Mavrodin, *Krestianskaia Voina v Rossii v 1773-1775 godakh: Vosstanie Pugacheva* (Leningrad: Izdatelstvo Leningradskovo Universiteta, 1966), II, 499.

[66]Ibid., 502.

[67]Professor Rudé believes that the Réveillon riots, which occurred in Paris in April 1789, indicate a trend in which "the older style of more popular, near-spontaneous protest tends to give way to a more organized armed revolt." George Rudé, *Paris and London in the Eighteenth Century: Studies in Popular Protest* (New York: Viking Press, 1971), p. 74.

[68]George Rudé, "Iz'iatie Oruzhia u Parizhskikh Oruzheinikov 12-14 Iulia 1789 goda," *Frantsuzskii Ezhegodnik 1968* (Moscow: Gosizdat, 1969), p. 74.

[69]Edward Gibbon, *The Decline and Fall of the Roman Empire* (New York: The Modern Library, n.d.), I, 53. In a similar vein Montesquieu wrote: "To prevent the executive power from being able to oppress, it is requisite that the armies with which it is entrusted should consist of the people, and have the same spirit as the people, as was the case in Rome until the time of Marius." Charles de Secondat, baron de Montesquieu, *The Spirit of the Laws*, translated by Thomas Nugent, with an introduction by Franz Neumann (New York: Hafner Publishing Co., 1949), I, 160-161.

[70] Joel Barlow, *Advice to the Privileged Orders in the Several States of Europe Resulting from the Necessity and Propriety of a General Revolution in the Principle of Government*, reprinted from the London editions of Parts I and II dated 1792 and 1795, respectively (Ithaca, N. Y.: Cornell University Press, 1956), pp. 45, 46.

[71] Frederick B. Artz, *Reaction and Revolution 1814-1832* (New York: Harper & Brothers, 1934), pp. 125-126.

[72] A recent authority has asserted that there was no serious arms control legislation in England from the time of the Six Acts (most of which soon lapsed) until the twentieth century. Colin Greenwood, *Firearms Control: A Study of Armed Crime and Firearms Control in England and Wales* (London: Routledge and Kegan Paul, 1972), p. 17. In France the period with least restrictions coincided with the Third Republic, particularly after the legislation of 1885. Alex Durr, "L'histoire de la législation des armes en France," part II, *Cibles*, no. 14 (April-May 1969): 79-80.

[73] It has also found expression in scholarly circles. See, for example, Werner Gembruch, "Zum Gedanken der Volksbewaffnung in der Neueren Geschichte," *Wehrwissenschaftliche Rundschau* 13, no. 4 (1963): 185-197.

Chapter 2

[1] Oscar Handlin, "The Significance of the Seventeenth Century," in *Seventeenth-Century America*, edited by James M. Smith (Chapel Hill: University of North Carolina Press, 1959), pp. 5-6.

[2] Howard M. Jones, *O Strange New World* (New York: Viking Press, 1964), pp. 1-70. Louis B. Wright, *The Dream of Prosperity* (New York: New York University Press, 1965), pp. 1-88. Clarence L. VerSteeg, *The Formative Years, 1607-1763* (New York: Hill and Wang, 1964), p. 121.

[3] Harold L. Peterson, *Arms and Armor in Colonial America, 1526-1783* (New York: Bramhall House, 1956), p. 24.

[4]Wesley Frank Craven, *The Southern Colonies in the Seventeenth Century, 1607-1689* (Baton Rouge: Louisiana State University Press, 1949), pp. 27-182. VerSteeg, *The Formative Years, 1607-1763*, pp. 20-28. Edmund Morgan, "The First American Boom: Virginia, 1618 to 1630," *William and Mary Quarterly*, 3d Series, 28 (April 1971): 174, 181-182. L. Harrison Matthews, *British Mammals* (London: Coldeir, 1968), pp. 218-221.

[5]Daniel Boorstin, *The Americans: The Colonial Experience* (New York: Random House, 1958), pp. 347-349. John R. Galvin, *The Minute Men* (New York: Hawthorn Books, Inc., 1967), pp. 34-35.

[6]Philip B. Sharpe, *The Rifle in America* (New York: William Morrow, 1938), p. 4.

[7]Darrett Rutman, "Militant New World" (Ph.D. dissertation, University of Virginia, 1959), pp. 375-376.

[8]Carl P. Russell, *Guns on the Early Frontier* (New York: Bonanza Books, 1957), pp. 4, 9, 11. Peterson, *Arms and Armor in Colonial America*, pp. 19-20. Charles E. Chapel, *Guns of the Old West* (New York: Coward-McCann, Inc. 1961), p. 51.

[9]The difference between a snaphance and flintlock is mainly in the protection of the powder in the pan. The snaphance had a sliding cover and on the flintlock; the pan cover and frizzen were one piece. Russell, *Guns on the Early Frontier*, pp. 11-12. The colonists used the term *snaphance* to cover several stages of lock development. See Peterson, *Arms and Armor in Colonial America*, p. 28.

[10]Peterson, *Arms and Armor in Colonial America*, pp. 43-4. Rutman, "Militant New World," pp. 309-10, 452-453.

[11]Warren Moore, *Weapons of the American Revolution . . . the Accoutrements* (New York: Funk and Wagnalls Co., 1967), p. vi.

[12]Peterson, *Arms and Armor in Colonial America*, 159-160. Russell, *Guns on the Early Frontier*, pp. 68-69.

[13]John W. Oliver, *History of American Technology* (New York: Ronald Press, 1956), pp. 94-5. Peterson, *Arms and Armor in Colonial America*, pp. 192-193.

[14]Roger Burlingame, *March of the Iron Men* (New York: Charles Scribner's Sons, 1938), pp. 33, 123-125. Felix Reich-

man, "The Pennsylvania Rifle: A Social Interpretation of Changing Military Techniques," *Pennsylvania Magazine of History and Biography* 69 (January 1945): 8-10. Carl Bridenbaugh, *The Colonial Craftsmen* (Chicago: Phoenix Books, 1961), pp. 117-118. Russell, *Guns on the Early Frontier*, p. 44. Chapel, *Guns of the Old West*, pp. 2-3, 18-19. Joe Kindig, *Thoughts on the Kentucky Rifle in Its Golden Age* (Wilmington, Del.: G. N. Hyatt, 1960).

[15]Burlingame, *March of the Iron Men*, p. 125.

[16]Russell, *Guns on the Early Frontier*, pp. 234-235.

[17]A. Merwyn Carey, *American Firearms Makers* (New York: Thomas Y. Crowell, 1953), p. 143. March 28, 1628, *Minutes of Council and General Court of Virginia, 1622-1632, 1670-1876*, edited by H. R. McIlwaine (Richmond: Colonial Press, 1927), p. 169.

[18]W. W. Hening, compiler, *The Statutes at Large Being a Collection of All the Laws of Virginia from the 1st Session of the Legislature in the Year 1619* (13 vols., New York: R. & W. & C. Bartow, 1823), I, 151 (cited as Hening). Thomas Cooper and David J. McCord, editors, *The Statutes at Large of South Carolina* (10 vols., Columbia, S.C.: A. S. Johnston, 1836-1873), II, 20-21, 307. Arthur P. VanGelder and Hugo Schlatter, *History of the Explosives Industry in America* (New York: Columbia University Press, 1927), pp. 10-25.

[19]Douglas Leach, *Northern Colonial Frontier, 1607-1763* (New York: Holt, Rinehart, and Winston, 1966), p. 77.

[20]James F. Shepherd and Gary M. Walton, *Shipping, Maritime Trade, and the Economic Development of Colonial North America* (Cambridge: Cambridge University Press, 1972), p. 231.

[21]Hening, I, 199. William F. Sigler, *Wildlife Law Enforcement* (Dubuque, Iowa: W. C. Brown, 1957), p. 8. Phillip O. Foss, editor, *Conservation in the United States, A Documentary History* (New York: Chelsea, 1971), pp. 16-17. Virginia closed the season on deer from December to September, starting in 1706 except for frontiersmen. See *Hening*, I, 462. Jane Carson,

Colonial Virginians at Play (Charlottesville, Va.: University of Virginia Press, 1965), pp. 136-137.

[22]Quoted in Boorstin, *The Americans: The Colonial Experience*, p. 351.

[23]Harold F. Williamson, *Winchester, The Gun That Won the West* (New York: A. S. Barnes & Co., 1970), p. 3.

[24]Quoted in Boorstin, *The Americans: The Colonial Experience*, p. 350.

[25]Ibid., p. 353.

[26]Ibid., p. 354. Rutman, "Militant New World," pp. 402-403.

[27]Bernal Díaz del Castillo, *The Discovery and Conquest of Mexico, 1517-1521*, translated by A. P. Maudslay (New York: Grove Press, 1958), pp. 58-59. Bernard DeVoto, *The Course of Empire* (Boston: Houghton, Mifflin Co., 1952), p. 83.

[28]Quoted in Rutman, "Militant New World," p. 75.

[29]Ibid., p. 114. George F. Willison, *Saints and Strangers* (New York: Reynal and Hitchcock, 1945), p. 189.

[30]Rutman, "Militant New World," pp. 78, 95-96, 145-151, 205, 291-295; Peterson, *Arms and Armor in Colonial America*, p. 43.

[31]Martial Laws of Virginia, 1611, quoted in Peterson, *Arms and Armor in Colonial America*, p. 38-39.

[32]Kenneth Coleman "The Southern Frontier: Georgia's Founding and the Expansion of South Carolina," *Georgia Historical Quarterly* 56 (Summer 1972): 166, 172-173.

[33]Rutman, "Militant New World," p. 530.

[34]Carson, *Colonial Virginians at Play*, pp. 136-137. Hening, I, 199.

[35]Douglas Leach, *Flintlock and Tomahawk* (New York: W. W. Norton & Co., 1958), pp. 106-107.

[36]Peterson, *Arms and Armor in Colonial America*, pp. 178-179. Boorstin, *The Americans: The Colonial Experience*, pp. 354-355. Rutman, "Militant New World," p. 271, 528. *United States* v. *Miller*, 307, U.S. 180. Brooke Hindle, "The March of the Paxton Boys," *William and Mary Quarterly*, 3d Series, 3 (October 1946): 461-486. R.L.D. Davidson, *War Comes to Quaker Pennsyl-*

vania, 1682-1756 (New York: Columbia University Press, 1957), p. 169.

[37]Peterson, *Arms and Armor in Colonial America*, p. 179.

[38]John Shy, *Towards Lexington* (Princeton: Princeton University Press, 1965), p. 40.

[39]Wilcomb Washburn, *The Governor and the Rebel* (Chapel Hill: University of North Carolina Press, 1957), pp. 17-40. VerSteeg, *The Formative Years, 1607-1763*, pp. 133-137.

[40]Quoted in Boorstin, *The Americans: The Colonial Experience*, p. 353.

[41]VerSteeg, *The Formative Years, 1607-1763*, pp. 140-144, 273.

[42]George Rudé, *The Crowd in History* (New York: John Wiley & Sons, Inc., 1964), pp. 5-15.

[43]Patricia U. Bronomi, *A Factious People* (New York: Columbia University Press, 1971), pp. 217-221. Lee R. Boyer, "Lobster Backs, Liberty Boys, and Laborers in the Streets," *New York Historical Society Quarterly*, 57 (October 1973): 300. Hiller B. Zobel, *The Boston Massacre* (New York: W. W. Norton & Co., 1970), pp. 202-205. New York City also experienced a series of riots in the late eighteenth century. In these riots there was a distinct lack of firearms in use; see Sidney I. Pomerantz, *New York, An American City, 1783-1803* (Port Washington, N.Y.: Ira J. Friedman, Inc., 1965), p. 300.

[44]Nathaniel B. Shurtleff, editor, *Records of the Governor and Company of the Massachusetts Bay in New England* (5 vols., New York: AMS Press, 1968, reprint of 1852-1853 edition, Boston, William White), I, 211-212.

[45]Abbot E. Smith, *Colonists in Bondage* (Chapel Hill: University of North Carolina Press, 1947), p. 239.

[46]Hening I, 226.

[47]Cooper and McCord, editors, *Statutes at Large of South Carolina*, VII, 352-357, 396. Hening II, 481, contains a Virginia statute expressing similar sentiments, entitled "An Act for Preventing Insurrections."

[48]Don Higginbotham, *The War of American Independence* (New York: Macmillan Co., 1971), p. 4.

[49]Cooper and McCord, editors, *The Statutes at Large of South Carolina*, VII, 395-396. Boorstin, *The Americans: The Colonial Experience*, pp. 355-356. Winthrop D. Jordan, *White Over Black* (Baltimore: Penguin Books, 1969), pp. 125-126. Benjamin Quarles, "Colonial Militias and Negro Manpower," *Mississippi Valley Historical Quarterly* 45 (1959): 643, 646-648.

[50]DeVoto, *The Course of Empire*, p. 95. Allen W. Trelease, *Indian Affairs in Colonial New York* (Ithaca, N.Y.: Cornell University Press, 1960), pp. 94-96. Russell, *Guns on the Early Frontier*, p.v.

[51]A. B. Benson, editor, *The America of 1750; Peter Kalm's Travels in North America* (2 vols., New York: Wilson-Erickson, Inc., 1937), II, 519.

[52]Leach, *The Northern Colonial Frontier*, p. 97. The Puritans actually whipped and branded a firearms smuggler.

[53]Russell, *Guns on the Early Frontier*, p. 42.

[54]Alden T. Vaughan, *New England Frontier* (Boston: Little, Brown and Co., 1965), pp. 89-91, 100-101.

[55]Trelease, *Indian Affairs in Colonial New York*, pp. 96-100. Russell, *Guns on the Early Frontier*, p. 113.

[56]Trelease, *Indian Affairs in Colonial New York*, p. 100.

[57]Peterson, *Arms and Armor in Colonial America*, p. 46.

[58]Benson, editor, *The America of 1750; Peter Kalm's Travels in North America*, II, 519.

[59]Russell, *Guns on the Early Frontier*, pp. 14, 47. 20 February 1676/7 M. R. McIlwaine, editor, *Journal of the Virginia House of Burgesses, 1649/60-1693* (12 vols., Richmond, 1904-1915), II, 68.

[60]Rutman, "Militant New World," p. 378.

[61]Quoted in Russell, *Guns on the Early Frontier*, p. 19.

[62]Ibid., p. 14.

[63]Berkeley R. Lewis, *Small Arms in the United States Service*, vol. 129 of the Smithsonian Miscellaneous Collection (Washington, D.C.: Smithsonian Institution, 1956), p. 36. Alvin Josephy, Jr., *The Patriot Chiefs* (London: Eyre and Spottswoode, 1962), p. 107. Howard Peckham, *Pontiac and the Indian Uprisings* (Princeton: Princeton University Press, 1947),

p. 11. Russell, *Guns on the Early Frontier*, pp. 20-23.

[64]George Masselman, *The Cradle of Colonialism* (New Haven: Yale University Press, 1963), pp. 47, 62-3, 211-213, 219-225, 462-465.

[65]Philip Longworth, *The Cossacks* (New York: Holt, Rinehart and Winston, 1970), pp. 2-10. Gunther E. Rothenberg, *The Austrian Military Boarder in Croatia, 1522-1747* (Urbana: University of Illinois Press, 1960), pp. 124-126. James R. Scobie, *Argentina, A City and a Nation* (New York: Oxford University Press, 1964), pp. 67-71. Richard O. Perry, "The Argentine Frontier, The Conquest of the Desert, 1878-1879," (Ph.D. dissertation, University of Georgia, 1971), pp. 68-90, 94. The adoption of the Remington Rolling-Block Rifle by Argentina and its dispersion on the frontier brought a rapid downfall of the Indians.

[66]Henry B. Parkes, *A History of Mexico* (Boston: Houghton, Mifflin Co., 1938), pp. 73, 80-83. Edward H. Spicer, *Cycles of Conquest* (Tucson: University of Arizona Press, 1962), pp. 285-306.

[67]W. J. Eccles, *France in America* (New York: Harper & Row, Publishers, 1972), pp. 69-70, 115, 186. Richard A. Preston and Sydney F. Wise, *Men in Arms* (New York: Praeger Publishers, 1970), pp. 167-170.

[68]Jack S. Radabaugh, "The Military System of Colonial Massachusetts, 1690-1740)" (Ph.D. dissertation, University of Southern California, 1965), p. 3.

Chapter 3

[1]Ralph Waldo Emerson, "Concord Hymn," in *The Complete Works of Ralph Waldo Emerson*, edited by Edward Waldo Emerson (12 vols., Boston: Houghton, Mifflin Co., 1903-1906), IX, 158.

[2]Second Amendment, United States Constitution.

[3]There is a real disparity in the figures because of the inaccuracies of the records. The potential available is estimated at a

ratio of 1 militiaman to every 5 1/3 persons. See *The Statistical History of the United States from Colonial Times to the Present* (Stamford, Conn.: Fairfield Publishers, Inc., 1965), pp. 743, 756. See also Don Higginbotham, *The War of American Independence* (New York: Macmillan Co., 1971), pp. 7, 10, 389-390. Victor Hicken, *The American Fighting* (New York: Macmillan Co., 1969), p. 7. Robert A. Sprecher, "The Lost Amendment," *American Bar Association Journal* 51 (June 1965): 536.

[4]Allen French, *The First Year of the American Revolution* (Reprinted, New York: Octagon Books, Inc., 1967), p. 35. Higginbotham, *The War of American Independence*, p. 9. John K. Mahon, *The American Militia, Decade of Decisions, 1789-1800*, in University of Florida Monographs, Social Science, No. 6, Spring 1960 (Gainesville, Fla.: University of Florida Press, 1960), pp. 2-3.

[5]James T. Flexner, *George Washington, The Forge of Experience, (1732-1775)* (Boston: Little, Brown and Co., 1965), pp. 107-109.

[6]Quoted in Daniel Boorstin, *The Americans: The Colonial Experience* (New York: Random House, 1958), p. 365.

[7]French, *The First Year of the American Revolution*, pp. 34-35. John Shy, *Towards Lexington* (Princeton: Princeton University Press, 1965), pp. 182-183.

[8]Pauline Maier, *From Resistance to Revolution* (New York: Alfred A. Knopf, 1972), p. 28.

[9]Ibid., pp. 33-35, 38.

[10]Bernard Bailyn, *The Ideological Origins of the American Revolution* (Cambridge: Belknap Press of Harvard University Press, 1967), p. 113.

[11]Ibid., p. 114.

[12]Ibid., p. 119.

[13]Ibid., pp. 36, 62-63.

[14]Clinton Rossiter, *Seedtime of the Republic* (New York: Harcourt, Brace, 1953), p. 387.

[15]Higginbotham, *The War of American Independence*, p. 11.

[16]Ibid., p. 13. Sprecher, "The Lost Amendment," pp. 554-555.

[17]Walter Millis, *Arms and Men* (New York: G. P. Putnam's Sons, 1956), p. 27.

[18]Thomas Jefferson, *Declaration of Independence*. For a discussion of the individual clauses, see Carl Becker, *The Declaration of Independence* (New York: Vintage Books, 1922), pp. 188-189.

[19]French, *The First Year of the American Revolution*, pp. 37-41. Merrill Jensen, *The Founding of a Nation* (New York: Oxford University Press, 1968), pp. 536-541.

[20]Jensen, *The Founding of a Nation*, p. 542.

[21]Millis, *Arms and Men*, pp. 34-35.

[22]Jensen, *The Founding of a Nation*, pp. 591-592.

[23]Higginbotham, *The War of American Independence*, pp. 213, 390. E. C. Burnett, *The Continental Congress* (New York: Macmillan Co., 1941), pp. 75-76. Mahon, *The American Militia*, p. 3. Marcus Cunliffe, *Soldiers and Civilians* (Boston: Little, Brown and Co., 1968), p. 40-43.

[24]Felix Reichman, "The Pennsylvania Rifle," *Pennsylvania Magazine of History and Biography* 69 (January 1945): 4-13.

[25]*Amateurs At War*, edited by Ben A. Williams (Boston: Houghton, Mifflin Co., 1943), p. vii. Warren Moore, *Weapons of the American Revolution . . . and Accoutrements* (New York: Funk and Wagnalls, 1967), pp. 61-62.

[26]Jensen, *The Founding of a Nation*, p. 542.

[27]*Virginia Gazette* (Dixon and Hunter), 22 July 1775, p. 3.

[28]Boorstin, *The Americans: The Colonial Experience*, p. 357. Roger Burlingame, *March of the Iron Men* (New York: Charles Scribner's Sons, 1938), pp. 126-127, 133. Higginbotham, *The War of American Independence*, pp. 4, 102-103, 120.

[29]Tristan P. Coffin, *Uncertain Glory, Folklore and the American Revolution* (Detroit: Folklore Association, 1971), p. 187. Charles E. Chapel, *Guns of the Old West* (New York: Coward-McCann, Inc., 1961), p. 16. Moore, *Weapons of the American Revolution . . . and Accoutrements*, pp. 59-60. Boorstin, *The Americans: The Colonial Experience*, pp. 350-353. Harold L. Peterson, *Pageant of the Gun* (Garden City, N.Y.: Doubleday and Co., 1967), p. 43.

[30]Harold L. Peterson, *Arms and Armor in Colonial America, 1576-1783* (New York: Bramhall House, 1956), p. 200.

[31]French opinion of the American militia is found in Orville T. Murphy, "French Contemporary Opinion of the American Revolutionary Army (Ph.D. dissertation, University of Minnesota, 1957).

[32]Peter B. Feller and Karl L. Gotting, "The Second Amendment: A Second Look," *Northwestern University Law Review* 61 (March-April 1966): 48-49.

[33]George Mason, "Final Draft of the Virginia Declaration of Rights [12 June 1776]," in *The Papers of George Mason*, edited by Robert A. Rutland (3 vols., Chapel Hill: University of North Carolina Press, 1970), I, 288. The original text was composed as a committee of the Virginia Convention debated Mason's original draft. According to Rutland, the wording is "characteristically" Mason's; see I, 286.

[34]Feller and Gotting, "The Second Amendment: A Second Look," p. 67.

[35]F. N. Thorpe, *The Federal and State Constitutions* (7 vols., Washington, D.C.: U.S. Government Printing Office, 1907), V, 3083.

[36]Feller and Gotting, "The Second Amendment: A Second Look," p. 55.

[37]"Delaware Declaration of Rights, 1776," in *The Bill of Rights: A Documentary History*, edited by Bernard Schwartz (3 vols., New York: Chelsea House Publishers, 1971), I, 277. Thorpe, *The Federal and State Constitutions*, III, 1688; IV, 2455.

[38]Articles of Confederation, Article VI.

[39]Cunliffe, *Soldiers and Civilians*, p. 410. Mahon, *The American Militia, Decade of Decision*, p. 6. Higginbotham, *The War of American Independence*, pp. 441-444.

[40]Millis, *Arms and Men*, pp. 38-39.

[41]Higginbotham, *The War of American Independence*, pp. 442-444.

[42]Ibid., p. 447-448. Cunliffe, *Soldiers and Civilians*, pp. 43-44. Marion L. Starkey, *A Little Rebellion* (New York: Alfred A. Knopf, 1955), pp. 1-6.

[43]Mahon, *The American Militia, Decade of Decision*, p. 9.

[44]Section 8, Clause 15-16, United States Constitution.

[45]Jackson T. Main, *The Antifederalists* (Chapel Hill: University of North Carolina Press, 1961), pp. 158-160, 204-205.

[46]Jonathan Elliot, *The Debates in the Several State Conventions on the Adoption of the Federal Constitution as Recommended by the General Convention at Philadelphia in 1787* (5 vols., Philadelphia: J. B. Lippincott Co., reprinted in 1941), I, 326.

[47]*The Bill of Rights: A Documentary History*, edited by Schwartz, II, 628.

[48]Feller and Gotting, "The Second Amendment: A Second Look," pp. 58-59.

[49]Ibid., p. 59. *The Bill of Rights: A Documentary History*, edited by Schwartz, II, 758.

[50]"Proposed Amendments Agreed Upon by the Antifederal Committee of Richmond and Dispatched to New York [ca. 11 June 1788]," *The Papers of George Mason*, edited by Rutland, III, 1070.

[51]"Militia Duty May Become Onerous Unless the Power of Congress is Amended [16 June 1788]," ibid., 1081.

[52]"New York Proposed Amendments, 1788" in *The Bill of Rights: A Documentary History*, edited by Schwartz, II, 912.

[53]*United States* v. *Miller*, 307 U.S. 181.

[54]Stuart R. Hays, "The Right to Bear Arms, A Study in Judicial Misinterpretation," *William and Mary Law Review* 2 (1960): 393.

[55]Joseph Story, *Commentaries on the Constitution of the United States* (3 vols., New York: Reprinted DeCapo Press, 1970), III, 746.

[56]Elliot, *The Debates in the Several State Conventions . . .*, I, 371.

[57]8 June 1789, *Annals of Congress*, I, 1026. *The Bill of Rights: A Documentary History*, edited by Schwartz, II, 1006-1009.

[58]Elbridge Gerry, [17 August 1789] in *The Bill of Rights: A Documentary History*, edited by Schwartz, II, 1107.

[59]Second Amendment, United States Constitution. The first two amendments were not ratified, so the fourth became the Second Amendment.

[60]Edward Dumbauld, *The Bill of Rights* (Norman: University of Oklahoma Press, 1957), pp. 60-61.

[61]Daniel J. McKenna, "The Right to Keep and Bear Arms," *Marquette Law Review* 12, no. 2 (February 1928): 143.

[62]Millis, *Arms and Men*, pp. 48-49.

[63]Dumbauld, *The Bill of Rights*, p. 62.

[64]*City of Salina* v. *Blaksley* (1905), 72 Kan 230. Ronald B. Levine and David B. Saxe, "The Second Amendment: The Right to Bear Arms," *Houston Law Review* 7 (September 1969): 17-18.

[65]Nicholas V. Olds, "The Second Amendment and The Right to Keep and Bear Arms," *Michigan State Bar Journal* 46 (October 1967): 22-23. Lucilius A. Emery, "The Constitutional Right to Keep and Bear Arms," *Harvard Law Review* 28 (1914-1915): 477.

[66]*U.S. Code Annotated* (St. Paul: West Publishing, 1972), p. 358. Ralph J. Rohner, "The Right to Bear Arms: A Phenomenon of Constitutional History," *Catholic University Law Review* 16 (September 1966): 66. George D. Newton and Franklin E. Zimring, *Firearms and Violence in American Life* (Washington, D.C.: U.S. Government Printing Office, 1970), p. 259.

[67]*U.S.* v. *Cruikshank*, (1876) 92 U.S. 553.

[68]*Presser* v. *Illinois*, (1886) 116 U.S. 252.

[69]*Patsone* v. *Commonwealth*, (1914), 232 U.S. 138.

[70]*U.S.* v. *Miller*, (1939), 307 U.S. 174. *U.S.* v. *Tot*, (1942), 317 U.S. 623.

[71]Bartlett Rummel, "To Have and Bear Arms," *The American Rifleman* 112, no. 6 (June 1964): 41.

[72]McKenna, "The Right to Keep and Bear Arms," pp. 141-142.

[73]For a sampling of cases dealing with various aspects of the firearms problem, see: *State* v. *Burgoyne*, 75 Tenn. (7 Lea) 173 (1881). *State* v. *Workman*, 35 W. Va. 367. *Dobbs* v. *State*, 39 Ark. 353 (1882). *Presser* v. *Illinois* 116 U.S. 252 (1886). *State* v. *Shelby*, 90 Mo. 302 (1886). *Hill* v. *State* 53 Ga. 472 (1874).

[74]*People ex rel. Ferris* v. *Horton* (1933), 269 NYS. 579. *Glasscock*

v. *City of Chattanooga*, (1933), 157 Tenn. 518. *People* v. *Seale*, (1969), 78 Cal. Rptr. 811.

[75]Mahon, *The American Militia, Decade of Decision*, pp. 20-21.

[76]Millis, *Arms and Men*, p. 51. Jacob E. Cooke, "The Whiskey Insurrection: A Re-evaluation," *Pennsylvania History* 30 (July 1963): 323.

[77]Story, *Commentaries on the Constitution of the United States*, II, 741.

[78]Boorstin, *The Americans: The Colonial Experience*, p. 352.

Chapter 4

[1]One enthusiastic observer calculated that the Pennsylvania gunmakers could turn out the staggering number of 100,000 muskets per year at a price of twenty-eight shillings each. Berkeley R. Lewis, *Small Arms and Ammunition in the United States Service*, Vol. 129 of the *Smithsonian Miscellaneous Collections* (Washington D.C.: Smithsonian Institution, 1956), p. 41.

[2]John C. Miller, *Origins of the American Revolution* (Boston: Little,and Co., 1943), p. 429.

[3]On the state of gunmaking during the Revolution, see Harold Peterson, *Arms and Armor in Colonial America, 1526-1783* (New York: Bramhall House, 1956), pp. 159-222.

[4]Charles Knowles Bolton, *The Private Soldier Under Washington* (Port Washington, N.Y.: Kennikat Press, Inc., 1964), p. 113. This is a reprint of the original edition of 1902.

[5]Felicia Deyrup, *Arms Makers of the Connecticut Valley: A Regional Study of the Economic Development of the Small Arms Industry, 1798-1870*, Vol. XXXIII of *Smith College Studies in History* (Northampton, Mass., 1948), pp. 37-38, 41-42.

[6]This innovative spirit can be seen in the experimentation leading to the adoption of the percussion system, in which the powder charge was ignited by means of substances that would explode on the impact of a hammer blow. For American contributions here, see, *passim*, Lewis Winant, *Early Percussion*

Firearms: A History of Early Firearms Ignition—From Forsyth to Winchester 44/40 (New York: Bonanza Books, 1959).

[7]The government's relations with its contractors are treated in Deyrup, *Arms Makers*, pp. 39-67.

[8]Jeannette Mirsky and Allan Nevins, *The World of Eli Whitney* (New York: Collier Books, 1952), p. 214.

[9]Robert S. Woodbury, "The Legend of Eli Whitney and Interchangeable Parts," in *Technology and Culture: An Anthology*, edited by Melvin Kranzberg and William H. Davenport (New York: Schocken Books, 1972), pp. 318-336. This article originally appeared in *Technology and Culture* 1, no. 3 (1960): 235-254.

[10]Gene S. Cesari, "American Arms-Making Machine Tool Development, 1798-1855" (Ph.D. dissertation, University of Pennsylvania, 1970), p. 92.

[11]A qualification should be made here. The government contracts called for parts that could be "readily fitted," that is, with a minimum of finishing work in assembly (ibid., p. 64). Even during the Civil War arms had to be "tuned" at assembly for proper working of their components. Complete interchangeability as a general practice came only afterward. One of the first instances of complete interchangeability on a large scale was in the 650,000 rifles which the Providence Tool Company made for the Turkish government in the 1870s. Though each weapon was composed of sixty-nine pieces, a contemporary noted "the first instance has yet to be made known of any one part being unfitted to take its particular place in any one whole." Charles B. Norton, *American Inventions and Improvements in Breech-Loading Small Arms, Heavy Ordnance, Machine Guns, Magazine Arms, Fixed Ammunition, Pistols, Projectiles, Explosives, and other Munitions of War, Including a Chapter on Sporting Arms*, 2d ed. (Boston: James R. Osgood and Co., 1882), p. 65.

[12]For American contributions to machine tool development, see Joseph Wickham Roe, *English and American Tool Builders* (New Haven, Conn.: Yale University Press, 1916), pp. 109-215.

[13]Deyrup, *Arms Makers*, p. 148. The author continues: "Thus Colt, opening his London revolver factory in 1853, found England so retarded in the machine tool industry that he was forced to take both men and machines with him from the United States."

[14]W. Paul Strassmann, *Risk and Technological Innovation: American Manufacturing Methods During the Nineteenth Century* (Ithaca, N.Y.: Cornell University Press, 1959), p. 135.

[15]P. B. McDonald, "Charles Ethan Billings," *Dictionary of American Biography*, II, 264-265.

[16]On the contributions of this firm, see its *Accuracy for Seventy Years, 1860-1930* (Hartford, Conn.: For Pratt & Whitney, 1930).

[17]Colt also made shoulder arms on the revolving cylinder principle which were equally unsuccessful. For his early career, see William B. Edwards, *The Story of Colt's Revolver. The Biography of Colonel Samuel Colt* (Harrisburg, Pa.: The Stackpole Co., 1953), pp. 15-135.

[18]Walker had witnessed a celebrated engagement of 1844, in which sixteen Texas Rangers armed with Colts had defeated eighty Comanches, killing about half that number.

[19]Colt revolvers were part of the American small arms display at the Great Exhibition held in London in 1851. The display was so impressive that one London newspaper was prompted to rhapsodize: "The sceptre is fast passing from England: westward the Star of Empire takes its way." John W. Oliver, *History of American Technology* (New York: Ronald Press, 1956), p. 256.

[20]His London factory was visited by Charles Dickens in 1855. Dickens' account of the visit has been reproduced in Charles T. Haven and Frank A. Belden, *A History of the Colt Revolver and Other Arms Made by Colt's Patent Fire Arms Manufacturing Company from 1836 to 1940*, with an introduction by Stephen V. Grancsay (New York: Bonanza Books, n.d.), pp. 345-349.

[21]Ronald Cox, *A Manual of Trade Mark Cases*, 2d ed., revised and enlarged (Boston: Houghton, Mifflin Co., 1892), p. 142. The variant spelling "derringer," used by other gunmakers

hoping to avoid a lawsuit, has become the generic term for a small pistol of large caliber.

[22]Peter N. Johnson, *Parker: America's Finest Shotgun* (Harrisburg, Pa.: The Stackpole Co., 1961), pp. 14-15.

[23]Harold F. Williamson, *Winchester: The Gun That Won the West*, 1st ed. (Washington, D.C.: Combat Forces Press, 1952), pp. 19-21.

[24]Lewis, *Small Arms*, p. 63.

[25]Union purchasing policies are covered in Daniel M. Roche, "The Acquisition and Use of Foreign Shoulder Arms by the Union Army, 1861-1865" (Ph.D. dissertation, University of Colorado, 1949).

[26]Albert S. Bolles, *Industrial History of the United States, from the Earliest Settlements to the Present Time* (Norwich, Conn.: The Henry Bill Publishing Co., 1881), p. 259.

[27]For a recent survey of southern armaments problems, see Henry I. Kurtz, "Arms for the South," *Civil War Times* 4, no. 1 (1960): 12-19.

[28]William B. Edwards, *Civil War Guns: The Complete Story of Federal and Confederate Small Arms; Design, Manufacture, Identification, Procurement, Issue, Employment, Effectiveness, and Postwar Disposal* (Harrisburg, Pa.: The Stackpole Co., 1962), pp. 25-59.

[29]Lincoln's personal interest in armament matters has been studied by Robert V. Bruce, *Lincoln and the Tools of War* (New York: Bobbs-Merrill, Inc., 1956).

[30]Norton, *American Inventions*, p. 19. Many of the wartime patents were inspired more by patriotism than by practicality. Two gentlemen of Waterloo, N.Y., proposed a plow incorporating a cannon barrel for repelling "surprises and skirmishing attacks." Lewis Winant, *Firearms Curiosa* (New York: St. Martin's Press, 1955), p. 266.

[31]Alden Hatch, *Remington Arms in American History* (New York: Rinehart and Co., 1956), p. 82.

[32]On the problems created by surplus sales see Edwards, *Civil War Guns*, pp. 400-412.

[33]These shipments have been the subject of a recent monograph: Pierre Lorain, *Les armes américaines de la Défense*

Nationale, 1870-1871 (Paris: Librairie Pierre Petitot, 1970).

[34]"Henry O. Peabody," in Robert Gardner, *Small Arms Makers: A Directory of Fabricators of Firearms, Edged Weapons, Cross Bows, and Polearms* (New York: Crown Publishers, Inc., 1963), p. 148.

[35]Alexander Tarsaidze, "Berdanka," *Russian Review* 4, no. 1 (January 1950): 30-36.

[36]"Providence Tool Company," in Gardner, *Small Arms Makers*, p. 155.

[37]A partial list of Remington's arms sales abroad includes: Chile—12,000, Egypt—50,000, France—145,000, Mexico —50,000, Spain—130,000. "Remington Arms Company," in ibid., p. 160.

[38]Robert J. Neal and Roy G. Jenks, *Smith and Wesson, 1857-1945* (New York: A. S. Barnes & Co., 1966), pp. 158, 162, 173.

[39]Paul Wahl and Donald R. Toppel, *The Gatling Gun* (New York: Arco Publishing Co., 1965), pp. 39-94 *passim*.

[40]*A New Chapter in an Old Story, Being an Interesting Account of the Strange Steps by which a Great Modern Business Has Grown out of Ancient Conditions, Together with a Look into the Future* (New York: Remington Arms-Union Metallic Cartridge Co., 1912), no pagination. This booklet also relates how a Remington-U.M.C. employee named Alfred C. Hobbs astonished the British by picking the lock on the main vault of the Bank of England.

[41]Williamson, *Winchester*, pp. 52-54.

[42]*A New Chapter.*

[43]L. Sprague de Camp, *The Heroic Age of American Invention* (New York: Doubleday & Co., 1961), p. 90.

[44]Williamson, *Winchester*, p. 63; Hatch, *Remington Arms*, p. 109.

[45]Norton, *American Inventions*, p. 19.

[46]In the 1880s American machine tools sold for about half the price of comparable English products. Strassmann, *Risk and Technological Innovation*, p. 117.

[47]L.T.C. Rolt, *A Short History of Machine Tools* (Cambridge, Mass.: M.I.T. Press, 1965), p. 161.

[48]*Accuracy for Seventy Years*, p. 29.

[49]The prolific Browning provided over forty designs for Winchester alone. By 1900 75 percent of the repeating sporting arms sold on the American market were his inventions. John Browning and Curt Gentry, *John M. Browning, American Gunmaker* (New York: Doubleday & Co., 1964), pp. 133-134.

[50]Though 300,000 arms had been made under his patents, Christian Sharps left an estate of $341.25. Frank M. Sellers, "Sharps 4-Barrel Pistols," *Gun Digest*, 17th ed. (1963), p. 156.

[51]Hatch, *Remington Arms*, pp. 167-183.

[52]These acquisitions are described *passim* in Williamson, *Winchester*.

[53]A similar agreement may have existed with Smith & Wesson. Ibid., pp. 30, 111-112.

[54]Ibid., pp. 122-124.

[55]Donald B. Webster, *Suicide Specials* (Harrisburg, Pa.: The Stackpole Co., 1958).

[56]On the development of mail-order sales, see the opening chapters of Boris Emmet and John E. Jeuck, *Catalogues and Counters: A History of Sears, Roebuck and Company* (Chicago: University of Chicago Press, 1950).

[57]Reproduced in ibid., facing p. 60.

[58]Williamson, *Winchester*, pp. 178-181.

[59]*New York Daily Tribune*, 12 September 1892, p. 4.

[60]Import and export figures are for the year ending 30 June 1899. U.S., Congress, House, *Monthly Survey of Commerce and Finance of the United States, July, 1899*, 56th Cong., 1st Sess., House Doc. 15, Part 1, pp. 653, 673.

[61]Williamson, *Winchester*, p. 247.

[62]Ibid., pp. 286-367 *passim*.

[63]"Contrary to the general impression, the Remington Arms Company has always prospered more in peacetime than in war." Hatch, *Remington Arms*, p. 62.

[64]Figures taken from the *Statesman's Year Book: Statistical and*

Historical Annual of the States of the World for the Year 1904 (London: MacMillan & Co., 1904).

[65]"Government Support of Industry in American History," *Social Research* 17, no. 3 (1950): 348.

[66]Richard F. Wacht, "A Note on the Cochran Thesis and the Small Arms Industry in the Civil War," *Explorations in Entrepreneurial History* 4, no. 1 (1966-1967): 60.

[67]The company's vicissitudes in the interwar period are recounted in Hatch, *Remington Arms*.

[68]John Buttrick, "The Inside Contract System," *Journal of Economic History* 12, no. 3 (Summer 1952): 205-226.

[69]William J. Helmer, *The Gun That Made the Twenties Roar* (New York: Macmillan Co., 1969), p. 67.

[70]Osgood Hardy, "The *Itata* Incident," *Hispanic American Historical Review* 5 (May 1922): 195-226.

[71]John E. Wiltz, *In Search of Peace: The Senate Munitions Inquiry, 1934-36* (Baton Rouge: Louisiana State University Press, 1963), p. 4.

Chapter 5

[1]Charles E. Chapel, *Guns of the Old West* (New York: Coward-McCann, Inc., 1961), p. 15. John W. Ward, *Andrew Jackson, Symbol for an Age* (New York: Oxford University Press, 1955), pp. 3-10, 16-23.

[2]The lyrics were written by Samuel Woodward. See Ward, *Andrew Jackson, Symbol for an Age*, pp. 13-14.

[3]Chapel, *Guns of the Old West*, pp. 15-16.

[4]Harold F. Williamson, *Winchester, The Gun That Won the West* (Washington, D.C.: Combat Forces Press, 1952), p. 3.

[5]Thomas D. Clark, *Frontier America* (New York: Charles Scribner's Sons, 1969), p. 389.

[6]Harold L. Peterson, *Pageant of the Gun* (Garden City, N.Y.: Doubleday & Co., 1967), pp. 127-128. Charles E. Hanson, Jr., *The Plains Rifle* (Harrisburg, Pa.: The Stackpole Co., 1960), p.

1. Carl Russell, *Firearms, Traps, & Tools of the Mountain Men* (New York: Alfred A. Knopf, 1967), pp. 56-57, 63.

[7]Roger Burlingame, *March of the Iron Men* (New York: Charles Scribner's Sons, 1938), p. 429.

[8]Ibid., pp. 430-431. Carl Russell, *Guns on the Old Frontier* (New York: Bonanza Books, 1957), pp. 172-173.

[9]Carroll L. Holloway, *Texas Gun Love* (San Antonio: The Naylor Co., 1951) pp., 30, 34. Russell, *Guns on the Old Frontier*, p. 194. Colt even plied congressmen with Madeira trying to secure their support for a government contract. See Burlingame, *March of the Iron Men*, p. 351.

[10]Russell, *Guns on the Old Frontier*, p. 95.

[11]Walter P. Webb, *The Great Plains* (New York: Ginn and Co., 1931), p. 175.

[12]Ibid., p. 167.

[13]William B. Edwards, *The Story of Colt's Revolver* (Harrisburg, Pa.: The Stackpole Co., 1953), p. 259.

[14]Russell, *Firearms, Traps & Tools*, pp. 58-59, 63. Hanson, *The Plains Rifle*, p. 2. Russell, *Guns on the Old Frontier*, p. 180.

[15]Russell, *Guns on the Old Frontier*, p. 76.

[16]Charles Askins, *Texas, Guns & History* (New York: Winchester Press, 1970), pp. 6-8, 133. Williamson, *Winchester*, p. 102.

[17]Hanson, *The Plains Rifle*, pp. 6, 29-30, 53, 105. Russell, *Guns on the Old Frontier*, p. 96. James E. Serven, "San Francisco Gunmakers," *American Rifleman* 98 (September 1950): 11-14. Russell, *Firearms, Traps & Tools*, pp. 39-73. Philip D. Jordan, *Frontier Law and Order* (Lincoln: University of Nebraska Press, 1970), p. 7. Serven, "The Gunmakers of Denver," *American Rifleman* 97 (September 1949): 17-20. John Barsotti, "Freund & Bro., Gunmakers on the Frontier," *Gun Digest Treasury*, edited by John T. Amber (Chicago: Follett Publishing Co., 1961), pp. 35-52. Jerald T. Tersdale, "The Gunmaking Industry in Wisconsin," *Wisconsin Magazine of History* 32 (March 1949): 302-311.

[18]Chapel, *Guns of the Old West*, p. 154. Russell, *Guns on the Old Frontier*, p. 191. Joint resolution of 14 February 1849,

Congressional Globe, 30th Cong., 2d Sess. (Washington, D.C., 1850), p. 535.

[19]22 February 1849, *Congressional Globe*, 30th Cong., 2d Sess. p. 580. This emigrant bill provided for $50,000 to underwrite the cost of arming settlers; see Edwards, *The Story of Colt's Revolvers*, pp. 250-251.

[20]Bernard Mayo, "The Man Who Killed Tecumseh," *The American Mercury* 19 (April 1930): 446-453.

[21]Clark, *Frontier America*, pp. 693-722.

[22]See discussion in Chapter 2 on the Indians originally acquiring firearms.

[23]John E. Parsons, "Gunmakers for the American Fur Company," *New York Historical Society Quarterly* 36 (April 1952): 181-193. Ora B. Peake, *A History of the U.S. Indian Factory System, 1795-1822* (Denver: Sage Books, 1954), pp. 2, 63, 74. Russell, *Guns on the Old Frontier*, pp. 38-40, 57, 97-98, 104-105, 130-136.

[24]Estwick Evans, "A Pedestrian's Tour: 1818," reprinted in *Early Western Travels*, edited by R. G. Thwaites (32 vols., Cleveland: The Arthur H. Clark Co., 1904-1907), VIII, 230-231.

[25]Robert M. Utley, *Frontiersmen in Blue, The U.S. Army and the Indians, 1848-1865* (New York: Macmillan Co., 1967), p. 25. Jack Hornbeck, "A Brief Historical Introduction to Oregon Firearms," *Oregon Historical Quarterly* 50 (March 1949): 45-46. Chapel, *Guns of the Old West*, p. 257.

[26]Williamson, *Winchester*, pp. 43, 51-52.

[27]George A. Custer, *My Life on the Plains*, edited by Edgar I. Stewart (Norman: University of Oklahoma Press, 1962), p. 33.

[28]Williamson, *Winchester*, p. 52.

[29]Ibid., p. 67.

[30]Harold M. Hollingsworth and Sandra L. Myers, *Essays on the American West* (Austin: University of Texas Press, 1969), p. 73.

[31]Ibid., pp. 81-82. Fred Kimble and Charles B. Roth, "Burning Powder," in *Field and Stream Treasury*, edited by Hugh Grey and Ross McClusky (New York: Holt, Rinehart and Winston, 1961), p. 219. The story relates that in the 1860s and 1870s

every little village had its "champion duck shooter of the world." To this man, the town owed its loyalty.

[32]Chapel, *Guns of the Old West*, pp. 271, 273-274. Don Russell, *The Life and Legends of Buffalo Bill* (Norman: University of Oklahoma Press, 1960), pp. 164-165. Kent Ladd Steckmesser, *The Western Hero in History and Legend* (Norman: University of Oklahoma Press, 1965), p. 177.

[33]Natt N. Dodge, "Wildlife of the American West," in *The Book of the American West*, edited by Jay Monaghan (New York: Julian Messner, Inc., 1960), p. 436. Harold McCracken, "Quick Triggers," in *Field and Stream Treasury*, edited by Grey and McClusky, pp. 326-328. Henry H. Randall, *Across the Plains and Over the Divide: A Mule Train Journey from East to West, 1862* (Reprinted, New York: Argosy-Antiquarian Ltd., 1964), p. 178. Russell, *The Life and Legends of Buffalo Bill*, p. 94. *Conservation in the United States: A Documentary History: Recreation*, edited by Phillip O. Foss (New York: Chelsea, 1971), p. 16.

[34]Russell, *The Life and Legends of Buffalo Bill*, p. 90.

[35]Pat T. Tucker, "Buffalo in the Judith Basin," in *Way Out West*, edited by H. G. Merriam (Norman: University of Oklahoma Press, 1969), p. 69. William Sigler, *Wildlife Law Enforcement* (Dubuque, Iowa: W. C. Brown, 1957), p. 9.

[36]Chapel, *Guns of the Old Frontier*, p. 119.

[37]Nyle H. Miller and Joseph W. Snell, *Great Gunfighters of the Kansas Cowtons, 1867-1886* (Lincoln: University of Nebraska Press, 1963), p. 4.

[38]Robert Easton, "Guns of the American West," in *The Book of the American West*, edited by Monaghan, p. 408.

[39]Joe B. Frantz and Julian E. Choate, Jr., *The American Cowboy, the Myth and the Reality* (Norman: University of Oklahoma Press, 1955), p. 85.

[40]Easton, "Guns of the American West," in *The Book of the American West*, edited by Monaghan, p. 408.

[41]Washington Irving, *The Adventures of Captain Bonneville and Wolfert's Roost* (2 vols., New York: G. P. Putnam's Sons, 18—), I, 12.

[42]Joseph G. Rosa, *The Gunfighter: Man or Myth?* (Norman: University of Oklahoma Press, 1969), pp. 30-33, 36-39.

[43]The price of a Dragoon model was over $300 in gold and pocket pistols sold for $200; see Edwards, *The Story of Colt's Revolver*, p. 259. Rosa, *The Gunfighter: Man or Myth?*, pp. 33, 39.

[44]Hinton R. Helper, *The Land of Gold* (Baltimore: Henry Taylor, 1855), p. 158. The Colt salesman in California, A. B. Eaton, sold around 10,000 pistols between 1851 and 1855; see Edwards, *The Story of Colt's Revolver*, pp. 260-266.

[45]John E. Parsons, *Henry Deringer's Pocket Pistol* (New York: Morrow Co., 1952), p. 129.

[46]Rosa, *The Gunfighter: Man or Myth?* p. 39. Frantz and Choate, *The American Cowboy*, pp. 76-78.

[47]Frantz and Choate, *The American Cowboy*, pp. 76-77.

[48]Chapel, *Guns of the Old West*, p. 218. Allison quoted in Rosa, *The Gunfighter: Man or Myth?*, p. viii.

[49]Rosa, *The Gunfighter: Man or Myth?*, p. vii.

[50]Steckmesser, *The Western Hero in History and Legend*, pp. 133-134. Robert E. Riegel, *America Moves West* (Boston: Henry Holt and Co., 1947), p. 534. Rosa, *The Gunfighter: Man or Myth?*, p. 63.

[51]Steckmesser, *The Western Hero in History and Legend*, p. 138. This statement was made by J. W. Buell in his 1880 biography of Hickok.

[52]Rosa, *The Gunfighter: Man or Myth?*, p. 4.

[53]Ibid., p. 115.

[54]Wayne Gard, *Frontier Justice* (Norman: University of Oklahoma Press, 1949), p. 261.

[55]Burlingame, *March of the Iron Men*, p. 355. Gard, *Frontier Justice*, pp. 46, 235-253.

[56]Rosa, *The Gunfighter: Man or Myth?*, p. 49. Steckmesser, *The Western Hero in History and Legend*, pp. 85, 89-90.

[57]Harold Preece, *The Dalton Gang* (New York: Hastings House Publishers, 1963), pp. 231-253. Wayne Gard, "The Law of the American West," in *The Book of the American West*, edited by Monaghan, pp. 298-307. Richard M. Brown, "Historical Patterns of Violence in America" and "American Vigilante

Tradition," in *The History of Violence in America*, edited by Hugh Davis and Ted R. Gurr (New York: Frederick A. Praeger, 1969), pp. 67-71, 180-182.

[58]George L. Anderson, *Kansas West* (San Marino, Calif.: Golden West Books, 1963), pp. 151-174. Steckmesser, *The Western Hero in History and Legend*, p. 62.

[59]Wayne Gard, "The Law of the American West," in *The Book of the American West*, edited by Monaghan, pp. 283-296. Gard, *Frontier Justice*, pp. 40-145.

[60]Rosa, *The Gunfighter: Man or Myth?*, pp. 25-26. John D. Hicks, *The Populist Revolt* (Minneapolis: University of Minnesota Press, 1931), p. 294. Gard, "The Law of the American West," in *The Book of the American West*, edited by Monaghan, pp. 283-289.

[61]See Steckmesser, *The Western Hero in History and Legend, passim*. Vardis Fisher and Opal L. Holmes, *Gold Rushes and Mining Camps of the Early American West* (Caldwell, Idaho: Caxton Printers, 1968), pp. 7-10.

[62]Rosa, *The Gunfighter: Man or Myth?*, pp. 64, 125.

[63]Ramon F. Adams, *Western Words* (Norman: University of Oklahoma, 1968), pp. 9, 19, 24, 29, 40, 46, 136, 137, 225, 348.

[64]Richard Hofstadter, "America as a Gun Culture," *American Heritage* 21 (October 1970): 82.

Chapter 6

[1]*Los Angeles Daily Times* 6 December 1881, p. 2.

[2]"Yesterday; Slaughter Unlimited," *Sports Illustrated*, 24 October 1955, p. 59.

[3]Donald B. Russell, *The Lives and Legends of Buffalo Bill* (Norman: University of Oklahoma Press, 1960), pp. 285-310. James E. Serven, ed. and James B. Trefethen, comp., *Americans and Their Guns* (Harrisburg, Pa.: The Stackpole Co., 1967), p. 82. This range was at 260 Broadway and consisted of a 100-yard long tunnel.

[4]Harold F. Williamson, *Winchester: the Gun That Won the West*

(Washington, D.C.: Combat Forces Press, 1952), pp. 183-184. Pete Kuhlhoff, *Kuhlhoff on Guns* (New York: Winchester Press, 1970), pp. 64-66. Walter Havighurst, *Annie Oakley of the Wild West* (New York: Macmillan Co., 1954), p. 93. Harold L. Peterson, *The Remington Historical Treasury of American Guns* (New York: Grossett & Dunlap, 1966), p. 121. J. D. Brown, "The Rifle Called Daisy," *Sports Illustrated*, 29 April 1963, pp. 59, 62.

[5]Williamson, *Winchester*, pp. 159, 185, 189. Charles Askins, *Texas, Guns & History* (New York: Winchester Press, 1970), p. 7. *Field and Stream Treasury*, edited by Hugh Grey & Ross McClusky (New York: Holt, Rinehart and Winston, 1961), pictures of old advertisements between pp. 240-241.

[6]*The New York Times*, 11 July 1879, p. 6. *Chicago Tribune*, 5 July 1879, p. 6. *New York Tribune*, 21 August 1881, p. 6. *Alta Californian*, 5 July 1879, p. 1. For the development of fireworks in Europe, see Alan St. H. Brock, *A History of Fireworks* (London: George A. Harrap & Co., Ltd., 1949). James Flint, *Letters from America* (Edinburg, 1822), reprinted in *Early Western Travels*, edited by R. G. Thwaites (32 vols., Cleveland: Arthur H. Clark Co., 1904-1907), IX, 147, 151.

[7]Charles Seton Henry Hardee's "Recollections of Old Savannah, Edited by Martha G. Waring," *Georgia Historical Quarterly* 13 (1929): 34-35. Peterson, *The Remington Historical Treasury of American Guns*, pp. 93-94.

[8]Kuhlhoff, *Kuhlhoff on Guns*, pp. 60-61. Charles E. Chapel, *Guns of the Old West* (New York: Coward-McCann, Inc., 1961), p. 277. Peterson, *The Remington Historical Treasury of American Guns*, pp. 76-77, 84-85.

[9]Serven and Trefethen, *Americans and Their Guns*, pp. 20-56.

[10]A. C. Gould, *Modern American Pistols and Revolvers* (Boston: Bradley Whidden, 1894), p. 155. James Serven, "The Gunmakers of Denver," *American Rifleman*, 97 (September 1949): 20. Serven and Trefethen, *Americans and Their Guns*, pp. 88-89, 136.

[11]Serven and Trefethen, *Americans and Their Guns*, pp. 113-115.

[12]Ibid., pp. 128, 132.

[13]Ibid., pp. 134-141.

[14]Ibid., p. 142.

[15]Ibid., pp. 143-181.

[16]Ibid., p. 174. Arthur A. Ekirch, Jr., *The Civilian and the Military* (New York: Oxford University Press, 1956), p. 154.

[17]Hamilton Cochran, *Noted American Duels and Hostile Encounters* (New York: Chilton Books, 1963), pp. 38-39. Don C. Seitz, *Famous American Duels* (New York: Thomas Y. Crowell, 1929), p. 17. Walter Millis, *Arms and Men* (New York: G. P. Putnam's Sons, 1956), p. 73.

[18]John Hope Franklin, *The Militant South, 1800-1861* (Cambridge: Harvard University Press, 1956), p. 38.

[19]Cochran, *Noted American Duels and Hostile Encounters*, p. 11; John E. Parsons, *Henry Deringer's Pocket Pistol* (New York: William Morrow and Co., 1952), p. 29.

[20]Cochran, *Noted American Duels and Hostile Encounters*, pp. 102, 113, 122.

[21]Ibid., p. 186.

[22]Harnett T. Kane, *Gentlemen Swords and Pistols* (New York: William Morrow & Co., 1951), p. ix. Clement Eaton, *A History of the Old South* (New York: Macmillan Co., 1949), p. 283. *Correspondence of Andrew Jackson*, edited by John S. Bassett (7 vols., Washington, D.C.: Carnegie Institution, 1926-1935), I, 207-208, 317-318. Franklin, *The Militant South*, pp. 49-52.

[23]Cochran, *Noted American Duels and Hostile Encounters*, p. 130.

[24]Ibid., p. 19.

[25]Ibid., pp. 45, 48.

[26]Ibid., p. 131.

[27]Ibid., pp. 231-232.

[28]Franklin, *The Militant South*, p. 49.

[29]Vardis Fisher and Opal L. Holmes, *Gold Rushes and Mining Camps of the Early American West* (Caldwell, Idaho: Caxton Printers, 1968), p. 407. It should be noted that nineteenth-century American commentators stated that American dueling was a direct offshoot from Europe; see Franklin, *The Militant South*, p. 59.

[30]J. G. Milligan, *The History of Duelling* (London: n.p., 1841) in Cochran, *Noted American Duels and Hostile Encounters*, p. 287.

[31]Sam B. Warner, Jr., *The Private City* (Philadelphia: University of Pennsylvania Press, 1968), pp. 125-155. Richard Wade, *Urban Frontier* (Cambridge: Harvard University Press, 1959), p. 88. John Schneider, "Mob Violence and Public Order in the American City, 1830-1865," (Ph.D. dissertation, University of Minnesota, 1971), pp. 6-7. Leonard L. Richards, *Gentlemen of Property and Standing* (New York: Oxford University Press, 1970), pp. 8-9. Robbery report in *Daily Savannah Republican*, 2 February 1830, p. 2.

[32]Richards, *Gentlemen of Property and Standing*, pp. 8-9, 124-127. William J. Bopp and Donald O. Schultz, *A Short History of American Law Enforcement* (Springfield, Ill.: Charles C. Thomas, 1972), p. 33. Schneider, "Mob Violence and Public Order in the American City, 1830-1865," pp. 45, 66, 82, 132, 153. Schneider, in discussing various mob actions, indicated that no firearms were used in the New York riot of 1834. However, in the Philadelphia riot of 1844, arms were in use and evident; see Ray Allen Billington, *The Protestant Crusade, 1800-1860* (Chicago: Quadrangle Books, Inc., 1964), pp. 225-230. Later, in the St. Louis riot of 1854 and the Detroit draft riot of 1863 firearms were generally present.

[33]*A Philadelphia Perspective, The Diary of Sidney George Fisher Concerning the years, 1841-1871*, edited by Nicholas B. Wainwright (Philadelphia: Historical Society of Philadelphia, 1967), p. 168.

[34]Chicago Tribune, 26 July 1877, p. 1.

[35]Allan Nevins, *Ordeal of the Union* (2 vols., New York, 1947), II, 380-411.

[36]Ray Allen Billington, *Westward Expansion: A History of the American Frontier* (New York: Macmillan Co., 1970), p. 604.

[37]Paul Dolan, "The Rise of Crime in the Period 1830-1860," *Journal of Criminal Law and Criminology*, 30 (March-April 1946): 859-860, 864. *A Philadelphia Perspective*, edited by Wainwright, pp. 165, 167-168.

[38]*Chicago Tribune*, 4 August 1877, p. 8.

[39]*Chicago Tribune*, 30 January 1922, p. 6.

[40]Parsons, *Henry Deringer's Pocket Pistol*, p. 21.

[41]Dolan, "The Rise of Crime in the Period 1830-1860," pp. 859-860, 864. James P. McCabe, Jr., *Lights and Shadows of New York Life," or the Sights and Sensations of a Great City* (Philadelphia: National Publishing Co., 1872), p. 542.

[42]Raymond B. Fosdick, *American Police Systems* (New York: Century Co., 1922, reprinted Monclair, N.J.: Patterson Smith Publishing Co., 1972), pp. 59-61, 66-67. Roger Lane, *Policing the City, Boston 1822-1885* (Cambridge: Harvard University Press, 1967), pp. 3-13.

[43]Fosdick, *American Police Systems*, pp. 61, 66-67. Bopp and Schultz, *A Short History of American Law Enforcement*, pp. 33-47.

[44]Bopp and Schultz, *A Short History of American Law Enforcement*, pp. 33. Fosdick, *American Police Systems*, p. 11.

[45]*Our Police. A Study of the Baltimore Force from the First Watchmen to the Latest Appointee*, edited by DeFrancias Folsom (Baltimore: J. D. Ehlers & Co, 1888), p. 28; *The New York Times*, 12 November 1858, p. 8, 15 November 1858, p. 4.

[46]Lane, *Policing the City, Boston 1822-1885*, pp. 103-104, 118, 142-145, 187-188, 203. Blake McKelvey, *The Urbanization of America* [*1860-1915*] (New Brunswick: Rutgers University Press, 1963), p. 92. Otis A. Singletary, "The Negro Militia Movement During Radical Reconstruction" (Ph.D. dissertation, Louisiana State University, 1954), p. 98. James F. Richardson, *The New York Police Colonial Times to 1901* (New York: Oxford University Press, 1970), p. 263. Robert J. Neal and Roy G. Jenks, *Smith and Wesson, 1857-1945* (New York: A. S. Barnes & Co., 1966), p. 154. Howard O. Sprogle, *The Philadelphia Police, Past and Present* (Philadelphia: n.p., 1887), p. 169.

[47]Singletary, "The Negro Militia Movement During Radical Reconstruction," p. 1. Wade, *Urban Frontier*, pp. 88-89. Wade, *Slavery in the Cities* (New York: Oxford University Press, 1964), p. 98. For a clear statement that the rioting of the 1830s and

1840s escalated the development of police forces, see David Grimsted, "Rioting in Its Jacksonian Setting," *American Histori-cal Review* 77 (April 1972): 395-396.

[48]June Purcell Guild, *Black Laws of Virginia* (Reprinted New York: Negro Universities Press, 1969), pp. 96-97. *State* v. *Newson*, 27 N.C. 250 (1844).

[49]Franklin, *The Militant South*, pp. viii, 2-3, 7, 69, 72, 104, 132-136, 173, 184.

[50]Ibid., p. 196.

[51]Chapel, *Guns of the Old West*, p. 155. William D. Edwards, *The Story of Colt's Revolver* (Harrisburg, Pa.: The Stackpole Co., 1953), pp. 372-373. Claud E. Fuller and Richard D. Steuart, *Firearms of the Confederacy* (Huntington, W. Va.: Standard Pub-lications, 1944), pp. 14, 45, 52, 98, 155. Phillip S. Paludan, "The American Civil War Considered as a Crisis in Law and Order," *American Historical Review* 77 (October 1972): 1013-1034.

[52]Douglas S. Freeman, *R. E. Lee* (4 vols., New York: Charles Scribner's Sons, 1934-1937), IV, 138.

[53]*Macon* (Georgia) *American Union*, 19 March 1869, in E. Merton Coulter, *The South During Reconstruction, 1865-1877* (Baton Rouge: Louisiana State University Press, 1947), pp. 49-50.

[54]Allen W. Trelease, *Reconstruction: The Great Experiment* (New York: Harper & Row, 1971), p. 23.

[55]Singletary, "The Negro Militia Movement During Radical Reconstruction," p. 2.

[56]John Hope Franklin, *Reconstruction: After the Civil War* (Chicago: University of Chicago Press, 1961), p. 49.

[57]Singletary, "The Negro Militia Movement During Radical Reconstruction," pp. 4-6.

[58]Trelease, *Reconstruction: The Great Experiment*, p. 66. James G. Randall and David Donald, *The Civil War and Reconstruction* 2d ed. (Boston: D. C. Heath and Co., 1961), pp. 689-690. After the Civil War, black Militia units could not carry arms in Baltimore; see William A. Paul, "The Shadow of Equality: The

Negro in Baltimore" (Ph.D. dissertation, University of Wisconsin, 1972), p. 195.

[59]Chapel, *Guns of the Old West*, p. 144. Frank Wesson termed one of his small models a "Ladies' Friend." Peterson, *The Remington Historical Treasury of American Guns*, pp. 57-61. After 1865 Remington produced 50,000 pistols called the vest-pocket. Colt introduced a pocket pistol; see Edwards, *The Story of Colt's Revolvers*, p. 247. *The New York Times*, 20 April 1875, p. 6. Lewis Winant, *Firearms Curiosa* (New York: St. Martin's Press, 1955), pp. 100, 113.

[60]Winant, *Firearms Curiosa*, p. 264.

[61]Ibid., p. 110.

[62]Charles A. Worman, "Alarm and Trap Guns," *Hobbies* 74 (September 1969): 150-151.

[63]Donald B. Webster, Jr., *Suicide Specials* (Harrisburg, Pa.: The Stackpole Co., 1958), p. 1.

[64]Ibid., p. 33. *The New York Times*, 26 March 1879, p. 4.

[65]*The New York Times*, 31 January 1882, p. 4. *Chicago Tribune*, 4 August 1877, p. 8.

[66]Anon., *The Pistol as a Weapon of Defense in Its Home and on the Road. How to Choose It and How to Use It.* (New York: Industrial Publications Co., 1875), pp. 7, 10.

[67]Edward Crapsey, *The Nether Side of New York; or, the Vice, Crime and Poverty of the Great Metropolis* (New York: Sheldon & Co., 1872), p. 29.

[68]Clement Eaton, *The Growth of Southern Civilization, 1790-1860* (New York: Harper & Row, 1961), pp. 273-274.

[69]Philip D. Jordan, *Frontier Law and Order* (Lincoln: University of Nebraska Press, 1970), pp. 2-3, 13-14.

[70]William Blackstone, *Commentaries on the Laws of England* (4 vols., Oxford: Clarendon Press, 1768), III, 3.

[71]Jordan, *Frontier Law and Order*, p. 12.

[72]Ibid., p. 2. See also Benjamin L. Oliver, *The Rights of an American Citizen* (1832, reprinted Freeport, New York: Books for Libraries Press, 1970), pp. 177-178. The author touches on the beginnings of the challenge that the Second Amendment

prevents states from restraining citizens from being armed. He labels the practice of concealed weaponry "cowardly and disgraceful."

[73]Jordan, *Frontier Law and Order*, pp. 2-3, 5, 12. See also *Arizona Penal Code*, compiled by Henry D. Ross (6 vols., Indianapolis: Bobbs-Merrill, 1940), III, Ch. 43, Art. 22.

[74]Jordan, *Frontier Law and Order*, p. 7.

[75]Coulter, *The South During Reconstruction*, p. 381.

[76]Jordan, *Frontier Law and Order*, p. 14. *Bliss* v. *Commonwealth*, 2 Litt (Ky) 90 (1822).

[77]Prasan Wongyai, "Right to Bear Arms" (Master's Thesis, University of Georgia, 1969), pp. 10-12. *Nunn* v. *State*, 1 Ga. 243-244, 257 (1846). See also *State* v. *Workman*, 35 W. Va. 367 (1891).

[78]*The State* v. *Reid*, I Ala. 612, cited in Jordan, *Frontier Law and Order*, p. 15.

[79]*English* v. *State*, 35 Texas 476 (1872). Wongyai, "Right to Bear Arms," p. 9. See also *State* v. *Shelby*, 90 Mo. 302 (1886), *Andrews* v. *State*, 50 Tenn (3 Heisk), 165, (1871), *Fife* v. *State*, 31 Ark 455 (1876). They are representative cases upholding the militia association.

[80]Jordan, *Frontier Law and Order*, pp. 17-22; Wongyai, "Right to Bear Arms," pp. 13-14.

[81]Reports Respecting Laws in European Countries as to the Carrying of Fire-Arms by Private Persons, Sessional Papers (1889), *passim*.

Chapter 7

[1]"Is the Pistol Responsible for Crime?" *Journal of the American Institute of Criminal Law and Criminology* 15 no. 5 (January 1911): 793-794.

[2]Lucilius A. Emery, "The Constitutional Right to Bear Arms," *Harvard Law Review* 28, no. 5 (March 1915): 476.

[3]Editorial in *The Nation*, 25 July 1907, p. 161.

[4]Alabama, *Code* (1897), I, Sec. 27, Ch. 110.

[5]Texas, *Complete Texas Statutes* (1928), Art. 7068.

[6]Oregon, *An Act Forbidding the Sale, Barter, Giving Away, Disposal of or Display for Sale of Pocket Pistols and Revolvers and Fixing a Penalty for the Violation thereof, Laws* (1913), p. 497. The law required those seeking permits to purchase pistols to furnish affidavits "from at least two reputable freeholders as to the applicant's good moral character."

[7]"The 'Bar' Bars the Pistol," *Literary Digest*, 2 September 1922, p. 17; William McAdoo, "Crime and Punishment: Causes and Mechanisms of Prevalent Crimes," *Scientific Monthly* 24 (May 1927): 418.

[8]George W. Walling, *Recollections of a New York Chief of Police* (New York: Caxton Book Concern, Ltd., 1887), p. 84; James F. Richardson, *The New York Police: Colonial Times to 1901* (New York: Oxford University Press, 1970), p. 113. According to Richardson (p. 263), the New York Police were not issued a standard revolver until Theodore Roosevelt became president of the Board of Police in the 1890s.

[9]As quoted in James McCague, *The Second Rebellion: The Story of the New York City Draft Riots of 1863* (New York: Dial Press, Inc., 1968), pp. 140-141.

[10]New York, *An Act to Prevent the Furtive Possession and Use of Slung Shot and other Dangerous Weapons, Laws* (1866), II, 1523.

[11]New York, *Laws* (1881), III, 103.

[12]This was merely a restatement of an ordinance dating back to 1839. It was apparently not well enforced, since it was called to the attention of city police in 1851. *Rules and Regulations for the Government of the Police Department of the City of New-York; with Instructions as to the Legal Powers and Duties of a Policeman* (New York: Bourne and Co., 1851), pp. 50-51. Well into the 1870s there were complaints about people firing at dogs in the city streets.

[13]*New York Tribune*, 22 February 1878, p. 4; 24 March 1895, p. 6.

[14]Ibid., 30 January 1881, p. 7.

[15]*The New York Times*, 8 July 1879, p. 4.

[16]*Tribune*, 20 April 1892, p. 18.

[17]Ibid., 6 January 1905, p. 7; 20 February 1905, p. 1.

[18]*Times*, 17 August 1910, p. 6.

[19]*Tribune*, 13 February 1906, p. 6.

[20]*The Independent*, 11 August 1910, p. 280.

[21]It also prompted a commentary by John W. Broadman in *Frank Leslie's Weekly*, 13 October 1910, pp. 374, 384.

[22]*Times*, 17 August 1910, p. 6.

[23]Ibid., 19 August 1910, p. 6.

[24]Ibid., 15 August 1910, p. 1. This same organization engaged in a revolver battle with railroad police a few weeks later. *Tribune*, 4 September 1910, p. 12.

[25]*Times*, 20 August 1910, p. 3.

[26]For a hostile but essentially accurate portrait of Sullivan, see Jac Weller, "The Sullivan Law," *The American Rifleman* 110, no. 4 (April 1962): 33-36.

[27]*Times*, 24 January 1911, p. 1.

[28]*Tribune*, 30 January 1911, p. 3.

[29]Ibid., 2 February 1911, p. 8.

[30]That spring it was alleged that a Gun Trust lobbyist had entertained members of the New Jersey Fish and Game Committee at a lavish dinner in order to influence their decisions on hunting regulations. *Times*, 24 March 1911, p. 2.

[31]*Tribune*, 11 May 1911, p. 1.

[32]Sullivan's political skills may account in part for the bill's easy passage, but there is some truth in later allegations that the measure did not get sufficient study. This was less the result of political maneuvering than of circumstance. The 1911 session was one of the most distracted in the state's history. For three months the legislators were deadlocked over choice of a United States senator. Hardly was this problem solved when the capitol caught fire, forcing an interruption in proceedings. When the session resumed, the legislators were besieged by an angry delegation of Suffragettes.

[33]*Tribune*, 11 May 1911, p. 1.

[34]Ibid., 3 February 1911, p. 8.

[35]*Times*, 17 August 1910, p. 6.

[36]Ibid., 15 February 1911, p. 3; 16 March 1911, p. 1.

[37]These charges led the adjutant general of the New York National Guard to lament the decline of the nation's martial spirit, a decline he placed at the door of "female school-teachers," "Suffragettes," and "socialists." *Times*, 12 March 1911, p. 8.

[38]*Tribune*, 4 May 1911, p. 1.

[39]Ibid., 14 January 1911, p. 1.

[40]*Times*, 14 February 1911, p. 6.

[41]*Tribune*, 19 November 1903, p. 6.

[42]Ibid., 21 June 1903, Sec. II, p. 1.

[43]New York, *An Act to Amend the Penal Code, Relative to the Sale and Possession of Dangerous Weapons, Laws* (1905), I, 128-129.

[44]*Times*, 26 August 1910, p. 6.

[45]Ibid., 23 August 1910, p. 6.

[46]Ibid., 18 May 1911, p. 10.

[47]*Tribune*, 21 June 1903, Sec. II, p. 1.

[48]Charles E. Van Loan, "Disarming New York," *Munsey's Magazine* 46 (February 1912): 691.

[49]*Times*, 10 August 1910, p. 1.

[50]*Tribune*, 21 June 1903, Sec. II, p. 1.

[51]Ibid., 11 January 1911, p. 7.

[52]*Times*, 27 March 1911, p. 8. Similar chases that spring mobilized as many as 1,500 persons, some of whom fired at the fleeing suspects. At least one bystander was wounded in this way.

[53]Ibid., 20 March 1911, p. 1.

[54]Opponents of the Sullivan Law would later argue that the disarming of the city's inhabitants had produced a general apathy in the face of crime. If New Yorkers repealed the Sullivan Law and rearmed, "there would be no such things as a daylight payroll holdup with a crowd looking on." *Times*, 25 August 1923, p. 8.

[55]New York, *An Act to Amend the Penal Law, in Relation to the Sale and Carrying of Dangerous Weapons, Laws* (1911), pp. 442-445.

[56]*Tribune*, 2 September 1911, p. 3.

[57]Ibid., 13 September 1911, p. 3.

[58]Ibid., 6 September 1911, p. 3.

[59]*Times*, 1 September 1911, p. 6.

[60]Ibid., 28 September 1911, p. 8.

[61]Ibid., 6 September 1911, p. 8.

[62]*Tribune*, 10 September 1911, p. 5.

[63]Ibid., 1 September 1911, p. 6; 19 September 1911, p. 6.

[64]Ibid., 12 September 1911, p. 14.

[65]Van Loan, "Disarming New York," p. 692.

[66]*Tribune*, 10 September 1911, p. 14.

[67]Ibid., 8 September 1911, p. 1.

[68]Van Loan, "Disarming New York," p. 692.

[69]*Times*, 26 February 1913, p. 12.

[70]*Tribune*, 30 January 1911, p. 3; *Times*, 27 January 1913, p. 20.

[71]*Times*, 23 May 1913, p. 9.

[72]Ibid., 12 April 1914, Sec. III, p. 9.

Chapter 8

[1]By 1925 eleven states had prohibited or restricted the use of firearms by aliens; much of the legislation dated from the early 1920s. "Report of the Committee on an Act to Regulate the Sale and Possession of Firearms," *Handbook of the National Conference of Commissioners on Uniform State Laws*, 1925, p. 886.

[2]Kansas, *An Act Relating to the Flag, Standard, or Banner of Bolshevism, Anarchy, or Radical Socialism, Declaring Any Violation thereof a Felony, and Providing Penalties therefor, Laws* (1919), p. 244.

[3]*The People* v. *Camperlingo*, 69 CA 466 (1924).

[4]*Biffer* v. *City of Chicago*, 278 ILL 562 (1917).

[5]*Chicago Daily Tribune*, 16 November 1924, p. 1.

[6]*The New York Times*, 23 October 1921, Sec. II, p. 1.

[7]A National Crime Commission was created in 1925. For these movements, see Virgil W. Peterson, *Crime Commissions in the United States* (Chicago: Chicago Crime Commission, 1945).

[8]*Chicago Tribune*, 8 February 1922, p. 3.

[9]See, for example, *The New York Times*, 9 June 1921, p. 25.

[10]*Chicago Tribune*, 15 January 1922, p. 1.

[11]Ibid., 25 January 1922, p. 1.

[12]Ibid., 8 February 1922, p. 1.

[13]Ibid., 14 February 1922, p. 5.

[14]Ibid., 8 February 1922, p. 1.

[15]"Saying It with Pistols," *Literary Digest*, 23 August 1924, p. 32.

[16]U.S., Congress, House, Committee on the Post Office and Post Roads, *Carrying of Pistols, Revolvers, and other Firearms Capable of Being Concealed on the Person in the Mails, Hearings*, before a subcommittee of the Committee on the Post Office and Post Roads, House of Representatives, on H.R. 4502, 69th Cong., 1st Sess., 1926, p. 17.

[17]Atlanta, Ga., *Code* (1924), Secs. 1861, 1866.

[18]Pistol legislation was also the subject of a debater's handbook, a sure sign of its vogue: Lamar T. Beman, *Outlawing the Pistol* (New York: H. W. Wilson Co., 1926).

[19]William McAdoo, "Crime and Punishment: Causes and Mechanisms of Prevalent Crimes," *Scientific Monthly* 24 (May 1927): 419. McAdoo also wrote a book which dealt extensively with firearms and crime: *When the Court Takes a Recess* (New York: E. P. Dutton & Co., 1924).

[20]Among the scores of works Hoffman wrote on mortality rates, one in particular might be cited: *The Homicide Problem* (Newark, N.J.: Prudential Press, 1925). See particularly pp. 4-5, 54-59.

[21]"For a Better Enforcement of the Law," *American Bar Association Journal* 8, no. 9 (September 1922): 591.

[22]*Chicago Tribune*, 11 February 1922, p. 1.

[23]*The New York Times*, 9 November 1925, p. 21.

[24]The Uniform Firearms Act was revised several times. For its history see the two articles by Charles V. Imlay in the *American Bar Association Journal*: "The Uniform Firearms Act," 12, no. 11 (November 1926), 767-769; and "Uniform Firearms Act Reaffirmed," 16, no. 12 (December 1930), 799-801.

[25]See in this connection Carl Bakal, *The Right to Bear Arms*

(New York: McGraw-Hill Book Co., 1966), pp. 161-164.

[26]*Firearms and Violence in American Life. A Staff Report Submitted to the National Commission on the Causes and Prevention of Violence*, prepared by George D. Newton, Jr., and Franklin E. Zimring (Washington, D.C.: U.S. Government Printing Office, 1970), pp. 202-240 *passim.*

[27]Arkansas, *An Act to Regulate the Ownership of Pistols and Revolvers, Acts* (1923), p. 379.

[28]Michigan, *An Act to Regulate the Possession and Sale of Pistols, Revolvers, and Guns, to Provide a Method of Licensing the Carrying of Such Weapons Concealed, and to Provide Penalties for Violations of Such Legislation, Laws* (1925), p. 473.

[29]South Carolina, *An Act to Regulate the Sale and Carrying of Pistols, Acts* (1910), p. 718. The law remained on the books for a half-century.

[30]*The New York Times*, 8 April 1922, p. 3.

[31]*The People* v. *O'Donnell*, 223 Ill. App. 161 (1921).

[32]*City of Chicago* v. *Thomas*, 228 Ill. App. 65 (1923).

[33]*Glasscock* v. *City of Chattanooga*, 157 Tenn. 518 (1928).

[34]House, *Hearings*, 1926, p. 21.

[35]As early as 1915, Sears had tried to police its sales of handguns by announcing that it kept careful records that were available to the police. It also asked purchasers to give their age and occupation, and to furnish the names of two character references. David L. Cohn, *The Good Old Days: A History of American Morals and Manners as Seen Through the Sears, Roebuck Catalogs, 1905 to the Present*, with an introduction by Sinclair Lewis (New York: Simon and Schuster, 1940), pp. 441-442.

[36]*Chicago Tribune*, 8 February 1922, p. 3.

[37]An executive of a New York mail-order house admitted to William McAdoo that his firm had made $400,000 in three years through pistol sales. U.S., Congress, House, Committee on Interstate and Foreign Commerce, *Firearms, Hearings*, before a subcommittee of the Committee on Interstate and Foreign Commerce, House of Representatives, on H.R. 2569, H.R. 3665, H.R. 6606, H.R. 6607, H.R. 8633, and H.R. 11325, 71st Cong., 2d Sess., 1930, p. 24.

[38]Horace Kephart, "Arms for Defense of Honest Citizens," *Outing* 79 (September 1921): 259, 286.

[39]Imlay, "Firearms Act Reaffirmed," p. 801.

[40]U.S., Congress, House, Representative Thomas Blanton of Texas speaking in opposition to H.R. 9093, 68th Cong., 2d Sess., 17 December 1924, *Congressional Record*, LXVI, 728.

[41]*The New York Times*, 17 January 1924, p. 19.

[42]Ibid., 23 April 1922, Sec. VI, p. 12.

[43]Ibid., 7 April 1922, p. 1.

[44]Ibid., 3 May 1923, p. 18.

[45]U.S., Congress, Senate, Committee on Commerce, *To Regulate Commerce in Firearms, Hearings*, before a subcommittee of the Committee on Commerce, Senate, on S. 885, S. 2258, and S. 3680, 73d Cong., 2d Sess., 1934, p. 41.

[46]Lynn G. Adams, "Adequate and Proper Restriction on Sale and Ownership of Firearms," *Annals of the American Academy of Political and Social Science*, 125 (May 1926): 153. But at a meeting sponsored by the National Crime Committee one year later, "sixteen police chiefs gave it as their unanimous opinion that nothing could be gained by allowing citizens to arm themselves against bandits." "The Battle to Disarm the Gunman," *Literary Digest*, 19 February 1927, p. 9.

[47]"Denver Meeting Breaks Attendance Records," *American Bar Association Journal* 12, no. 8 (August 1926): 564.

[48]See its *Handbook, 1925*, pp. 854-893.

[49]*The New York Times*, 21 March 1932, p. 4.

[50]*An Act to Control the Possession, Sale, Transfer, and Use of Pistols and Other Dangerous Weapons in the District of Columbia, to Provide Penalties, to Prescribe Rules of Evidence, and for Other Purposes, Statutes at Large*, XLVII, pt. 1, 650 (1932).

[51]This was the explanation he gave his colleagues when he spoke in support of his bill. U.S., Congress, Senate, 67th Cong., 1st Sess., 24 June 1921, *Congressional Record*, LXI, 3021.

[52]*The New York Times*, 29 June 1921, p. 14.

[53]The bill was actually reported out with amendments while Brandegee happened to be absent from the Judiciary Committee. On his return he asked that it be returned to the committee

and this was done. U.S., Congress, Senate, 67th Cong., 1st Sess., 16 May 1921, *Congressional Record*, CXI, 1512.

[54]*Chicago Tribune*, 24 February 1922, p. 5.

[55]House, *Hearings*, 1926, p. 9.

[56]Ibid., p. 21.

[57]See his speech in opposition to H.R. 9093, U.S., Congress, House, 68th Cong., 2d Sess., 17 December 1924, *Congressional Record*, LXVI, 730.

[58]Ibid., p. 727.

[59]Ibid., p. 728.

[60]*An Act Declaring Pistols, Revolvers, and Other Firearms Capable of Being Concealed on the Person Nonmailable and Providing Penalty, Statutes at Large*, XLIV, 1059 (1927).

[61]For deliberations on protection of the small arms industry, see U.S., Congress, House, 67th Cong., 2d Sess., 7 June 1922, *Congressional Record*, LXII, 8326-8327; and Senate, 71st Cong., 1st Sess., 8 November 1929, *Congressional Record*, LXXI, 5357-5357.

[62]*The New York Times*, 14 October 1925, p. 1.

[63]"Firearms and the Gunman," *Saturday Evening Post*, 31 October 1925, p. 28.

[64]*Chicago Tribune*, 5 February 1922, p. 3.

[65]*The New York Times*, 21 October 1925, p. 25.

[66]"How the Gunman Goes into Battle," *Literary Digest*, 17 November 1928, p. 42.

[67]George Watrous, *The History of Winchester Firearms, 1866-1966*, 3d ed., edited by Thomas E. Hall and Pete Kuhlhoff (n.p.: Winchester-Western Press, 1966), p. 52.

[68]"An 'American Atrocity,'" *Literary Digest*, 19 October 1918, p. 13.

[69]John Toland, *The Dillinger Days* (New York: Random House, 1963), p. 39.

[70]William J. Helmer, *The Gun That Made the Twenties Roar* (New York: MacMillan Co., 1969), p. 18.

[71]*Chicago Tribune*, 19 January 1922, p. 2.

[72]U.S., Congress, House, Committee on Military Affairs, *Miscellaneous Bills, Hearings* before the Committee on Military

Affairs, House of Representatives, 69th Cong., 1st Sess., 1926, p. 88.

[73]Helmer, *Gun*, p. 74.

[74]House, *Hearings*, 1934, p. 152.

[75]Helmer, *Gun*, p. 53.

[76]Ibid., pp. 80, 89. Sales were also made to respectable citizens; thus, a number of wealthy Denver, Colorado, residents purchased them for protection after a celebrated kidnapping in their town. *The New York Times*, 19 March 1933, Sec. IV, p. 6.

[77]*The New York Times*, 21 March 1932, p. 4.

[78]Ibid., 18 July 1933, p. 7.

[79]The investigations ran from 1934 to 1936. Regarding them see John E. Wiltz, *In Search of Peace: The Senate Munitions Inquiry, 1934-36* (Baton Rouge: Louisiana State University Press, 1963).

[80]In 1926 arms and ammunition makers had formed a trade association called the Sporting Arms and Ammunition Manufacturers' Institute (SAAMI). By the time of the 1934 hearings, there were fifteen manufacturers of small arms and approximately 70,000 dealers in them.

[81]"C. B. Lister Dies," *American Rifleman* 99, no. 6 (June 1951): 13.

[82]Ibid.

[83]*Firearms and Violence*, p. 244.

[84]By that time over 100,000 boys had been enrolled in the program. "Anniversary of N.R.A. Junior Program," *American Rifleman* 99, no. 8 (August 1951): 33.

[85]Senate, *Hearings*, 1934, p. 16.

[86]U.S., Congress, House, Committee on Ways and Means, *National Firearms Act, Hearings*, before a subcommittee of the Committee on Ways and Means, House of Representatives, on H.R. 9066, 73d Cong., 2d Sess., 1934, p. 13.

[87]Senate, *Hearings*, 1934, pp. 1-5.

[88]Ibid., p. 32.

[89]House, *Hearings*, 1934, p. 157.

[90]Senate, *Hearings*, 1934, p. 73.

[91]House, *Hearings*, 1934, pp. 63-64.

[92]Senate, *Hearings*, 1934, p. 63.

[93]Ibid., p. 12. General Reckord said the money had come from a "central organization" of manufacturers, presumably the SAAMI.

[94]Ibid., p. 30.

[95]House, *Hearings*, 1934, pp. 124-125.

[96]Ibid., pp. 110, 160.

[97]"Club-Women Mapping War on Gangsters," *Literary Digest*, 16 June 1934, p. 19.

[98]Toland, *Dillinger Days*, pp. 286-287.

[99]*National Firearms Act, Statutes at Large*, CXLVIII, Pt. 1, 1236 (1934).

[100]U.S., Congress, House, Committee on Interstate and Foreign Commerce, *Firearms, Hearings*, before a subcommittee of the Committee on Interstate and Foreign Commerce, House of Representatives, on S.3, 75th Cong., 1st Sess., 1937.

[101]*Federal Firearms Act, Statutes at Large*, LII, 250 (1938).

[102]The speech, delivered on 5 October 1937, is reproduced in *Selected Papers of Homer Cummings, Attorney General of the United States, 1933-1939*, edited by Carl Brent Swisher (New York: Charles Scribner's Sons, 1939), pp. 83-89.

[103]"Club-Women," p. 19.

[104]*Papers of Homer Cummings*, p. 88.

[105]See, for example, "Man the Walls! Again!" *Country Life* 73 (March 1938): 76.

[106]*Firearms and Violence*, p. 104, n. 40.

[107]H. C. Engelbrecht, who popularized the term "merchants of death" to describe arms manufacturers, made the Remington representative's remarks the point of departure for a book on the subject: *"One Hell of a Business"* (New York: Robert McBride and Co., 1934).

[108]The charge against Morgan produced a book-length disclaimer: R. Gordon Wasson, *The Hall Carbine Affair: A Study in Contemporary Folklore* (New York: Pandick Press, Inc., 1948).

[109]Radio address of George Aubrey Hastings, 27 February 1932, text reproduced in U.S., Congress, Senate, Committee on the District of Columbia, *Control of Firearms Sales, Hearings*,

before the Committee on the District of Columbia, Senate, on S. 2751, 72d Cong., 1st Sess., 1932.

[110]Reproduced in U.S., Congress, Senate, 72d Cong., 1st Sess., 15 January 1932, *Congressional Record*, LXXV, 2000.

[111]"Should a Boy Have a Gun?" *Parents' Magazine* 9, no. 10 (October 1934): 26, 77.

[112]Ibid., 27.

Chapter 9

[1]In 1942 *Parents' Magazine* assured readers who were "gun-shy" that rifle clubs were worthwhile organizations for boys. H. DeWitt Erk, "Are You a Gun-Shy Parent?" 17, no. 8 (August 1942): 31, 64.

[2]*The New York Times*, 31 August 1918, p. 14.

[3]"Bigger Than the Government," *The Nation*, 8 May 1935, p. 524.

[4]Carl R. Hellstrom, *"S. & W." 100 Years of Gunmaking! (1852-1952)* (New York: The Newcomen Society of America, 1952), p. 16. This is the text of an address delivered before the Newcomen Society on 21 October 1952.

[5]John E. Wiltz, *In Search of Peace: The Senate Munitions Inquiry, 1934-36* (Baton Rouge: Louisiana State University Press, 1963), p. 55.

[6]U.S., Department of Commerce, Bureau of the Census, *Biennial Census of Manufacturers, 1923*, p. 366; *1935*, p. 893.

[7]The company published a book on its production achievements during the war: *In Abundance and on Time, 1939-1943. A Record of Remington Arms Company's Share in the Production of Small Arms and Ammunition for the Armed Forces of the United States and Her Allies* (Bridgeport, Conn.: Remington Arms Co., Inc., 1944).

[8]Hellstrom, "S. & W.", p. 24.

[9]*Firearms and Violence in American Life. A Staff Report Submitted to the National Commission on the Causes and Prevention of Violence*, prepared by George D. Newton, Jr., and Franklin E. Zimring

(Washington, D.C.: U.S. Government Printing Office, 1970), p. 12.

[10]The development of shooting sports after the war is traced in James E. Serven, ed., and James B. Trefethen, comp., *Americans and Their Guns. The National Rifle Association Story —Through Nearly a Century of Service to the Nation* (Harrisburg, Pa.: Stackpole Press, 1967), pp. 250-289.

[11]Ashley Halsey, Jr., "All-American Weapon, Kentucky Long Rifle," *Saturday Evening Post*, 26 November 1955, pp. 44-45. See also "Most Fatal Widow and Orphan Maker in the World," *Life*, 30 May 1955, pp. 58-60.

[12]"Films Go Gun-Happy and a Great Fighter Offers Some Advice," *Life*, 2 July 1956, pp. 28-29.

[13]David Cort, "Arms and the Man," *The Nation*, 7 May 1959, p. 476.

[14]Dorothy Barclay, "Behind All the Bang-Bang," *New York Times Magazine*, 22 July 1962, p. 47.

[15]Colt representatives helped organize many of these clubs. Huston Horn, "High Noon for the Fast Draw," *Sports Illustrated*, 11 December 1961, pp. 98-108.

[16]Charles Edward Chapel, *Gun Collecting* (New York: Coward McCann, Inc., 1939), p. 180.

[17]Ibid., p. 5.

[18]James E. Serven, "The Business of Collecting Colts," *American Rifleman* 111, no. 9 (September 1963): 23.

[19]Carl Bakal, "This Very Day a Gun May Kill You," *McCall's*, 86, no. 10 (July 1959): 86.

[20]*Firearms and Violence*, pp. 172-173.

[21]"Two Gun Makers with Opposite Views," *Business Week*, 19 November 1955, p. 60.

[22]Ray Riling, "The Arms Library for Collector-Hunter-Shooter-Outdoorsman," *Gun Digest*, 1963, pp. 327-335.

[23]On the NRA's growth see Serven and Trefethen, *Americans and Their Guns*, pp. 250-289.

[24]Merritt Edson, "Target for Tomorrow," *American Rifleman* 100, no. 12 (December 1952): 12.

[25]Serven and Trefethen, *Americans and Their Guns*, p. 258.

[26]"The Quick-Draw Craze," *American Rifleman* 109, no. 2 (February 1959): 14.

[27]A bill calling for registration of firearms was introduced by Senator Alexander Wiley of Wisconsin in 1947 but subsequently withdrawn. In 1957 the Treasury Department filed notice of its intention to alter the regulations implementing the Federal Firearms Act. The NRA and other shooters' groups successfully challenged some of the changes. Carl Bakal, *The Right to Bear Arms* (New York: McGraw-Hill Book Co., 1966), pp. 180-186; "The Proposed Federal Firearms Regulations," *American Rifleman* 105, no. 7 (July 1957): 33, 39.

[28]The Pittman-Robertson Act of 1937 levied an excise tax on sporting arms and ammunition, the proceeds being made available for state conservation efforts. In addition, beginning in 1935 the small arms and ammunition industry began to underwrite such efforts with its own funds. It contributes to the National Wildlife Federation and the Wildlife Management Institute.

[29]"The Greatest Danger," *American Rifleman* 103, no. 6 (June 1955): 16.

[30]Stanley Meisler, "Dodge City Syndrome," *The Nation*, 4 May 1964, p. 40.

[31]Alfred M. Lansing, "Moose or Man?" *Collier's* 29 (October 1954): 30-33; Allen Rankin, "Hunters or Hoodlums?" *Coronet* 39 (February 1956): 89-92.

[32]Al Look, "Hunted Hunters," *American Rifleman* 117, no. 6 (June 1949): 13.

[33]Serven and Trefethen, *Americans and Their Guns*, pp. 260, 262.

[34]Paul Schubert, "A Hunter's Greatest Peril," *Saturday Evening Post*, 25 October 1958, pp. 37, 95-98; Donald E. Feltz, "Speaking Out, Boobs in the Woods," ibid., 13 October 1962, p. 8; Jhan and June Robbins, "Shot While Hunting," *Reader's Digest*, October 1962, pp. 117-119.

[35]"A Hunter's Heartbreak," *Life*, 30 November 1959, p. 41.

[36]Gene Caesar, "Anatomy of the Hunter," *Holiday* 28, no. 5 (November 1960): 24.

[37]Edmund Gilligan, "Why I Quit Hunting," *Saturday Evening Post*, 1 December 1962, p. 67.

[38]Durward L. Allen, "Growing Antagonism to Hunting," *Field and Stream* 68, no. 5 (September 1963): 12-16.

[39]"Sale of Firearms," *The New Republic*, 18 June 1956, p. 2.

[40]A deactivated or "dewat" machine gun was one made incapable of firing by welding its breech, etc. Such altered arms did not fall under the provisions of the National Firearms Act.

[41]Ashley Halsey, Jr., "Murder Weapons for Sale," *Saturday Evening Post*, 8 February 1958, p. 100. Halsey became editor of the *National Rifleman* in 1966.

[42]Bakal, "This Very Day," p. 84.

[43]Arthur Grahame, "Gallup's Poll on Guns," *Outdoor Life* 124, no. 4 (October 1959): 12; "Gallup Poll Hits Gun Owners," *American Rifleman* 107, no. 10 (October 1959): 12.

[44]"Let's Take the Offensive," *American Rifleman* 106, no. 9 (September 1958): 16.

[45]For the membership and avowed purposes of the organization, see the statement of Howard Carter, Jr., in U.S., Congress, Senate, Committee on the Judiciary, *Juvenile Delinquency, Hearings*, before the Subcommittee to Investigate Juvenile Delinquency, Committee on the Judiciary, Senate, pursuant to S. Res. 63, Pt. 14 (Interstate Traffic in Mail-Order Firearms), 88th Cong., 1st. Sess., 1963, pp. 3495, 3499-3500. Hereafter cited as Dodd Committee, *Hearings*, 1963.

[46]On Cummings and the surplus arms business see George Thayer, *The War Business: International Trade in Armaments* (New York: Simon and Schuster, 1969), pp. 43-112.

[47]U.S., Congress, Senate, Committee on the Judiciary, *Federal Firearms Act, Hearings*, before the Subcommittee to Investigate Juvenile Delinquency, Committee on the Judiciary, Senate, pursuant to S. Res. 52, 89th Cong., 1st Sess., 1965, pp. 689, 717-719. Hereafter cited as Dodd Committee, *Hearings*, 1965.

[48]The firms of High Standard, Marlin, Sturm Ruger, Remington, Colt, Mossberg, and Winchester are located in Connec-

ticut; Massachusetts has Smith & Wesson, Harrington & Richardson, Iver Johnson, Noble, and Savage.

[49]U.S., Department of Commerce, Business and Defense Services Administration, *The United States Small Arms Industry* (Washington, D.C.: U.S. Government Printing Office, 1959). The study seems to indicate that the industry suffered more from a decline in military contracts than anything else.

[50]U.S., Congress, House, 85th Cong., 2d Sess., 15 April 1958, *Congressional Record*, CIV, 6471.

[51]*The New York Times*, 2 November 1959, p. 1.

[52]"Small Arms Manufacturers Ask Surplus Sales Curbs," *American Rifleman* 106, no. 12 (December 1958): 4; "Foreign Military Arms Embargo," ibid., 108, no. 9 (September 1960): 6.

[53]See, for example, the editorial "Why Arm Potential Killers?" *Saturday Evening Post*, 6 October 1962, p. 98; Jack Anderson, "Where Johnny Gets His Gun," *Reader's Digest*, July 1963, pp. 138-140.

[54]The Mutual Security Act of 1954 had given the Department of State licensing powers for the importation and exportation of armaments. The committee was quite critical of its Office of Munitions Control, which handled the licensing. See its grilling of Robert N. Margraves, then director of the Office, Dodd Committee, *Hearings*, 1965, pp. 126-133.

[55]Statement of John W. Coggins, Alcohol and Tobacco Tax Division, Internal Revenue Service, Dodd Committee, *Hearings*, 1963, pp. 3411, 3426.

[56]Ibid., p. 3483.

[57]Ibid., p. 3481.

[58]Ibid., p. 3496.

[59]Ibid., p. 3497.

[60]"Mail Order Guns," *American Rifleman* 111, no. 8 (August 1963): 17.

[61]Text reproduced in U.S., Congress, Senate, Committee on Commerce, *Interstate Shipment of Firearms, Hearings*, before the Committee on Commerce, Senate, 88th Cong., 1st and 2d

Sess., 1963-1964, pp. 2-5. Hereafter cited as Commerce Committee, *Hearings*.

[62]Still another amendment would have required purchasers to supply a supporting letter from his local law enforcement chief. Ibid., pp. 5-7.

[63]Ibid., p. 280.

[64]"Realistic Firearms Controls," *American Rifleman*, 112, no. 1 (January 1964): 14.

[65]Commerce Committee, *Hearings*, pp. 262-268.

[66]Statement of William G. Gibson, ibid., p. 253.

[67]Hearings were held in 1963, 1964, 1965, 1967, and 1968.

[68]Commerce Committee, *Hearings*, p. 229.

[69]Ibid., p. 234.

[70]*Patterns in Criminal Homicide* (Philadelphia: University of Pennsylvania Press, 1959).

[71]Dodd Committee, *Hearings*, 1965, p. 390.

[72]The belief that England's restrictive legislation reduced her defense capacity in 1940 is still frequently cited in pro-gun circles. See on this question Serven and Trefethen, *Americans and Their Guns*, pp. 244-245; Bakal, *Right to Bear Arms*, pp. 275, 279-280.

[73]The NRA strongly supported this bill. "Current Gun Legislation," *American Rifleman* 113, no. 5 (May 1965): 18.

[74]"Gun Law: A Step Toward Sanity," *Life*, 10 May 1968, p. 4. *Life* stated its own position a few weeks later: "We favor registration of all firearms, long or short" ("High Noon for the Gun Lobby," 28 June 1968, p. 4).

[75]Statement of Burr D. Marley, Commerce Committee, *Hearings*, p. 243.

[76]James Ridgeway, "The Kind of Gun Control We Need," *The New Republic*, 22 June 1968, p. 11.

[77]"Gun Control: Melodrama, Farce and Tragedy," *Christian Century*, 26 June 1968, p. 832.

[78]"Editor's Firing Point," *American Rifleman* 115, no. 5 (May 1967): 111.

[79]Dodd Committee, *Hearings*, 1965, p. 447.

[80]Richard Starnes, "147 Gun Laws," *Field and Stream* 77, no. 10 (February 1973): 8.

[81]A paperback edition appeared in 1968 under the title *No Right To Bear Arms*.

[82]Dodd Committee, *Hearings*, 1965, p. 622.

[83]*The New York Times*, 7 May 1967, p. 1; 16 May 1967, p. 28.

[84]Elizabeth Brenner Drew, "The Gun Law That Didn't Go Off," *Reporter*, 8 October 1964, p. 34.

[85]Roger Caras, *Death as a Way of Life* (Boston: Little, Brown and Co., 1970), p. 122.

[86]"First Memorial," *The Nation*, 22 April 1968, p. 522.

[87]*Beat the Heat: A Radical Survival Handbook*, by the Berkeley Liberation School and the People's Law Book Collection, with the Help of Bay Area Members of the National Lawyers' Guild (San Francisco: Ramparts Press, 1972), p. 6.

[88]Between 1959 and 1967 the Gallup and Harris organization conducted six polls on the subject of guns. These are reproduced in U.S., Congress, Senate, *Federal Firearms Act, Hearings*, before the Subcommittee to Investigate Juvenile Delinquency, Committee on the Judiciary, Senate, 90th Cong., 1st. Sess., 1967, pp. 520-527. Hereafter cited as Dodd Committee, *Hearings*, 1967.

[89]"Gun Control: Melodrama, Farce and Tragedy," p. 831.

[90]About one gun owner in forty belonged to the organization.

[91]The National Council for a Responsible Firearms Policy and the Emergency Committee for Gun Control tried to fill this function. For their efforts see Maurice Christopher, "Guns, Congress, and the Networks," *The Nation*, 19 August 1968, pp. 115-116; *Legislators and the Lobbyists*, 2d ed. (Washington, D.C.: Congressional Quarterly Service, 1968), p. 87; and testimony of James V. Bennett and others in U.S., Congress, Senate, *Federal Firearms Legislation, Hearings*, before the Subcommittee to Investigate Juvenile Delinquency, Committee on the Judiciary, Senate, 90th Cong., 2d Sess., 1968, pp. 575-584.

[92]The Senate censured Dodd in 1967 for misuse of campaign funds.

[93]On the leadership problems in Congress, see Don Stephen Cupps, "Bullets, Ballots, and Politics: The National Rifle Association Fights Gun Control" (Ph.D. dissertation, Princeton University, 1970), pp. 188-190.

[94]See, for example, "McCarthy on Guns," *The New Republic*, 29 June 1968, pp. 10-11; and on Hubert Humphrey, "The Crawfisher," *The Nation*, 26 October 1970, pp. 387-388.

[95]Bakal, *Right to Bear Arms*, p. 127; Richard Starnes, "You Might Call It 'CBS Distorts,' " *Field and Stream* 69, no. 5 (September 1964): 20.

[96]In 1965, the *Washington Post* published editorials on the gun problem for seventy-seven consecutive days.

[97]The conservative *National Review* generally sympathized with pro-gun positions but acknowledged that it had little company: "It is extremely unfashionable nowadays to do or say anything that suggests that arms might conceivably be necessary against organized enemies of the United States." William F. Buckley, Jr., "Stampede," *National Review*, 23 August 1966, p. 821.

[98]"Operations in 1965," *American Rifleman* 113, no. 6 (June 1965): 25.

[99]Statement of Samuel R. Maxwell, Dodd Committee, *Hearings*, 1965, p. 682.

[100]Richard Starnes, "Handbook for Arm Twisters: Letters to Legislators," *Field and Stream* 70, no. 11 (March 1966): 22.

[101]Political figures who spoke or wrote in favor of gun control were amazed at the deluge of hostile mail they immediately received. See the case of Representative John Lindsay, Commerce Committee, *Hearings*, 1963-1964, p. 233. Senator Frank Church of Idaho received petitions opposing rigid gun controls signed by 44,000 of his constituents. He was convinced they were "not the work of any lobbying organization." Dodd Committee, *Hearings*, 1967, p. 515.

[102]See, for example, the statements of James L. Linford of the Suffolk County Fish and Game Association of New York,

and Ben Avery of the Arizona State Rifle & Pistol Association, Commerce Committee, *Hearings*, 1963-1964, pp. 194, 200.

[103]See, for example, the statement of William B. Edwards in U.S., Congress, House, Committee on Ways and Means, *Proposed Amendments to Firearms Acts, Hearings*, before the Committee on Ways and Means, House of Representatives, 88th Cong., 1st Sess., 1965, Pt. 2, pp. 681-682.

[104]The government announced the construction of a huge electric furnace to melt down its surplus arms.

[105]"New DCM Cuts Hit Senior Clubs Most," *American Rifleman* 116, no. 8 (August 1968): 40.

[106]For a survey of this legislation, see "New U.S. Gun Laws Piled High by Now," ibid., pp. 43-46.

[107]Ibid., 116, no. 9 (September 1968): 34.

[108]*Statutes at Large*, XC, 351 (1968).

[109]*Statutes at Large*, XC, 618 (1968).

[110]The legislative maneuvering that preceded congressional action is traced in Cupps, "Bullets, Ballots, and Politics."

[111]*The New York Times*, 16 June 1968, p. 1.

[112]"New U.S. Law Limits All Gun Sales," *American Rifleman* 106, no. 12 (December 1968): 17.

[113]U.S., Congress, House, 90th Cong., 2d Sess., 24 July 1968, *Congressional Record*, CXIV, 23095-23096.

Conclusion

[1]Robert Ardrey, *African Genesis: A Personal Investigation into the Animal Origins and Nature of Man* (New York: Atheneum, 1968), p. 316.

[2]James Jones, *The Pistol* (New York: Charles Scribner's Sons, 1958), p. 35.

[3]*Washington Post*, 1 July 1973, Sect. C, p. 1.

[4]*Wall Street Journal*, 7 June 1972, p. 14.

Bibliographical Notes

The gun as an element in American life is not an easy theme to pursue. In this respect it is less understood than the cotton gin and the automobile. As the notes indicate, much of the material used in this study occurred incidentally in such scattered sources as newspapers, government reports, diaries, legal compilations, and court decisions. Rather than listing these random materials again in a formal bibliography, we have preferred to comment on some of the most useful works we encountered.

The few historians who have written on guns have largely had an antiquarian or technological bent. Richard Hofstadter's brief "America as a Gun Culture," which appeared in *American Heritage*, October 1970, is a recent and rare exception. But the heated debates of the 1960s have inspired a number of works on the gun in American life which do make some historical references. First in the field was Carl Bakal's *The Right to Bear Arms* (New York: McGraw-Hill Book Co., 1966). Richard Harris' "If You Love Your Guns" took up most of the 20 April 1968, issue of *The New Yorker*. More recent is Robert Sherrill, *The Saturday Night Special* (New York: Charter House, 1973). These men are all professional writers, and their works are ringing indictments of the gun. Also hostile but more sober and "official" in its tone is *Firearms and Violence in American Life*, a staff report submitted to the National Commission on the Causes and Prevention of Violence, and prepared by George D. Newton and Franklin E. Zimring (Washington, D.C.: U.S. Government Printing Office, 1970). The gun has also had its defenders, though their books have generally not been so well known: Bill Davidson, *To Keep and Bear Arms* (New York: Arlington House, 1969); H. Charles Defensor, *Gun Registration Now—Confiscation Later?* (New York: Vantage Press, 1970); and Louis B. Whisker, *Our Vanishing Freedom—The Right to Keep and Bear Arms* (McLean, Va.: Heritage House Publishers, 1972).

Statistics figure prominently in many of the writings on the gun problem and are one of the most fashionable avenues of argument. Yet we have used them very sparingly, an omission that calls for some explanation. In the first place there are no meaningful national figures on gun deaths before the 1930s. Local calculations for the earlier period tend to be incomplete and imprecise about the weapons involved. In some cases they can at least serve to establish a profile of criminality, as in Roger Lane, "Crime and Criminal Statistics in Nineteenth-Century Massachusetts," *Journal of Social History* 2, no. 2 (Winter 1968): 156-163. A second reason for the limited use of statistical data in the present study was our feeling that the fluctuating tolerance of firearms has not depended so much on the sheer incidence of misuse as on other factors. The so-called crime wave, with which this tolerance is no doubt linked, may in turn take its origin from something other than the raw incidence of violence. See in this connection Fred P. Graham, "A Contemporary History of American Crime," in *Violence in America: Historical and Comparative Studies* (Washington, D.C.: U.S. Government Printing Office, 1969), pp. 371-385.

A good introduction to statistical correlations between guns and violence is offered in *Firearms and Violence in American Life*. Much of the national data is drawn from the FBI's *Uniform Crime Reports*. The role of the gun in recent urban riots has been measured in Arnold Kotz, "Firearms, Violence and Civil Disorders," a research paper issued by the Stanford Research Institute in 1968. The debate over statistics is part of the debate over guns; for recent examples of varying interpretations, see Alan A. Krug, "The True Facts on Firearms Legislation: Three Statistical Studies," published as a pamphlet by the

National Shooting Sports Foundation (Riverside, Conn., 1968); and Franklin E. Zimring, "Games with Guns and Statistics," *Wisconsin Law Review*, no. 2 (1968): 1113-1126.

Much can be gleaned from the large number of studies on guns themselves. The older literature is listed in Ray Riling, *Guns and Shooting: A Selected Chronological Bibliography* (New York: Greenberg, 1951). More recent books are conveniently analyzed in the bibliography of the annual *Gun Digest*. The best account of the industry in general until 1870 is still Felicia Deyrup, *Arms Makers of the Connecticut Valley: A Regional Study of the Economic Development of the Small Arms Industry, 1798-1870*, Vol. 33 of *Smith College Studies in History* (Northampton, Mass., 1948). Another work of importance is Russell I. Frees, "A Comparative Study of the British and American Arms Industry, 1790-1890" (Ph.D. dissertation, Johns Hopkins, 1972). Harold L. Peterson's *Arms and Armor in Colonial America 1526-1783* (New York: Bramhall House, 1956) is excellent for the armament of the colonial period. Carl P. Russell has written two books on frontier firearms: *Guns on the Early Frontier* (New York: Bonanza Books, 1957); and *Firearms, Tools and Traps of the Mountain Men* (New York: Alfred A. Knopf, 1967). Useful for the same period is Charles E. Chapel, *Guns of the Old West* (New York: Coward-McCann, Inc., 1961). William B. Edwards, *Civil War Guns* (Harrisburg, Pa.: The Stackpole Co., 1962) is valuable for the arms of that era. Among company histories the most useful was H. F. Williamson's *Winchester: The Gun That Won the West* (Washington, D.C.: Combat Forces Press, 1952), the work of an economic historian. More anecdotal but still of importance are Alden Hatch, *Remington Arms in American History* (New York: Rinehart and Co., 1956); and John E. Parsons, *Henry Deringer's Pocket Pistol* (New York: Morrow Co., 1952). Books on Samuel Colt and his guns are legion. Two of the most useful to us were William B. Edwards, *The Story of Colt's Revolver* (Harrisburg, Pa.: The Stackpole Co., 1953); and C. T. Haven and F. A. Belden, *A History of the Colt Revolver* (New York: Bonanza Books, 1967). The Thompson submachine gun has been treated in the excellent book by

William J. Helmer *The Gun That Made the Twenties Roar* (New York: Macmillan Co., 1969). Studies have also been made of distinctive types of arms. On the Pennsylvania-Kentucky Rifle an exceptionally good work is Henry J. Kauffman, *The Pennsylvania-Kentucky Rifle* (New York: Bonanza Books, 1968). Also recommended are Charles E. Hanson, Jr., *The Plains Rifle* (Harrisburg, Pa.: The Stackpole Co., 1960); and Donald B. Webster, Jr., *Suicide Specials* (Harrisburg, Pa.: The Stackpole Co., 1958). Finally, Lewis Winant's *Firearms Curiosa* (New York: St. Martin's Press, 1955) is a repertory of unusual weapons designed for sometimes bizarre uses.

The legal problems concerning firearms have been discussed by authors both in Europe and in America. These sources on European Legislation are helpful: Colin Greenwood, *Firearms Control: A Study of Armed Crime and Firearms Control in England and Wales* (London: Routledge and Kegan Paul, 1972); Pierre Bourgoin, *De la fabrication, de la détention, du port et du commerce des armes* (Paris: Presses continentales, 1946); Jacob Meulen, *Het Wapenbruick van de Politie in Nederland* (Alphen aan den Rijn: N. Samson, 1966); F. Kunze, *Das Waffenrecht im Deutschen Reiche* (Berlin: Parey, 1938); and Gerhard Potrykus, *Waffenrecht* (Munich: C. H. Beck, 1973).

For comparative purposes the following sources on American law are most valuable. *The Corpus Juris Secundum* (101 vols., Brooklyn, N.Y.: American Law Book Co., 1936—), under the headings of "weapons" and "militia," contains entries regarding the continuing interpretation of American firearms law. For a list of pertinent cases, consult the *American Digest* (318 vols., St. Paul, Minn.: West Publishing Co., 1898—). It has been published every ten years since 1896. The first set to 1896 deals with cases since 1658. Under the general rubric of "weapons," one can locate most of the American court cases affecting the bearing, possession, ownership, and use of firearms. In addition, the compilers of the volumes have cross-referenced other important points of law that have an impact on firearms.

Using these sources as background, we must turn to the

commentators on the legal background and judicial decisions affecting firearms. The Second Amendment has, of course, drawn considerable attention. An early discussion on state protection of the "Right to Bear Arms" is David J. McKenna, "The Right to Keep and Bear Arms," *Marquette Law Review* 12 (February 1928): 138-149. He points out that legal decisions change and that it is conceivable that future judges might deny that man has "any inherent right to keep and bear arms" (p. 149).

Of recent years, even more discussions of the Second Amendment have emerged. Many authors have viewed the amendment from several different perspectives. For a representative sampling, the reader should consider the articles that follow here. Stuart R. Hays, "The Right to Bear Arms, A Study in Judicial Misinterpretation," *William and Mary Law Review* 2 (1960): 381-406. Hays believes that the courts have always been too restrictive in their interpretations; he develops a case to support the right to bear arms. Ronald B. Levine and David B. Saxe, "The Second Amendment: The Right to Bear Arms," *Houston Law Review* 7 (September 1969): 1-19 contend that "the reserve of federal power to regulate the right to bear arms is minimal" (p. 1). Nicholas V. Olds, "The Second Amendment and the Right to Keep and Bear Arms," *Michigan State Bar Journal* 46 (October 1967): 15-25, supports the view that the Second Amendment upholds the individual's right to firearms. Robert A. Sprecher, "The Lost Amendment," *American Bar Association Journal* 51 (June-July 1965): 554-557, 665-669, develops the premise that the right to bear arms could be made absolute. Ralph J. Rohner, "The Right to Bear Arms: A Phenomenon of Constitutional History," *Catholic University Law Review* 16 (September 1966): 53-84, takes the position that "the right to bear arms should be expressed in terms of the purposes for which firearms can conceivably be used" (p. 78). He also includes an appendix containing the provisions of the thirty-five states that uphold in some fashion the right to bear firearms. Finally, Peter B. Feller and Karl L. Gotting, "The Second Amendment: A Second Look,"

Northwestern University Law Review 61 (March-April 1966): 46-71, limits the concept to the collective group of people. However, with the change in modern military weaponry, they believe that the Second Amendment protection of the states is obsolete.

For a listing of individual state laws, one should turn to the Wisconsin Legislative Reference Library, "The Regulation of Firearms by the States," *Research Bulletin*, 130 (Madison, July 1960). One should also consult New York State Commission of Investigation, *Report of New York State Commission Concerning Pistol Licensing Laws and Procedures in New York State*, November 1964. For the use that can be made of these laws by historians, one should read the excellent commentatory on concealed weapons found in Philip Jordan, *Frontier Law and Order* (Lincoln: University of Nebraska Press, 1970).

Since the legal use of firearms is closely linked with the militia, books concerning that topic are important. Bernard Bailyn in his *Ideological Origins of the American Revolution* (Cambridge: Belknap Press of the Harvard University Press, 1967), alludes to the concept of the independent militiaman as opposed to the professional soldier. In the years prior to the American Revolution, there was much debate about these two approaches to military organizations. Further discussion of this problem can be found in John Shy, *Towards Lexington* (Princeton: Princeton University Press, 1965). The early history of how Americans became so attached to the militia concept can be found in Darrett Rutman, "Militant New World" (Ph.D. dissertation, University of Virginia, 1959). In addition the fine chapter on the militia by Daniel Boorstin in his *The Americans: The Colonial Experience* (New York: Random House, 1958) develops many aspects of the problem. Don Higginbotham, *The War of American Independence* (New York: Macmillan Co., 1971) is also very useful. For latter aspects of the military and the militia, see John K. Mahon, *The American Militia: Decade of Decisions, 1789-1800*, in University of Florida Monographs, Social Science, No. 6., Spring 1960 (Gainesville, Fla.: University of Florida Press, 1960); Walter Millis, *Arms and*

Men (New York: G. P. Putnam's Sons, 1956); and Arthur A. Ekirch, *The Civilian and the Military* (New York: Oxford University, 1965). For a study of the distinctive characteristics of one section concerning the military, see John Hope Franklin, *The Militant South* (Cambridge: Harvard University Press, 1956).

The emerging social aspects of the use of firearms which Franklin alludes to in his study are important to the entire nation. The upheavals of the period 1830-1860 are discussed by a number of authors. Leonard L. Richards, *Gentlemen of Property and Standing* (New York: Oxford University Press, 1970); Ray Allen Billington, *The Protestant Crusade* (Chicago: Quadrangle Books, Inc., 1964); John Schneider, "Mob Violence and Public Order in the American City, 1830-1865," (Ph.D. dissertation, University of Minnesota, 1971); and David Grimstead, "Rioting in Its Jacksonian Setting," *American Historical Review* 77 (April 1972): 361-397, all discuss problems concerning mob violence in the United States. A 1967 colloquium on urban violence sponsored by the University of Chicago is the source of a collection of essays relevant to the topic: *Urban Violence* (Chicago: University of Chicago Press, 1969). Through these studies one can trace the progressive steps towards arming the urban people.

As the urban society became increasingly complex in the 1830s, cities started to realize the necessity of creating a police force. Although the history of the police in America has not been thoroughly developed, there are several very competent city police histories. Roger Lane, *Policing the City, Boston 1822-1885* (Cambridge: Harvard University Press, 1967) discusses Boston during this developmental period. James T. Richardson, *The New York Police: Colonial Times to 1901* (New York: Oxford University Press, 1970) covers that city. For a very brief history of the police in America, consult William J. Bopp and Donald O. Schultz, *A Short History of American Law Enforcement* (Springfield, Ill.: Charles C. Thomas, 1972).

Another aspect of the use of firearms by the society is hunting. Most hunting accounts are true adventure and there is no real scholarly account of hunting. A new book, very attractively illustrated by Charles F. Waterman, *Hunting in America* (New York: Holt, Rinehart and Winston, 1973), gives a brief account of the history of hunting in America. Michael Brander, *Hunting and Shooting, From Earliest Times to the Present Day* (New York: G. P. Putnam's Sons, 1971) is another example of that type of book. With hunting such an important business and sport, the necessity of conservation became important too. Phillip O. Foss, editor, *Conservation in the United States, A Documentary History* (New York: Chelsea, 1971) is a good summary of the movement toward conservation, including aspects about hunting. As the potential for hunting declined because of increasing population, Americans turned toward substitute institutions such as target and trap shooting. The book *Americans and Their Guns*, edited by James E. Serven and compiled by James B. Trefethen (Harrisburg, Pa.: Stackpole Press, 1967) is a self-history of the National Rifle Association. See also for another view, Donald G. Lefave, "The Will to Arm: The National Rifle Association in American Society, 1871-1970" (Ph.D. dissertation, University of Colorado, 1970).

While the East was responding to a changing society in terms of the use of firearms, the West, of course, developed a considerable reputation as the weapons-bearing section of the country. For a good overview of the West, including discussions of firearms, outlaws, cowboys, and other pertinent topics, see *The Book of the American West*, edited by Jay Monaghan (New York: Julian Messner, Inc., 1960). For studies on individual topics concerning the West, see K. L. Steckmesser, *The Western Hero in History and Legend* (Norman: University of Oklahoma Press, 1965); Joe B. Frantz and Julian E. Choate, Jr., *The American Cowboy, The Myth and the Reality* (Norman: University of Oklahoma Press, 1955); and Don Russell, *The Life and Legends of Buffalo Bill* (Norman: University of Oklahoma Press, 1965). For studies about the practitioners of the art of gunfighting, see Joseph G. Rosa, *The Gunfighter: Man or Myth?* (Norman: University of Oklahoma Press, 1969); and Nyle H. Miller and

Joseph W. Snell, *Great Gunfighters of the Kansas Cowtowns, 1867-1886* (Lincoln: University of Nebraska Press, 1963).

Corresponding to the use of firearms by gunfighters was the nineteenth-century practice of dueling. For studies of this phenomenon, see Hamilton Cochran, *Noted American Duels and Hostile Encounters* (New York: Chilton Books, 1963); Don C. Seitz, *Famous American Duels* (New York: Thomas Y. Crowell, 1929); and Harnett T. Kane, *Gentlemen Swords and Pistols* (New York: William Morrow & Co., 1951).

Dueling was very prevalent in the South, and firearms were in evidence particularly in the Reconstruction period. The use of firearms was a peculiar problem in the South because of the racial connotations associated with it. For a discussion of firearms in the South, see Allen W. Trelease, *Reconstruction: The Great Experiment* (New York: Harper & Row, 1971); and Otis A. Singletary, "The Negro Militia Movement During Radical Reconstruction" (Ph.D. dissertation, Louisiana State University, 1954).

As has been indicated in many of these sources, firearms have been an integral part of the American society for many years. For a contemporary reaction to modern society, see George Hunter, *How to Defend Yourself, Your Family and Your Home* (New York: David McKay, 1967); and Garry Wills, *The Second Civil War; Arming for Armageddon* (New York: New American Library, 1968).

Index